Constructivist Psychotherapy

Psychotherapy has undergone major changes in recent years, with a variety of new approaches including cognitive-behavioural therapy joining the more traditional and widespread schools of thought. These new approaches all share the epistemological assumption of constructivism, which states that there are alternative ways of looking at events and that we interpret events according to how we see the world.

Constructivist Psychotherapy reviews the constructivist trends in psychotherapy which link these new approaches, allowing the reader to enter an entirely new dialogue. The book traces constructivist thought, elaborating on Kelly's personal construct theory and the implications for psychotherapeutic theory and practice.

Areas of discussion include:

- The therapist's understanding of the client's narrative.
- A constructivist understanding of the person.
- Psychological constructivism and constructivist trends in psychotherapy.

Setting constructivist psychotherapy within its therapeutic, social and philosophical context and using case studies throughout, the book revisits 'Kellyan' ideas and theories, bringing them up to date, to explore what it is to be a constructivist psychotherapist today. As such this book will be of interest to all psychotherapists, as well as anyone with an interest in the psychotherapeutic field.

Gabriele Chiari is Co-Director and Professor at the Centre for Studies in Constructivist-oriented Cognitive Psychotherapy in Florence, and Lecturer in Clinical Psychology at the University of Florence. He is an editorial board member of *The Journal of Constructivist Psychology*.

Maria Laura Nuzzo (1946–2005) was a clinical psychologist and chartered psychotherapist, and President of the Italian Association of Constructivist Psychology and Psychotherapy (AIPPC).

Advancing Theory in Therapy
Series Editor: Keith Tudor

Most books covering individual therapeutic approaches are aimed at the trainee/student market. This series, however, is concerned with *advanced* and *advancing* theory, offering the reader comparative and comparable coverage of a number of therapeutic approaches.

Aimed at professionals and postgraduates, *Advancing Theory in Therapy* will cover an impressive range of theories. With full reference to case studies throughout, each title will

- present cutting-edge research findings
- locate each theory and its application within its cultural context
- develop a critical view of theory and practice.

Titles in the series

Constructivist Psychotherapy

A narrative hermeneutic approach

Gabriele Chiari and
Maria Laura Nuzzo

Routledge
Taylor & Francis Group
LONDON AND NEW YORK

First published 2010 by Routledge
2 Park Square, Milton Park, Abingdon, Oxon, OX14 4RN

Simultaneously published in the USA and Canada
by Routledge
711 Third Avenue, New York NY 10017

Routledge is an imprint of the Taylor & Francis Group, an Informa Business

Typeset in Times by Garfield Morgan, Swansea, West Glamorgan
Paperback cover design by Sandra Heath

British Library Cataloguing in Publication Data
A catalogue record for this book is available from the British Library

Library of Congress Cataloging-in-Publication Data
Chiari, Gabriele.
  Constructivist psychotherapy : a narrative hermeneutic approach /
Gabriele Chiari & Maria Laura Nuzzo.
      p. ; cm. – (Advancing theory in therapy)
  Includes bibliographical references and indexes.
  ISBN 978-0-415-41312-1 (hardback) – ISBN 978-0-415-41313-8 (pbk.)
  1.Constructivism (Psychology) 2. Personal construct therapy. 3. Cognitive
therapy. I. Nuzzo, Maria Laura. II. Title. III. Series: Advancing theory in
therapy.
  [DNLM: 1. Personal Construct Theory. 2. Psychotherapy–methods.
3. Narration.
  WM 420 C532c 2009]
  RC489.P46C55 2009
  616.89'1425–dc22
                                                            2009013225

ISBN: 978–0–415–41312–1 (hbk)
ISBN: 978–0–415–41313–8 (pbk)

To Maria Laura,
who co-authored my life
as well as the life of the many people
who had the chance to tell her their stories.

Contents

Series preface

This series focuses on advanced and advancing theory in psychotherapy. Its aims are: to present theory and practice within a specific theoretical orientation or approach at an advanced, postgraduate level; to advance theory by presenting and evaluating new ideas and their relation to the particular approach; to locate the orientation and its psychotherapeutic applications within cultural contexts, both historically in terms of the origins of the approach, and contemporarily in terms of current debates about philosophy, theory, society and therapy; and, finally, to present and develop a critical view of theory and practice, especially in the context of debates about power, organisation and the increasing professionalisation of therapy.

Having lived in Italy for two years in the mid 1980s, I have a particular connection with the country and, in recent years, have enjoyed making and developing professional contacts there in the field of psychotherapy, and, in doing so, have had the pleasure of meeting Gabriele Chiari, one of the authors of this book. I am only sorry that I did not also get to meet his late wife, Maria Laura Nuzzo, who stands as a posthumous co-author.

As were a number of schools or approaches to psychotherapy and psychology, personal construct psychology was developed in the 1950s. Its founder, George A. Kelly, was explicit about his view of the person as scientist or, as Bannister and Fransella later put it, 'Inquiring man'; and about the need for clarity about the philosophical assumptions which informed his theory of personality and practice. This present volume stands in this tradition and, in line with the brief of the series, advances it. *Constructivist Psychotherapy: A Narrative Hermeneutic Approach* is philosophical and theoretical, and challenging yet accessible. In their preface the authors make their approach clear, and explain why they take and develop a narrative and hermeneutic approach to what they describe as a constructivist psychotherapy, based, respectively, on the notion of a 'construction system', on the importance of a continuous process of interpretation, and on the concept of 'constructive alternativism'. Chiari and Nuzzo have carefully constructed a book which takes the reader through a logical progression of ideas and concepts: from the fundamental postulate of personal construct theory and a number of corollaries, through various constructivist trends in psychotherapy, a constructivist understanding of the person, and the therapist's understanding and construction of the client's narrative, to the psychotherapeutic process itself. In doing so, the authors invite and challenge the reader to think about epistemology or theory of knowledge and about ontology or the essence of things which we embody in our psychotherapeutic practice. I am delighted to introduce this advancing and challenging book and the tenth volume in the series.

Keith Tudor

Preface

After 32 years of psychotherapeutic practice and 27 years of teaching experience, a plan that we had thought about for some time, but repeatedly postponed, has been realised – namely writing a book that describes both our way of conceiving psychotherapy and the theory that guides its praxis.

One might think that the transition from intention (of writing a book) to action had been determined by the accumulation of evidence, though relative, about the subject. This is not so. Neither are we saying that our notions about psychotherapy are foggy, rather, the experience of these years has produced a change in the dimension of appraisal of the acquired knowledge, it is more in the direction of a prevailing of questions and doubts over answers and certainties. Expressed positively the previous point of view shows that we became much more aware of the complexity of the psychological understanding of the person (in particular the suffering person), and of the resulting difficulty in comprehending the psychotherapeutic process. On the other hand, we felt the necessity to rearrange our ideas, putting them in an organised fashion as much as possible; a necessity difficult to satisfy through the daily psychotherapeutic practice, informed as it is by yet another one, that of engaging oneself in the relationship with the client in ways that do not allow a conscious enough reflection upon one's acting. The teaching activity is different from the therapeutic one, since the effectiveness of the training intention is closely connected with the clarity of exposition, in turn related to the teacher's clarity of ideas.

Our practising and teaching activities move within the constructivist perspective. In the last two or three decades, the fields of psychology and psychotherapy have been witnessing an increasingly high number of works making reference to what is labelled as 'psychological constructivism' or 'social constructionism'. Furthermore, some developments of both the perspectives convene on the common final path of narrative therapy, where they also meet contributions coming from psychodynamic approaches. The present book fits into this corpus as an umpteenth proposal, with the hope that it provides an original contribution.

A book that proposes to outline a systematic approach to psychotherapy cannot omit describing the psychological theory such an approach belongs to. Without a theory which defines the prevailing subject matters (the person as a whole, or people's behaviours, cognitions, emotions) the possible relationships among them, the importance or not of personal development and its modality, the criteria of change, the importance of interpersonal relationships as a means of development and change and so forth the psychotherapeutic praxis would be casual, and therefore hardly therapeutic.

We are aware of the aversion some colleagues have towards what appears to them a lingering over theorisation. The alternative is seen as 'starting from the clinic', or 'from the bottom'. But we do consider it inevitable that the very same colleagues include the 'data of clinical observation' within theories which are more or less articulate and explicit. Theirs may, therefore, be interpreted as an invitation, with which we agree, not to halt the theorisation at the threshold of its applicability in the clinical and psychotherapeutic area. Having said that, we believe that the necessity of a clear exposition of the assumptions from which the psychotherapeutic praxis derives should be extended from the theoretical to the epistemological level. Epistemology is unavoidable for psychologists, in that, whether aware or not, they cannot leave it aside not even when it is rejected.

George A. Kelly had the same opinion, in that he put an analysis of the differences between the philosophical assumptions of 'accumulative fragmentalism' and 'constructive alternativism' before the exposition of his theory of personality and his psychotherapeutic proposal.

Choosing the title for the book *Constructivist Psychotherapy: A Narrative Hermeneutic Approach* represents the attempt to mark a significant differentiation from the more orthodox expositions of Kelly's personal construct psychotherapy on which we heavily base our approach, and at the same time to specify as much as possible our metatheoretical and theoretical references. A brief justification of the terms adopted may be useful to the reader, so as to draw the conceptual boundaries of our psychotherapeutic approach.

Why constructivist?

We met Kelly's personal construct theory in the early 1980s. In that period a few theory groups, prevailingly academic, in the United States, Great Britain and Canada had embraced personal construct theory and were cultivating it. The social and clinical psychologists using personal construct psychology and psychotherapy as their specific approach were probably no more than a few dozen, and constructivism was not yet an acknowledged and distinct orientation in psychology.

We were struck by the image of the person depicted by Kelly: that of the person as a scientist, who formulates hypotheses on the world and verifies them through their behaviour, in turn regarded as an experiment, according to a continuous circularity between knowledge and action, a revolution compared to the cognitive-behavioural perspective we were familiar with, but also compared to the already established cognitive therapies. The implications of Kelly's ideas were even more innovative: the focus on the anticipations implied by personal constructions rather than on environmental antecedents; the disorder viewed as a never-ending testing and retesting of the same hypotheses rather than as learned maladaptive habits or irrational beliefs; the role of the psychotherapist as the supervisor of the client's research program rather than a pedagogue.

All this theoretical structure rests on Kelly's philosophical assumption of constructive alternativism. Only later would we realise that that assumption – dating back to the 1950s – fits very well into the contemporary constructivist metatheory. Actually, the reference to a constructivist metatheory has now become inadequate to define a specific approach. Many attempts have been made to point out relevant differences under the umbrella of psychological constructivism. We too contributed by discriminating between epistemological and hermeneutic constructivism. While many authors interpret personal construct theory in terms of an epistemological constructivism, for years we have been striving to elaborate it in the direction of a hermeneutic constructivism.

Why hermeneutic?

To the extent that psychological constructivism views the person as a meaning-generating being, an interpreter, it has a point of contact with hermeneutics, defined, as it is, as the theory of interpretation of meaning. However, the relationship between constructivism and hermeneutics can go even further.

In recent years, many discourses in the field of social and human sciences appear to share a similar criticism in regard to the traditional, rationalistic view of knowledge, where two distinct phenomenological domains are given: the objective world of physical reality, and the subjective, mental world of individuals' thoughts and feelings. These discourses have given rise to several approaches – occasionally labelled as postmodernist, post-structuralist, neo-pragmatist, deconstructivist, narrativist, discursive, conversationalist, constructionist, enactivist and constructivist – which can be seen as specific elaborations of a common metatheoretical framework in the application to different fields of inquiry. In fact, what characterises them is their attempt to transcend the subject/object separation, the reason why almost all of them so frequently refer to phenomenological and hermeneutic reflections.

The ontological premise of phenomenology consists in the rejection of both an objectivist and a subjectivist position in favour of a consideration of the subject/object interdependence; of a mutual specification between knower and known. The terms of the relationship between subject and object are more easily understood, according to Gadamer (1976), by referring to the process of interpreting a text. The text has no intrinsic meaning, independent of an interpretation. The latter arises from the interaction between the 'horizon' supplied by the text, and the 'horizon' given to it by the interpreter. Each person, in understanding the world, themselves and others, can be regarded as continuously involved in a similar process of interpretation. This view is particularly relevant to the understanding of the psychotherapeutic relationship and process, to the extent that it guides the therapist's understanding of the client and their efforts to open conversational spaces aimed at encouraging a movement in the client's constructions.

Why narrative?

Kelly's (1991a/1955, 1991b/1955) use of the notion of 'construction system' as a metaphor for describing personal knowledge is very close to the contemporary notion of 'personal narrative', so much that he is sometimes credited as being the first narrative psychologist.

We can see no substantial difference between assuming that people anticipate events (particularly social events) by construing and reconstruing their lives, and assuming they ascribe meaning to their lives by plotting their experience into stories, and that these lived stories shape their relationship with other people. Even the psychotherapeutic applications of the above metaphors are very close to each other: in both cases, the therapist strives to favour the client's elaboration of alternative constructions, or the client's re-telling of experience.

It is our opinion, however, that the current narrative approaches to therapy often show a theoretical weakness and a scarcity of therapeutic techniques, not to mention the usually vague consideration of the role of the psychotherapeutic relationship. On the other hand, personal construct theory is expressed in a technical and rather cryptic language that makes it difficult to understand. Our main goal therefore is the elaboration of personal construct theory towards a hermeneutic constructivism, and its reformulation according to a narrative metaphor.

Acknowledgements

The first thought can only go to Maria Laura Nuzzo, who passed away shortly after we received the proposal to write this book. Although Maria Laura did not participate in the drafting of the book, she appears as a fully entitled co-author. It is not rhetorical to affirm that everything I wrote is the outcome of 26 years of the personal and professional life we fully shared.

In regarding this book as the crowning achievement of many years of psychotherapeutic experience, a thought must also go towards two other people, who passed away prematurely and who marked our professional adventure: they are Vittorio Guidano and Don Bannister. Vittorio was our first mentor: his enthusiasm and creativity taught us to be intellectually nonconformist and to always search for new paths to pursue. Don embodied intellectual transgression and, in his unique style, helped us to understand how personal construct theory represents a whole universe open to exploration and elaboration.

In time, other colleagues, through innumerable conversations and discussions, contributed in the elaboration of our way of considering constructivist psychotherapy. Among the first are Lorenzo Cionini and Gianluca Provvedi, with whom I founded in Florence the school of specialisation in constructivist-oriented cognitive psychotherapy at the *Center of Studies in Cognitive Psychotherapy* (CESIPc). We have also had contributions from some of our former students, who have become fine psychotherapists and teachers in the school: Simona Colombari, Alessandra Favaro, Mara Ognibeni, M. Cristina Ortu, Elena Sagliocco, Cristina Sassi, Mariaemanuela Timpano and Ombretta Zoppi.

Moreover, we owe a lot to our students, who, with at times embarrassing questions and sharp observations, have constantly put us in the position of having to look in-depth at the most controversial and obscure aspects of our way of interpreting constructivist psychotherapy. Of course we owe a lot to our clients, their narratives and their willingness to join us in those routes we traced walking together, step by step.

Our participation at international and European conferences has given us the opportunity to meet the community of personal construct psychology and to relate with many people who have enriched our formation in a decisive way. Among these, we like to remember particularly Richard Bell, Lluis Botella, Trevor Butt, Ana Catina, Pam Denicolo, Franz R. Epting, Guillem Feixas, Fay Fransella, Devorah Kalekin-Fishman, Larry M. Leitner, Miller Mair, James C. Mancuso, Spencer A. McWilliams, Robert A. Neimeyer, Jonathan D. Raskin, Joern W. Scheer, Linda L. Viney, Beverly M. Walker, Bill Warren and David A. Winter.

And now, a special thank you to our daughter Giulia who, according to many colleagues who have met her, embodies the constructivist epistemology, maybe because she was born and raised in hardly a traditional family and social environment; to Maria Laura's first child, Simone Nicolò, and his father Francesco, who were also involved in frequent family discussions on constructivism, and more recently ready to encourage me in bringing forth the writing of this book; to Marcello Cini, a friend, whose clearness of mind and intellectual honesty has represented to us a point of reference for many years; and to Elisabeth Takla, to whom I am grateful for reviewing my English, a bit lame, and especially for giving me back, together with family and friends, the chance of living an emotionally fulfilled life.

Gabriele Chiari

Chapter 1

Personal construct psychotherapy: forerunner of constructivist psychotherapies

Around the middle of the last century, Dr. George A. Kelly, a psychology teacher at the Ohio State University in Kansas, began to share, with about twenty colleagues on a weekly basis, hundreds of pages of notes he had been accumulating over the last twenty years. The original aim was to write a handbook of clinical procedures; but, when the author realised that the *hows* of clinical practice rested on many implicit basic assumptions taken for granted, he began coping with the necessity to explain the *whys*. When doing that, he discovered that 'in the years of relatively isolated clinical practice we had wandered far off the beaten paths of psychology, much farther than we had ever suspected' (Kelly, 1991a/1955, p. xi).

Much has been speculated about the reasons for Kelly's ideas on psychology and psychotherapy, which were uncommon in those times (Fransella, 1995): the importance placed on the tendency of people to invent and create has been related to Kelly's lonely childhood, being the only child of farming parents near Perth, Kansas (Rychlak, 1981); the emphasis on the human potential to live unconventionally, by bold experimentation rather than blind faith in authority, has been seen as the counterpoint to the religious ideology of his conservative Christian parents (Mair, 1985); the rigorous formal structure of **personal construct** theory and its more popular assessment technique, the repertory grid, have been supposed to derive from Kelly's former degree in physics and mathematics (Fransella, 1983, 2000); his view of personal identity in terms of socially embedded roles, as well as the therapeutic use of techniques such as role-playing and fixed-role therapy, have been connected to his former coaching in dramatics and to his reading of Moreno, the founder of psychodrama (Rychlak, 1981).

However, after three years of discussions with the so-called 'Thursday-nighters', *The Psychology of Personal Constructs* was published in 1955. Two volumes with a total of 1218 pages, the first entitled *A theory of personality*, and the second devoted to *Clinical diagnosis and psychotherapy*. The book had some authoritative, on the whole flattering, reviews (Bruner, 1956; McArthur, 1956; Rogers, 1956), but in practice soon fell into oblivion. After all, how could such a weighty tome, with a preface like the following, be successful?

> It is only fair to warn the reader about what may be in store for him. In the first place, he is likely to find missing most of the familiar landmarks of psychology books. For example, the term *learning*, so honourably embedded in most psychological texts, scarcely appears at all. That is wholly intentional; we are for throwing it overboard altogether. There is no *ego*, no *emotion*, no *motivation*, no *reinforcement*, no *drive*, no *unconscious*, no *need*. There are some words with brand-new psychological definitions, words like *foci of convenience, preemption, propositionality, fixed-role therapy, creativity cycle, transitive diagnosis*, and *the credulous approach*. *Anxiety* is defined in a special systematic way. *Role, guilt* and *hostility* carry definitions altogether unexpected by many; and, to make heresy complete, there is no extensive bibliography.
>
> (Kelly, 1991a/1955, p. xii, italics in original)

What kind of reader could ever be interested in these upsetting ideas? Kelly himself gives the answer:

> an adventuresome soul who is not one bit afraid of thinking unorthodox thoughts about people, who dares peer out at the world through the eyes of strangers, who has not invested beyond his means in either ideas or vocabulary, and who is looking for an *ad interim*, rather than an ultimate, set of psychological insights.
>
> (1991a/1955, p. xii, italics in original)

Such readers had yet to come. For many years, the psychology of personal constructs was to survive in small groups of followers dispersed in few countries (Neimeyer, 1985). Furthermore, most of the literature quoting Kelly's work has made use of forms of grid test (see section 4.4) in research and assessment, often with 'no logical relation to the principles of personal construct theory' (Adams-Webber, 1979, p. 20). Only with the spreading of psychological **constructivism** in the 1980s, was Kelly's work finally to find adequate readership.

In this chapter we shall briefly outline the basics of personal construct theory, as well as its application to various fields of psychology, particularly psychotherapy. Readers already familiar with these topics can skip this part of the book. In Chapters 3, 4, 5 and 6 we shall elaborate and advance some of Kelly's ideas by expounding our narrative hermeneutic interpretation of personal construct psychotherapy.

1.1 Personal construct theory

In our opinion, 'personal construct theory not only has been the first constructivist *theory* of personality, but it is to date the only constructivist theory of personality *and* psychotherapy' (Chiari & Nuzzo, 1996a, p. 27, italics in original).

By assuming that '*all of our present interpretations of the universe are subject to revision or replacement*', Kelly (1991a/1955, p. 11, italics in the original) uncovers the basic philosophical root of his theoretical position. Kelly was aware that philosophical speculation is inescapable for any scientific investigation, and consequently he chose to state his underlying assumptions at the very beginning of his work. He did that by coining two expressions that – consistent with his theoretical formulation – are shaped like the contrasting **poles** of a discrimination, a construct: *accumulative fragmentalism vs. constructive alternativism* (Chiari & Nuzzo, 2003a).

According to the prevailing epistemological assumption of accumulative fragmentalism, knowledge derives from the gathering of fragmented facts, that is, truth is collected piece by piece. On the other hand, in the modern debate on the nature of knowledge, the idea that all facts are theory-laden is increasingly widely held, thanks in particular to Popper's (1959/1934) and Kuhn's (1962) criticism of the inductive view of science. Science proceeds by means of conjectures and refutations: any person, as a scientist, does the same, according to Kelly. But Kelly goes even further, taking the stand that there are always some alternative constructions available to choose from in dealing with the world: 'No one needs to paint himself into a corner; no one needs to be completely hemmed in by circumstances; no one needs to be the victim of his biography' (1991a/1955, p. 11). Constructive alternativism 'leads one to regard a large accumulation of facts as an open invitation to some far-reaching reconstruction which will reduce them to a mass of trivialities' (1970a/1966, p. 2). In other words, Kelly believes in the possibility of interpreting the world in many, equally legitimate ways, since:

> we can no longer rest assured that human progress may proceed step by step in an orderly fashion from the known to the unknown. Neither our senses nor our doctrines provide us with the immediate knowledge required for such a philosophy of science. What we think we know is anchored only in our own assumptions, not in the bed rock of truth itself, and that world we seek to understand remains always on the horizons of our thoughts.
>
> (1977/1963, pp. 5–6)

On the other hand:

> to say that whatever exists can be reconstrued is by no manner or means to say that it makes no difference how it is construed. Quite the

contrary. It often makes a world of difference. Some reconstructions may open fresh channels for a rich and productive life. Others may offer one no alternative save suicide.

(1969b/1958, p. 228)

1.1.1 The stance of anticipation: the fundamental postulate

Grounded in this philosophical stance, personal construct theory opens with a fundamental postulate: 'a person's processes are psychologically channelized by the ways in which he anticipates events' (Kelly, 1991a/1955, p. 32).

The above is precisely a postulate, that is, an assumption, a tentative statement of truth to be meant as 'let us suppose, for the sake of the discussion which is to follow, that. . .'. What would ensue if people's processes were oriented by their ways to anticipate events?

The postulate represents the foundation for the whole theoretical building to follow. The person is the subject of the theory: 'the individual person rather than any part of the person, any group of people, or any particular process manifested in the person's behaviour' (ibid, p. 33). The choice of the person as the subject of psychology could appear obvious, but is not considered so by many psychologists.

Currently many psychologists feel that psychology should concern itself more with 'whole' people. It should centre more on 'real human experience'. This is comical in one sense – it is as if sailors suddenly decided they ought to take an interest in ships – but necessary in another. A variety of vanities have caused psychologists to turn their backs on the complete and purposeful person. A craving to be seen, above all, as scientists has led them to favour the clockwork doll, the chemical interaction or the environmentally imprisoned rat as their models of humanity.

(Bannister & Fransella, 1986, p. 1)

So, the person. And the person is presumed from the outset to be a process: 'the person is not an object which is temporarily in a moving state but is himself a form of motion' (Kelly, 1991a/1955, p. 33). One does not have to invoke any special notions (dynamics, drives, motivation or force) to explain why the object of psychology does not remain inert: as far as the theory is concerned, it is never inert.

The person's processes are 'channelized': a metaphor suitable for indicating that they are structured, not 'fluttering about' (ibid., p. 34). And they are channelised by the ways in which the person anticipates events. Here is one of the most revolutionary features of personal construct theory. People are not moved by occurrences of the past, be it as victims of reinforcement schedules or as victims of their infancy. Nor do people aim at achieving a pre-established state of mind. Instead, they strive to give personal meanings to the world, and to move in the world checking out how that meaning allows them to anticipate it.

The well-known metaphor of 'man-the-scientist' (ibid., p. 4) illustrates efficiently both the philosophy of constructive alternativism and the fundamental postulate. Just like a scientist, any person poses questions about the nature of the universe, observes the world, builds structures of meaning, and, behaving on the basis of such interpretive hypotheses, experiments with them in order to organise their experience and anticipate events. In doing so, the person is regarded as an 'inquiring man', to the extent that:

> construct theory sees man not as an infantile savage, nor as a just-cleverer-than-the-average-rat, nor as the victim of his biography, but as an inveterate inquirer, self-invented and shaped, sometimes wonderfully and sometimes disastrously, by the direction of his inquiries.
>
> (Bannister & Fransella, 1986, p. vii)

It is thanks to this image of the person that the theory shows its reflexivity, that is, personal construct theory is a construction which is accounted for by personal construct theory.

> One of the effects of this [treating scientists as persons and persons as scientists] is to make the model person of personal construct psychology look recognizable like you: that is, unless you are the very modest kind of person who sees themselves as the stimulus-jerked puppet of learning theory, the primitive infant of psychoanalytic theory or the perambulating telephone exchange of information theory.
>
> (Ibid., p. 4)

In the formulation of the fundamental postulate, there is an apparently odd grammatical construction: the choice to use the adverb 'psychologically' rather than the adjective 'psychological' ('a person's processes are psychologically channelized. . .' instead of 'a person's psychological processes are channelized. . .'). Of course, the choice is deliberate, and shows the consistency of Kelly's ideas about constructive alternativism:

> we do not conceive the substance of psychology to be itself psychological – or physiological, or sociological, or to be preempted by any system. A person's processes are what they are; and psychology, physiology, or what have you, are simply systems concocted for trying to anticipate them. Thus, when we use the term *psychologically*, we

mean that we are conceptualizing processes in a psychological manner, not that the processes are psychological rather than something else.

(Kelly, 1991a/1955, p. 33, italics in the original)

The following quotation appears to be effectively illustrative of what can be regarded also as a constructivist solution of the mind–body problem in terms of modes of construing events:

> If we contemplate a young lady crossing a bridge (a lay construction) then we may equally construe her as a 'series of moments of force about a point' (engineer's construing), as 'a poor credit risk' (banker's construing), as 'a mass of whirling electrons about nuclei' (physicist's construing), as 'a soul in peril of mortal sin' (theological construing) or as 'a likely dish' (young man's construing). We do not have to assume that she is *really* any of these. We can accept that they are all constructions which have some explanatory value and predictive utility, depending on the networks of constructs from which they stem.
>
> (Bannister, 1968, p. 229, italics in the original)

Relying upon the above metatheoretical foundation, the theory is then elaborated by means of eleven corollaries. We shall briefly expound them and, in doing that, we shall introduce other formal aspects of personal construct theory.

1.1.2 Knowledge as interpretation: the construction corollary

First, what are the ways in which people anticipate events, thus channelising their processes? The *construction corollary* states that '*a person anticipates events by construing their replications*' (Kelly, 1991a/1955, p. 35, italics in the original). If the person is a process, also the substance that a person construes is itself from the beginning 'an unending and undifferentiated process'. To explain what he means by 'replication', Kelly uses the analogy of listening to music, since it emphasises that the replication emerges because of our interpretation, rather than being something already out there to discover:

> Only when man attunes his ear to recurrent themes in the monotonous flow does his universe begin to make sense to him. Like a musician, he must phrase his experience in order to make sense out of it. The phrases are distinguished events. The separation of events is what man produces for himself when he decides to chop up time into manageable lengths.
>
> (1991a/1955, p. 36)

The 'recurrent themes' the person perceives represent the basis for the dichotomous nature of personal constructs, as will be explained in the following corollary.

1.1.3 People live in unique experiential worlds: the individuality corollary

In the *individuality corollary* Kelly gives his answer to the question, 'Why is it that two people in the same situation behave in different ways?' In line with the fundamental postulate, the answer is that they are not in the 'same' situation, to the extent that they interpret it differently. The situation appears the same only from the point of view of a third person looking at it through their construction. In the formulation of the corollary, *'persons differ from each other in their construction of events'* (ibid., p. 38, italics in the original).

1.1.4 The sharing of personal knowledge: the commonality corollary

The *commonality corollary* is the complement of the individuality corollary, stating that *'to the extent that one person employs a construction of experience which is similar to that employed by another, his psychological processes are similar to those of the other person'* (ibid., p. 63, italics in the original), or, more consistent with constructive alternativism, 'his processes are *psychologically similar* to those of the other person' (Kelly, 1970a/1966, p. 20, italics ours).

The preceding two corollaries suggest that when people are said to be different or similar, it is not necessarily because they have had different or similar experiences, but because they have placed, respectively, different or similar interpretations on their experiences. In the picturesque style of Bannister and Fransella:

> two bank clerks may work at adjoining counters and live what are, in objective terms, very 'similar' lives, but they may be entirely unable to make sense out of each other. Yet one of the bank clerks may well be corresponding with an aged missionary working out his or her life's significance in the jungles of some tropical country. The bank clerk and the missionary may find their exchange of letters full of mutual understanding, because they have basic similarities in their ways of construing events.
>
> (1986, p. 29)

1.1.5 Looking for an overall understanding: the organisation corollary

However, what characterises personality, even more than the differences between individual personal constructs, is their arrangement in hierarchical systems. According to the *organisation corollary*, '*each person characteristically evolves, for his convenience in anticipating events, a construction system embracing ordinal relationships between constructs*' (Kelly, 1991a/1955, p. 39, italics in the original).

Construction systems are more stable than the individual constructs of which they are composed, even though they are continually taking new configurations. These changes are made possible by re-organisations of the relations between the person's constructs, these being only 'ordinal'. By using this term, Kelly means that one construct may subsume another construct as one of its **elements**. For example, a person may subsume under the construct *self-confident vs. insecure* constructs like *relies on himself vs. depends on others* and *expresses himself vs. restrains himself*. In turn, the construct *self-confident vs. insecure*, together with *responsible vs. irresponsible*, may be the element of the construct *likely to be accepted by other people vs. likely to be rejected*.

When one construct subsumes another, it may be termed *superordinate construct*, the other becoming a **subordinate construct**. Within a construction system there may be several levels of ordinal relationships. A **regnant construct** is a kind of **superordinate construct** which assigns each of its elements to a category on an all-or-none basis, as in classical logic. It has the effect of making its subordinate constructs **constellatory** (see following section).

1.1.6 Meaning needs a contrast: the dichotomy corollary

In any case, '*a person's construction system is composed of a finite number of dichotomous constructs*', as stated in the *dichotomy corollary* (ibid., p. 41, italics in the original). At any instant, the alternatives that the person's processes can follow are finite, and they are represented by the person's repertory of constructs. Given the continual creation of new channels based on the old ones, these alternatives are finite but not definitive.

Moreover, the dichotomy corollary elaborates the notion that it might be useful to regard personal constructs as having a bipolar nature. This possibility indeed derives, as suggested previously, from implications of the construction corollary. Remember that 'the separation of events is what man produces for himself when he decides to chop up time into manageable lengths'. Kelly goes on: 'Within these limited segments, which are based on recurrent themes, man begins to discover the bases for likenesses and differences' (ibid., pp. 36–37). Once it is perceived that after a period of lightness follows one of darkness, and another of lightness, one can abstract the recurrent theme in terms of the rising and setting of the sun, that is, of a succession of days and nights. At least three events are needed to achieve this end: two of them construed as similar, the third as different. Until a new period of light follows that of darkness, there is no basis for the construction of a regularity.

Therefore, 'a construct is a way in which some things are construed as being alike and yet different from others' (ibid., p. 74). More precisely, a construct is an aspect by which at least two elements are construed as similar and, for the same aspect, different from at least a third one – the 'elements' being those things or events which are abstracted by a construct. Consequently, 'each construct involves two poles, one at each end of its dichotomy. The elements associated at each pole are like each other with respect to the construct and are unlike the elements at the other pole' (ibid., p. 96). The relationship between the two poles of a construct is one of **contrast**. When specifically referring to elements at one pole of a construct, Kelly suggests using the term *likeness end*, and the term *contrast end* when referring to the elements at the opposite pole. Another way of referring to the poles of a construct derives from the observation that usually one of them embraces most of the elements and can be explicitly mentioned. In this case, it may be useful to term it *emergent pole*, and the one contrasting with the former, *implicit pole*. Sometimes the latter is symbolised only implicitly by the emergent term.

The above distinctions relative to the poles of any personal construct (*likeness end vs. contrast end, emergent pole vs. implicit pole*) are in their turn personal constructs, and could not be otherwise. Yet, they have a peculiarity, being ways to refer to parts of personal constructs. We shall meet many other constructs that the clinician could use to subsume the clients' constructs, parts of them, their construction systems or particular processes in their personal construing. On the whole, they can be regarded as a system of *professional* or *diagnostic constructs*, which can be applied to personal construct systems in order to enable the clinicians to use the approach of personal construct psychology and psychotherapy in the relationship with their clients.

The possibility of using words as **symbols** of constructs represents the basis for another of such professional distinctions: that between *verbal* and *non-verbal constructs*. In fact, it is important not to confound construing with verbal formulation. The person's way of construing the world can be 'explicitly formulated or implicitly acted out, verbally expressed or utterly inarticulate, consistent with other courses of behaviour or inconsistent with them, intellectually reasoned or vegetatively sensed' (ibid., p. 7). A subset of non-verbal constructs is represented by the *preverbal constructs*: those which continue to be used even though they have no consistent word symbol, and that may or may not have been devised before the person had command of speech symbolism.

A particular set of professional constructs is relative to the nature of the control of personal constructs over their elements. A construct is used in a **pre-emptive** mode when it pre-empts its elements for membership exclusively in its own realm, according to a 'nothing-but' modality: 'if this man is gay, he is *nothing but* a gay'. A construct is used in a **constellatory** mode when it fixes the other realm membership of its elements, according to an 'if-then' modality: '*if* this man is gay, *then* he is also touchy, effeminate, and libertine'. Both the above modes are characteristic of prejudiced thinking. A construct is used in a **propositional** mode when it does not disturb the other realm memberships of its elements, that is, it carries no implications regarding the other realm membership of its elements, according to an 'as if' modality: 'I may look at this man *as if* he were (among many other things) gay'.

Propositionality and pre-emption have a central role in the person's process of decision-making. The **C-P-C** Cycle (*circumspection-pre-emption-control cycle*) is defined as 'a sequence of construction involving, in succession, circumspection, preemption, and control, and leading to a choice which precipitates the person into a particular situation' (ibid., p. 379). Circumspection enables the person to look at elements propositionally, or in a multidimensional manner. Subsequently, the person must choose the most relevant axis along which to construe the situation, selecting what they believe to be the crucial issue involved. Lastly, pre-emption is followed by the control, or choice, according to the choice corollary (see section 1.1.8).

1.1.7 Boundaries of convenience: the range corollary

According to the choice corollary (see section 1.1.8) the *range corollary* states that '*a construct is convenient for the anticipation of a finite range of events only*' (ibid., p. 48, italics in the original). Consequently, a personal construct has a **range of convenience** and a **focus of convenience**: they comprise those elements to which the user would find the construct respectively applicable or maximally applicable. To most of us, for instance, the construct *green vs. ripe* may be applied to people in relation to their age, and more suitably to fruits, but towels are out of its range of convenience. A construct which subsumes a wide variety of events is called **comprehensive** (e.g., for most people, the construct *good vs. bad*), whereas a construct which subsumes a narrow variety of events is termed **incidental** (e.g. the construct *serotonergic vs. dopaminergic*).

1.1.8 Decision is always for the best: the choice corollary

The answer to the key question as to what determines the application of one or the other pole of a construct to an element is given by the *choice corollary: 'a person chooses for himself that alternative in a dichotomized construct through which he anticipates the greater possibility for extension and definition of his system'* (ibid., p. 45, italics in the original). This corollary appears as a coherent implication of the fundamental postulate: 'If a person's processes are psychologically channelized by the ways in which he anticipates events, and those ways present themselves in dichotomous form, it follows that he must choose between the poles of his dichotomies in a manner which is predicted by his anticipations' (ibid., p. 45). In a more contemporary and plain terminology, we could say that people create and re-create their narratives while enacting their stories by choosing the version of the plot that appears to be more meaningful to their experiential world. Whichever the choice – either for a constricted certainty or for a broadened understanding – the decision is supposed to be essentially elaborative: the person always makes what Kelly calls an *elaborative choice*.

The relation of the person's processes with the environmental ones results in the continuous verification of the person's anticipations. Anticipation is inherent to any construction. 'By the very process of identifying the event as something replicated, we imply that it may happen again [. . .]. Thus it is impossible not to imply prediction whenever one construes anything' (ibid., p. 84). If I construe glass as fragile (an abstraction of repeated experiences), I anticipate it breaking should it fall. If it does, my anticipation is validated; otherwise not. '**Validation** represents the compatibility (subjectively construed) between one's prediction and the outcome he observes. *Invalidation* represents incompatibility (subjectively construed) between one's prediction and the outcome he observes' (ibid., p. 110, italics and bold ours). As one's anticipations are successively revised in the light of this verification, the construction system undergoes a progressive evolution.

1.1.9 Change as reconstruction: the experience corollary

Development is not the prerogative of children and adolescents: in greater or lesser extent, people continually develop. As stated by the *experience corollary*, *'a person's construction system varies as he successively construes the replications of events'* (ibid., p. 50, italics in the original). Therefore, it is not the mere succession of events that constitutes experience. It is worthwhile to mention the case, recounted by Kelly (ibid., p. 120), of a veteran school administrator who boasted having thirteen years of experience, whereas he effectively had only one year of experience repeated thirteen times. Actually:

a person can be a witness to a tremendous parade of episodes and yet, if he fails to keep making something out of them, he gains little in the way of experience from having been around when they happened. It is not what happens around him that makes a man experienced; it is the successive construing and re-construing of what happens, as it happens, that enriches the experience of his life.

(Ibid., p. 52)

1.1.10 The constraint on change: the modulation corollary

However, the change is not unbounded. As specified by the *modulation corollary*, '*the variation in a person's construction system is limited by the permeability of the constructs within whose range of convenience the variants lie*' (ibid., p. 54, italics in the original). This is to say that the variation itself must take place within a system, and therefore falls under the control of the constructs superordinate to it.

Even the changes which the person attempts within himself must be construed by him. The new outlook which a person gains from experience is itself an event; and, being an event in his life, it needs to be construed by him if he is to make any sense out of it.

(Ibid., p. 55)

This view is particularly outstanding, because it patently testifies that the assumption of personal construct theory implies what nowadays is defined by Maturana (1987) as structural determinism (see section 2.4.4). In Kelly's terms, 'one does not learn certain things merely from the nature of the stimuli which play upon one; one learns only what one's framework is designed to permit one to see in the stimuli' (Kelly, 1991a/1955, p. 55).

The notion of **permeability**, which appears in the modulation corollary, represents another professional construct. 'A personal construct is permeable if it will admit to its range of convenience new elements which are not yet construed within its framework' (ibid., p. 56). It is impermeable if it rejects elements on the basis of their newness. In the words of scientific method, a permeable construct has more of the qualities of a theoretical rather than of a hypothetical formulation. A theory is constructed in an open-ended form, so as to embrace and accept a wide variety of experimental results and to undergo progressive changes before being eventually rejected. A hypothesis is deliberately construed 'so that there can be no question about what it embraces and no doubt about its being wholly shattered or left intact at the end of an experiment' (ibid., p. 57). The relative degree of permeability and impermeability of a person's superordinate constructs has a central role in their conservation of an adaptation with the environment, and therefore in the clinical and psychotherapeutic field.

1.1.11 A system of alternatives: the fragmentation corollary

If the variation in a person's construction system is limited by the permeability of the constructs within whose ranges of convenience the variants lie, it does not need to be subordinate to all the preceding aspects of the system. As affirmed by the *fragmentation corollary*, '*a person may successively employ a variety of construction subsystems which are inferentially incompatible with each other*' (ibid., p. 58, italics in original). 'It is possible that what Willie thinks today may not be inferred directly from what he was thinking yesterday. His shift, nevertheless, [. . .] is consistent with the more stable aspects of his system' (ibid., p. 58). The relationship between the old and the new constructs can be collateral rather than lineal. 'A construct system is a hierarchy and also a series of subsystems having varying ranges of convenience. Therefore, conclusions about the "same" series of events can be drawn at levels which are not directly consistent with each other' (Bannister & Fransella, 1986, p. 16).

1.1.12 Understanding others for construing oneself: the sociality corollary

The last corollary described by Kelly, the *sociality corollary*, deserves a special consideration. It deals with a particular implication of the fundamental postulate, since the events anticipated by a person are represented here by the construction processes of another person. In this case, '*to the extent that one person construes the construction processes of another, he may play a role in a social process involving the other person*' (1991a/1955, p. 66, italics in the original). Therefore, in order to play a role, people have not so much to construe things as other people do, according to the commonality corollary, but they must construe the others' outlook, that is, subsume the other people's construing efforts: briefly, they must try to understand others.

Of course, there are different levels at which a person can construe other people's construction processes. In walking down a pavement, for instance, it is enough to anticipate the direction people heading toward us intend to take in order not to bump into them. For the more complex interplay of a couple, the understanding must cover a wider range of activities, so that the members can predict each other's behaviours in various situations. Furthermore, understanding does not have to be mutual; the therapist–client relationship exemplifies a greater understanding on behalf of one member than on the other. It is this very asymmetry that allows the therapists to play a role based upon their understanding of the client and the subsuming of this understanding under a system of professional constructs (see section 4.2), and to prevent the client from developing a role under certain conjectures about the therapist as a person (see section 6.3.2).

According to the preceding defined notion of role, people act in relationship with each other based on their reciprocal understanding: technically speaking, on the basis of their *role constructs*, defined as 'constructs which have the presumed constructs of other persons as elements in their **contexts**' (ibid, p. 145, bold our own).

Role constructs are not the only ones supposed to govern interpersonal relations. Long before the person is able to do the subsuming which is an essential feature of role construction, there are certain constructs which are supposed to relate the processes of nutrition and general survival to the peoples lives. 'For the young child the fact of having food is associated with the fact of having mother. The two are collected by means of a construct. [. . .] Similarly, the child construes other persons in relation to his survival' (Kelly, 1991b/1955, p. 79). The constructs by which certain people are construed in relation to one's survival are called *dependency constructs*. Given that they appear before the child has acquired language, dependency constructs are non-verbal constructs. Moreover, they cannot be easily applied to other people, thus showing a relative impermeability, as if the child could say 'only my mummy can feed me'. Finally, they tend to pre-empt their elements for membership exclusively in their own realm, as if the child could say 'my mummy is nothing but the person who feeds me'. Only through a progressive permeability and propositionality of dependency constructs, the adolescent, and later the adult, are likely to disperse their dependency through a greater number of people, thus acquiring a more mature sociality (see section 3.7.1).

1.2 Personal construct psychology

Personal construct psychology – including personal construct psychotherapy – is concerned with *professional* constructions about *personal* constructions. Namely, it can be considered a meta-science, 'a way of making sense out of the ways in which people make sense of their world' (Bannister & Fransella, 1986, p. 19). Under the preceding heading, we introduced some professional constructs designed to this aim. Many others have been suggested by Kelly, and among them those relative to particular transitions likely to occur within personal construct systems. They cover in a radically new manner what traditional psychologies describe under the heading of emotion, and we shall briefly outline them in the next section, given their relevancy to clinical psychology and psychotherapy.

Grounded in the basic tenets of personal construct theory, a whole psychology has been slowly but increasingly evolving. The difficulty in the spreading of personal construct psychology, in our opinion, can be attributed to several, intertwined causes (Chiari, 2000). To begin, personal construct theory's focus of convenience – as Kelly himself explicitly states – is psychotherapy, 'the psychological reconstruction of life' (1991a/1955, p. 17). Moreover, Kelly ignores his predecessors and caricatures competing theories, in particular psychoanalysis and behaviourism, thus opening the way for the intellectual isolationism still common among his followers (Neimeyer, 1985). The language of personal construct theory is very technical, and many terms are unfamiliar or acquire an unusual meaning. The epistemological assumption goes against common sense, and is difficult to grasp. The theory has a very rigorous formal structure that can discourage its further elaboration. Such difficulties, in some cases, result in a superficial understanding of personal construct theory, and in its application in terms of a trivial subjectivism that mortifies its revolutionary features (Mair, 1985).

Notwithstanding this, personal construct theory has been finding a lot of applications in the various fields of psychology, as testified by a recent, comprehensive review of the literature (Fransella, 2003a, 2005) and by some introductory works (Burr & Butt, 1992; Butt, 2008; Walker & Winter, 2007). On the whole, they contrast with the scientific criteria of naturalism, positivism and rationalism, which have marked the birth and development of psychology, opening an alternative which maintains the primacy of personal experience over any pretension of objective knowledge.

Thus, the peculiar epistemological assumption of personal construct theory leads to a radically new way of understanding knowledge and learning and consequently the process of teaching, seen as the struggle to enlarge mutual comprehension between people who have different world views. The application of Kelly's ideas to educational psychology is therefore particularly florid (Denicolo & Pope, 2001; Pope & Denicolo, 2001; Ravenette, 1999).

For similar reasons, personal construct theory can give fresh contributions to the field of developmental psychology (Butler & Green, 2007; Salmon, 1980, 1985). In this connection, the links between Kelly and Piaget are often pointed out (Mancuso & Hunter, 1985; Soffer, 1993).

There has been a considerable development in the application of personal construct theory to business (Stewart & Stewart, 1981), management (Purdy, 2000) and organisations (Cornelius, 2002), as well as to individuals in relation to culture and society (Chiari & Nuzzo, 2003b; Kalekin-Fishman & Walker, 1996; Stringer & Bannister, 1979). Promising signs of application of personal construct theory are relative to politics (du Preez, 1980; Scheer, 1996; Stojnov, 1996) and forensic psychology (Horley, 2003). The *Journal of Constructivist Psychology* (formerly *International Journal of Personal Construct Psychology*), has been publishing an increasing number of papers in which the various fields of psychology are dealt with according to a personal construct approach.

1.3 Personal construct psychotherapy

As already mentioned, Kelly conceived personal construct theory having in mind psychotherapy as its focus of convenience, and most of the literature on personal construct psychology is specifically (Epting, 1984; Faidley & Leitner, 1993; Fransella, 1972; Landfield, 1971, 1980; Leitner & Dunnett, 1993; Neimeyer & Neimeyer, 1987; Viney, 1996; Winter & Viney, 2005) or largely (Adams-Webber & Mancuso, 1983; Bannister, 1985; Beail, 1985; Bonarius *et al.*, 1981; Epting & Landfield, 1985; Landfield & Epting, 1987; Landfield & Leitner, 1980; Mair, 1989a) devoted to that, as well as to counselling (Epting, 1984; Fransella & Dalton, 1990) and clinical psychology (Button, 1985; Dunnett, 1988; Winter, 1992).

Given the peculiarity of the philosophical assumption of constructive alternativism, personal construct psychotherapy shows several features that make it different from nearly all of the traditional psychotherapeutic approaches.

First of all, the very notion of *disorder* changes dramatically (see section 6.2), turning from an entity which affects an individual and has intrinsic characteristics such those listed in the *Diagnostic and Statistical Manual of Mental Disorders*, DSM-IV-TR (American Psychiatric Association, 2000), into 'any personal construction which is used repeatedly in spite of consistent invalidation' (Kelly, 1991b/1955, p. 193). In their continuous interaction with the environment, people have the possibility to elaborate their constructions by verifying (validating or invalidating) their anticipations. The failure in reconstructing some aspects of their experiential reality results in a block of the personal process of elaboration, and consequently in the reapplication of the same, though invalidated, construction. Coherently, the whole psychotherapeutic process is aimed at encouraging the overcoming of the impasse, thus reinstating the movement of the personal construction system.

In order to accomplish this, personal construct psychotherapy demands of the therapist to show *acceptance* of the client (see section 4.2). Kelly technically defines acceptance as 'the movement of the therapist's mental processes in the construed direction of commonality with the client's construct system' (1991b/1955, p. 342). Metaphorically, acceptance is defined as 'the readiness to see the world through another person's eyes' (ibid., p. 421), or '[the therapist's attempt] to put himself in the client's shoes' (ibid., pp. 65–66). It is, apparently, the meaning given by some authors (Dymond, 1950; Mead, 1934) to the notion of empathy as the ability to assume the other's viewpoint, to understand the world according to the perspective of another person. And acceptance is, in Kelly's approach to psychotherapy, 'a precondition to the intentional adoption of role relationships' (1991a/1955, p. 277), and hence a precondition to any personal reconstruction.

In fact, according to the sociality corollary, by construing the construction processes of the clients, the therapists may play a role in their relationship with them. In particular, they can encourage the clients' experiencing of new ways of relating to others by extricating themselves from the constructions that the clients try to apply to them.

The therapist's construction of the client's construction processes, however, is only half of the affair of acceptance. As soon as the personal construct psychotherapists understand the client's perspective, they have to subsume it into their system of professional constructs.

In the preceding section we defined some professional constructs, such as *verbal vs. non-verbal* construct, *superordinate vs. subordinate* construct, *permeable vs. impermeable* construct. Now we have to outline other professional constructs that have a basic role in personal construct psychology and psychotherapy.

If any personal construct implies an anticipation, not every anticipation is equally precise. Thus, a distinction can be made between **tight constructs**, 'those which lead to unvarying predictions', and **loose constructs**, 'those which lead to varying predictions but which [. . .] may be said to retain their identity' (Kelly, 1991a/1955, p. 357). Like the other structural features of personal construing accounted for by professional constructs, also the dimension *tightness vs. looseness* can vary in time. Actually, in order to conserve adaptation with the environment, personal constructs can become looser or tighter. Moreover, a sequence of loosening and tightening is the basis of the **creativity cycle**, 'one which starts with loosened constructions and terminates with tightened and validated constructions' (ibid., p. 388, bold ours). Given that psychotherapy is regarded as a creative process, it involves a series of creativity cycles.

Another fundamental process is relative to the extension of the **perceptual field**, that is, the professional dimension **dilation vs. constriction**. 'Dilation occurs when a person broadens his perceptual field in order to reorganize it on a more comprehensive level'. On the other hand, 'constriction occurs when a person narrows his perceptual field in order to minimize apparent incompatibilities' (ibid., p. 391).

In an ever-changing personal construct system, not every variation has the same impact on the person's perspective. A distinction can be made between *core* and *peripheral* **constructs**. The former are 'those which govern a person's **maintenance processes**', that is, 'those by which he maintains his identity and existence'. By *maintenance processes* Kelly refers to those processes which lie outside the range of convenience of psychology, being better construed within a physiological construction system. The peripheral constructs are 'those which can be altered without serious modification of core structure' (ibid., p. 356). Psychotherapy usually deals with core constructs.

A set of professional constructs has to do with the person's awareness of a transition in their construct system, mostly relative to core constructs. As we previously anticipated, Kelly's notion of *transition* covers what the traditional psychologies deal with under the heading of emotion. There is however a fundamental difference between the two notions. Kelly remains faithful to his epistemological assumption by treating the topic in terms of professional constructs relative to the person's construction of particularly important transitions in their construct system. In doing so, Kelly also avoids falling into the dualistic (cognition/emotion) viewpoint held by most of the theories on emotion (Chiari & Nuzzo, 1985, 1988). This choice gives the impression, to those who had not thoroughly understood the theory and its epistemological assumption, that the subject emotion is not adequately dealt with, and that the theory is too intellectual. Kelly's following specification deserves being quoted:

> The psychology of personal constructs is built upon an intellectual model, to be sure, but its application is not intended to be limited to that which is ordinarily called intellectual or cognitive. It is also taken to apply to that which is commonly called emotional or affective and to that which has to do with action or conation. The classical threefold division of psychology into cognition, affection, and conation has been completely abandoned in the psychology of personal contructs.
>
> (1991a/1955, p. 91)

Curiously enough, Bruner reviewed *The Psychology of Personal Constructs* writing that 'these excellent, original, and infuriatingly prolix two volumes easily nominate themselves for the distinction of being the single greatest contribution of the past decade to the theory of personality functioning', even though 'the book fails signally [. . .] in dealing convincingly with the human passions' (1956, p. 355). Thirty years later, Bruner adopted a position similar to that of Kelly against what he called the 'tripartism' of cognition-affect-action:

> It seems far more useful to recognize at the start that all three terms represent abstractions, abstractions that have a high theoretical cost. The price we pay for such abstractions in the end is to lose sight of their structural interdependence. At whatever level we look, however detailed the analysis, the three are constituents of a unified whole. To isolate each is like studying the planes of a crystal separately, losing sight of the crystal that gives them being.
>
> (1986, p. 118)

Kelly's faithfulness to the constructivist stance is testified by his definition of *anxiety* as 'the recognition that the events with which one is confronted lie outside the range of convenience of one's construct system' (Kelly, 1991a/1955, p. 365). Anxiety is the awareness of a relative lack of structure in a given situation. 'We become anxious when we can only partially construe the events which we encounter and too many of their implications are obscure' (Bannister & Fransella, 1986, p. 22).

One of the most important constructs relating to transition is that of *threat*: 'the awareness of imminent comprehensive change in one's core structures' (Kelly, 1991a/1955, p. 361). That is, we are threatened when a large part of our major constructions of the world surrounding us is jeopardised; about to be invalidated. Thus, also the therapists can become threatening if they plunge their clients into too hasty an experimentation.

The transition of *guilt* has a particularly central role in clinical practice. In this case, it is the core role structure; the self that the person feels to be in danger. Defined as the 'perception of one's apparent dislodgment from one's core role structure' (ibid., p. 370), it leaves the more traditional meaning since it does not refer to particular moral codes or cultural standards. Instead, we suffer from guilt when 'we find ourselves doing, in important respects, those things we would not have expected to do if we were the kind of person we always thought we were' (Bannister & Fransella, 1986, p. 23).

When people, in the course of their experiences, put at risk too much of their construction system, they may recur to *hostility*, 'the continued effort to extort validational evidence in favour of a type of social prediction which has already proved itself a failure' (Kelly, 1991a/1955, p. 375). In Kelly's theory, hostility has a self-preserving rather than an antagonistic function: if the invalidated constructions are too central to the whole of one's system, and the person has no alternative way of viewing the situation, they can try any means to be proven right.

A kind of counterpart to hostility is represented by *aggressiveness*, that is, 'the active elaboration of one's perceptual field' (ibid., p. 374). 'We are being aggressive when we actively experiment to check the validity of our construing; when we extend the range of our construing (and thereby our activities) in new directions; when we are exploring' (Bannister & Fransella, 1986, p. 24).

The possibility to construe the client's awareness of personal transitions by means of the ideas outlined previously and other (McCoy, 1977) professional constructs relative to them (see section 5.3.7), gives the personal construct therapist a precious tool for understanding the client's construction systems and their movements. Together with the other professional constructs previously outlined, the constructs relating to transitions form a set of professional constructs that guide the therapist along the whole psychotherapy process.

In summary, it is on the basis of their understanding of the client, and the subsuming of this under a professional construction, that the therapists can arrive at the formulation of a *transitive diagnosis*, that is, a diagnosis 'concerned with transitions in the client's life' (Kelly, 1991b/1955, p. 153) rather than aimed at furnishing a static description of the patients' symptoms in the attempt of classifying them into a specific nosological category. The diagnosis can change during the course of the psychotherapy process, but the latter is always guided by the diagnosis so that the therapist can relate with the client in therapeutically effective ways. These ways, in turn, are represented by the techniques the therapist will choose to use in order to encourage some specific movement in the client.

Such techniques will be illustrated in Chapter 6. At this stage, it is enough to say that they are represented by particular ways to engage in therapeutic conversations with the client so as to provide reassurance or support, facilitate the elaboration of the complaint, of the construct system and of the emerging material, or to favour loosening or tightening of the client's personal constructs. The ultimate goal is that of producing a therapeutic movement that can allow the client to overcome the disorder as defined in the preceding sections.

Chapter 2

Psychological constructivism and constructivist trends in psychotherapy

2.1 Nature and varieties of psychological constructivism

At the time Kelly published his seminal work, the term 'constructivism' had no place in psychology and psychotherapy. It was only many years later that his work could be regarded as a main representative of psychological constructivism and of constructivist psychotherapy.

Constructivism today is the basis not only of a growing number of psychotherapeutic approaches and counselling, but even more so in new developments in educational psychology (von Glasersfeld, 1995; Phillips, 2000; Steffe and Gale, 1995). The rationale of this relation between therapy and learning lies in the interpretation of knowledge in a way that differs from the more traditionally diffused manner. In doing so, it modifies the outlook on the transformative relationship between therapist and client or teacher and student.

Broadly speaking, the similarities between psychologies and psychotherapies definable as constructivist are not a consequence of representing variations of a specific theory, but of referring to different theories (more or less complex and formalised) more or less coherent with a specific metatheory, that is, constructivist epistemology.

However, to plainly define 'constructivism' is not at all an easy task. Roughly speaking, constructivist epistemology considers knowledge not as a representation, even less as a reflection of an external reality, but as an interpretation. Actually, the term has and is still being used in psychology in ways that can be referred to as different meanings, so that defining oneself as a constructivist psychologist or psychotherapist says little about one's theoretical or metatheoretical approach.

Generally speaking, the matter refers to those kinds of complex and highly abstract issues traditionally dealt with in philosophy and epistemology. As in many other philosophical ideas constructivism has also been considered as being 'old wine in new bottles' (Matthews, 1992). We believe that this claim derives from considering the similarities with other thoughts, without appreciating the differences. In doing so, one can find resemblances between some assumptions of contemporary psychological constructivism and the line of thought of certain classical philosophers, generically definable as anti-foundationalist, who refute the idea that it is possible to base one's knowledge on a fundamental principle or conviction. Even more easily, one can find affinities between the constructivist view of the relation between knowledge and reality, and the various currents of modern philosophy particularly pragmatism, phenomenology and hermeneutics, which can now be regarded, in some of their developments, as expressions of the postmodern thought.

In *The Postmodern Condition* – considered the manifesto of postmodernism – Lyotard (1979) undermines the fundamental principles that generated the 'universalist' claims of the Enlightenment, and argues that our age is marked by an 'incredulity towards meta-narratives'; that is, grand, large-scale theories and philosophies of the world, such as the progress of history and the 'knowability' of everything by means of science, professing a preference for a plurality of small narratives that compete with each other. Because of this, postmodernism has often been interpreted as a form of relativism, presenting close relations with the anti-foundational philosophies. For the same reason, one can see many links between postmodern thought and psychological constructivism, which can be regarded as an expression of postmodernism in psychology (Kvale, 1992).

Substantially, we agree with von Glasersfeld when he writes that 'although the history of ideas can hardly be considered to have run along an orderly linear path, it is possible to isolate some details which, in retrospect, can be seen as a development' (1996b, p. 280) The following review aims to point out similarities and differences among these ideas, and between these and contemporary psychological constructivism.

2.2 Philosophical precursors and cognates of constructivist thought

It is difficult to trace the origin of the use of the term 'constructivism' in philosophy and psychology. It may be easier to suggest the philosophical ancestral proponents of what we regard today as a constructivist view of knowledge. However, we would rather not enter a debate for the nomination of the best candidate eligible as the first constructivist in the history of ideas. Given the difficulty in expressing an unambiguous definition of constructivism we chose to point out the contributions given by some philosophers to those features that appear, to a greater or smaller degree, akin to the contemporary psychological constructivisms.

It may be evocative to begin in von Glasersfeld's (1996b) footsteps, with the contrast dating back to the fifth century BC, between Socrates' and Protagoras' lines of thought; as forwarded by Plato in the form of a dialogue. In Plato's dialogue *Theaetetus* (line 160), Socrates declares that what is perceived must be there as perceivable beforehand. In a similar way, the mainstream of Western philosophy has always insisted that the results of perception and observation have to be images of things that exist in themselves, independently of the human subject. Opposed to this thesis, the sophist Protagoras argues that 'man is the measure of all things: of things which are, that they are, and of things which are not, that they are not' (Plato, *Theaetetus*, line 152a). One can interpret Protagoras' saying as an early form of phenomenology; in which what is or appears for a single individual is true or real for that individual. In addition to Protagoras' relativism of knowledge, there is an ethical relativism according to which the good varies from person to person on the basis of a utility criterion that in turn is reminiscent of modern pragmatism. In the absence of absolute truth and good, word becomes fundamental and may be put to work in a dialectic aimed at strengthening the weaker argument between two opposite theses.

Another sophist Gorgias recurred to rhetorics to argue that (1) nothing exists; (2) even if something exists, nothing can be known about it; and (3) even if something can be known about it, knowledge about it can't be communicated to others. Gorgias' argument could serve as epigram for today's radical constructivism, as well as the sentence of the Irish mystic John Scottus Eriugena (ninth century AD):

> For just as the wise artist produces his art from himself in himself and foresees in it the things he has to make [. . .] so the intellect brought forth from itself and in itself its reason, in which it foreknows and causally pre-creates all things it desires to make.
>
> (Quoted in Moran, 1985, p. 102)

Understandably, Eriugena's work was placed on the Vatican's *Index Librorum Prohibitorum* (*List of Prohibited Books*) almost as soon as it was published.

More recently, some psychologists familiar with the epistemological assumptions of psychology and psychotherapy indicate Immanuel Kant (1724–1804) as a main contributor of the constructivist metatheory (Mahoney, 1988; Rockmore, 2005; Rychlak, 1981, 1990). The reason is that, according to Kant's thought, knowledge does not simply appear out of the accumulation of sense perceptions; as claimed by the empiricists. Rather, knowledge develops in people's minds only through the organisation of information into fundamental built-in, a priori principles or 'categories of the understanding'. These categories operate on perceptions so as to organise experience, according to a top-down arrangement of meaning (Rychlak, 1981). Kant called himself a 'critical realist', in that he believed there is a reality out there (compounded by *noumena*), but that people could never know it directly: what people know about reality is what their senses and the categories of their understanding make it possible for them to know (the so-called *phenomena*). Thus, according to Kant, the 'objective' order of nature is a product of the mind in its interaction with what lies outside the mind (the 'thing-in-itself'), and 'objectivity' has to be understood as 'intersubjectively valid'. Even though Kant's (1929/1781) 'Copernican revolution' reshaped philosophy, metaphysical realism has remained strongly attractive: according to Putnam (1981), advocate of the anti-realist view of 'internal realism', we are still used to calling something 'true' only if we believe that it corresponds to an independent, 'objective' reality.

Another philosophical contribution to contemporary constructivism was given by the Italian Giambattista Vico (1668–1744) (Gash, 1983; Gash & von Glasersfeld, 1978; von Glasersfeld, 1984, 1996b; Rockmore, 2005). Vico turns his attention to knowledge construction more than half a century before Kant. In his *De antiquissima Italorum sapientia [On the most ancient wisdom of the Italians]* (1710), written in Latin, Vico proposes the dictum *verum ipsum factum* (the truth is the same as the made). In other words, truth is verified through creation or invention rather than through observation, as argued by Descartes. Vico's 'knowledge' is what, today, one might call an awareness of the operations that result in our experiential world. The world one experiences is what it is because one has put it together that way. Unlike Kant, in Vico there are no built-in principles to determine our ways of experiencing. Instead, the constraints 'spring from the history of our construction, because at any moment whatever has been done limits what can be done now' (von Glasersfeld, 1984, p. 30). There is, in Vico's thought the notion of knowledge as a recursive process that we shall encounter in Chapter 3 as a fundamental feature in some constructivist perspectives; particularly Piaget.

Some constructivist scholars maintain that there is no given reality independent of the observer. We can find a similar view in the Irish philosopher George Berkeley (1685–1753), whose extreme form of empiricism would later be known as 'subjective idealism'. In his dictum *esse est percipi* (to be is to be perceived), Berkeley (1710) argues that things only exist as a result of their being perceived by someone, challenging the prejudice 'accepted with the utmost tenacity by unreflecting people – i.e. by the great majority of people' (section 55) and 'that certain objects really exist outside the mind, having an existence distinct from being perceived, and our ideas are only images or resemblances of these objects, imprinted by the objects on the mind' (section 56). Berkeley's theory was welcomed mainly with derision, and his contemporaries debated whether or not a tree falling in a forest made a sound if no one was there to hear it. In a more modern phrasing, the question is whether sound is a quality of an underlying reality or it is dependent on the structure (the acoustic system) of the observer.

Berkeley, as well as some contemporary constructivists (at least, those sharing what we call hermeneutic constructivism), would agree to the latter.

Moving towards modern times, many other philosophers have been mentioned as contributors to constructivism. In particular, both the British Jeremy Bentham and the German Hans Vaihinger dealt with the notion of 'fiction', whose Latin root *fictio*, from *fingere*, implies to shape, to form, to invent, to pretend and to fabricate.

Bentham (1748–1832) is regarded as the founder of 'utilitarianism', stating that after first considering the consequences of our actions, we should make an appropriate choice that would then generate the greatest amount of happiness for the largest amount of people involved. However, of greatest relevance here is that he anticipated by about two centuries the linguistic turn in the analytic school of philosophy, whose most important characteristic is the focusing of language on constructing reality (Rorty, 1967). Mainly interested in seeing discourse as the necessary symbolic foundation of another symbolic system, that is, that of power relationships within society, Bentham came to see language not only as the instrument, but also as a constitutive part of thought. In his *Theory of Fiction*, Bentham concluded that 'to language, then – to language alone – it is, that fictitious entities owe their existence; their impossible, yet indispensable existence' (Bentham & Ogden, 1932, p. 15). According to von Glasersfeld (1991a, p. 15), Bentham's conceptual analyses anticipate the '"operational definitions" of Bridgman (1936) and consequently the operational analyses of Jean Piaget and the operational semantics of Silvio Ceccato (1964–66)'.

As to Vaihinger (1852–1933), he developed Kantian thought in the direction of an extreme form of pragmatism, sometimes called 'fictionism'. According to Vaihinger, the basic concepts and principles of natural science, mathematics, philosophy, ethics, religion and jurisprudence are pure fictions which, though lacking objective truth, are useful instruments of action. In his *Philosophy of 'As If'* (1965/1911), he argues that human beings can never know the underlying reality of the world, and that consequently we construct systems of thought and then we act 'as if' the real were what we assume it to be.

Vaihinger influenced Adler's individual psychology (Ellenberger, 1970), whose commonalities with constructivism have recently been outlined (see following quote). Above all, the philosophy of 'as if' can be associated to Kelly's personal construct theory (Wilkinson, 1981). The idea that 'the mind is not merely appropriative, it is also assimilative and constructive' (Vaihinger, 1965/1911, p. 2), is surprisingly akin to Kelly's notion of construing. Actually, Kelly himself credited Vaihinger in a paper in which he proposes the possibility of using language by casting verbs in the 'invitational mood', that is, 'in a form which would suggest to the listener that a certain novel interpretation of an object might be entertained' (1969/1964, p. 149). Kelly writes in this connection:

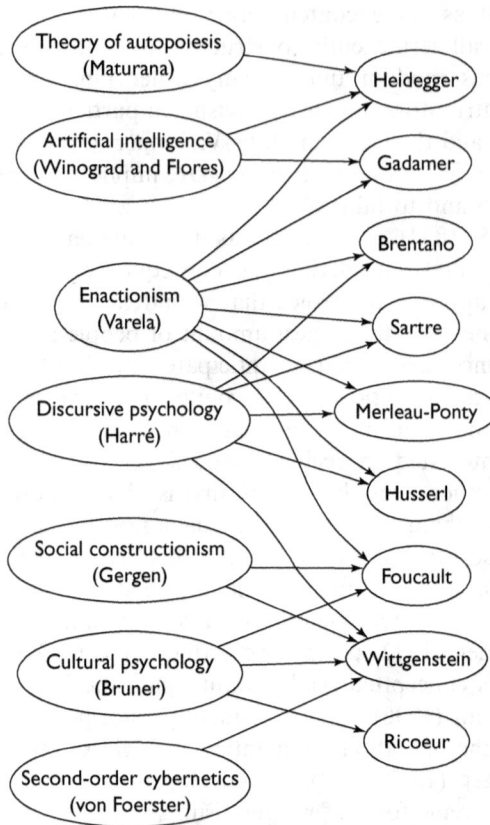

Figure 2.1 Links between forms of constructivism and pragmatist, phenomenologist and hermeneutic philosophers, derived from references in original work of representative authors.

> Vaihinger [. . .] offered a system of thought in which God and reality might best be represented as paradigms. This was not to say that either God or reality was any less certain than anything else in the realm of man's awareness, but only that all matters confronting man might best be regarded in hypothetical ways.
>
> (1969/1964, p. 149)

Maybe not coincidentally, Kelly's paper was addressed to the American Society of Adlerian Psychology.

A discussion on the philosophical precursors and cognates of constructivism cannot exempt itself from mentioning the close parallels to American pragmatism and European phenomenology (see Figure 2.1). Pragmatists and phenomenologists share with contemporary constructivists an anti-foundational view of knowledge and the rejection of several dualisms (theory/practice, mind/body, subject/object). This is proven in the many cross-references we shall point out, as appropriate, in the next section.

2.3 Early philosophical influences on constructivist thought

2.3.1 The path opened by pragmatism

The movement of pragmatism originated in the USA in the late 1800s under the influence of Darwinian theory of evolution. According to pragmatism, theories acquire meaning only in the struggle of intelligent organisms with the surrounding environment; and a theory becomes true only if it is successful in this struggle.

Pragmatists (Charles Peirce, John Dewey, William James, George H. Mead, to quote a few) therefore challenge the assumption that knowledge and action are two separate spheres, and that there exists an absolute or transcendental truth above and beyond the sort of enquiry that organisms use to cope with life. Though acknowledging an external world which must be dealt with, they regard 'real' and 'true' as labels that have a function in inquiry and cannot be understood outside that context.

> True ideas are those that we can assimilate, validate, corroborate and verify. False ideas are those that we can not. That is the practical difference it makes to us to have true ideas; that, therefore, is the meaning of truth, for it is all that truth is known as.
>
> (James, 1978/1907, p. 97)

The idea that there can be no truths without a conceptual scheme to express them, reminds us of Vico's and Piaget's idea of circularity between knowledge and action. Schiller (1907) used the analogy of a chair to make clear what he meant by saying that truth is made: just as a carpenter makes a chair out of existing materials and doesn't create it out of nothing, truth is a transformation of our experience, but that does not imply that reality is something we are free to construct or imagine as we please.

James (1890) resorts to the metaphor of the sculptor working on a block of stone to show how the mind is 'a theatre of simultaneous possibilities'.

> In a sense the statue stood there from eternity. But there were a thousand different ones beside it, and the sculptor alone is to thank for having extricated this one from the rest. Just so the world of each of us, howsoever different our several views of it may be, all lay embedded in the primordial chaos of sensations, which gave the mere *matter* to the thought of all of us indifferently. We may, if we like, by our reasonings

unwind things back to that black and jointless continuity of space and moving clouds of swarming atoms which science calls the only real world. But all the while the world *we* feel and live in will be that which our ancestors and we, by slowly cumulative strokes of choice, have extricated out of this, like sculptors, by simply rejecting certain portions of the given stuff. Other sculptors, other statues from the same stone! Other minds, other worlds from the same monotonous and inexpressive chaos! My world is but one in a million alike embedded, alike real to those who may abstract them. How different must be the worlds in the consciousness of ant, cuttle-fish, or crab!

> (1890, pp. 288–289, italics in original)

To a great extent, James argues, human beings largely agree as to the rejected and selected portions of the original world-stuff. In any one case, however, no two people are known to choose alike.

One great splitting of the whole universe into two halves is made by each of us; and for each of us almost all of the interest attaches to one of the halves; but we all draw the line of division between them in a different place. When I say that we all call the two halves by the same names, and that those names are '*me*' and '*not-me*' respectively, it will at once be seen what I mean.

> (1890, p. 289, italics in original)

'Each of us dichotomizes the Kosmos in a different place' (ibid., p. 290). The making of distinctions, so central in contemporary constructivist views on knowledge (see section 3.2), was already for James a fundamental psychological fact.

The affinities between the pragmatist theory of knowledge and constructivist epistemology have been emphasised by several authors (Chiari & Nuzzo, 2006; Knorr-Cetina, 1981; von Glasersfeld, 1995; Ludwig, 1998; Polkinghorne, 1992) or even critical in regard to constructivism (Bunge, 1999). Several resemblances between constructivism and pragmatism have been noted, particularly within the areas of educational psychology (Garrison, 1995; Neubert, 2001) and narrative psychology and therapy (Amundson, 2001; Stone, 2006).

The affinities we are more familiar with are those between pragmatism and personal construct psychology (Butt, 2000, 2001, 2006; Stevens, 1998; Stojnov & Butt, 2002). According to Warren (1998), Kelly was intellectually indebted to many, although he only credits a few of his intellectual ancestors. Kelly's most explicit debt is to pragmatism, particularly to Dewey, 'whose philosophy and psychology can be read between many of the lines of the psychology of personal constructs' (Kelly, 1991a/1955, p. 108), and specifically in relation to 'the anticipatory nature of behaviour and the person's use of hypotheses in thinking' (ibid., p. 90). Also Kelly's metaphor of the person-as-scientist has been supposed (Butt, 2001) to derive from Dewey:

> Even with his best thought, a man's proposed course of action may be defeated. But in as far as his act is a truly a manifestation of intelligent choice, he learns something:—as in a scientific experiment, an inquirer may learn through his experimentation, his intelligently directed action, quite as much, or even more, from a failure, than from a success.
>
> (1993/1928, pp. 133–134)

By contesting the individualistic view of personal construct psychology, Butt (2001) argues that Kelly's theory can be drawn on to complement the pragmatic social psychology of Mead (1934). Kelly's conceptualisation of choice would make it possible to theorise personal agency and its relationship to the context of social construction within which it is embedded.

2.3.2 The path opened by phenomenology and hermeneutics

The relationship and affinities between the many aspects that characterise phenomenology and constructivism appear so close as to dare to say that the constructivist movement is the present attempt to recover Husserl's (1976/1936) project of a re-foundation of science – and specifically psychology – without foundations, that is, on the basis of our lived, subjective experience of phenomena (Armezzani, 2002; Chiari & Nuzzo, 2000). We shall limit ourselves to a brief review, emphasising such affinities.

It was Dilthey, before Husserl, who criticised the application of the naturalistic method to the 'sciences of the spirit', on the basis of a distinction between natural sciences and human sciences, as well as a distinction between the ways to acquire knowledge: causal explanation and understanding, respectively. 'Die Natur erklären wir, das Seelenleben verstehen wir' (Dilthey, 1924, p. 144): we explain nature, understand psychic life. In the natural sciences, the phenomena are described in terms of cause and consequences, whereas the human sciences would be characterised by the search in understanding the relationship between the parts and the whole. It is from here that derives the necessity to recur to the hermeneutic method of interpretative research, similar to the one already proposed by Schleiermacher (1998/1828).

Brentano identifies the main characteristic of psychic phenomena in their intentionality, not present in physical phenomena. Every mental phenomenon, every psychological act has a content and is directed at an object, the intentional object. 'In presentation something is presented, in judgement something is affirmed or denied, in love loved, in hate hated, in desire desired and so on' (1995/1874, p. 89). Brentano also suggests defying perceptions. The external, sensory perception could not tell us anything about the existence of the perceived world, whereas we can be absolutely sure of our internal perception. When I hear a tone, I cannot be completely sure that there is a tone in the real world, but am absolutely certain I do hear it. Opposed to internal perception, external perception can only yield hypotheses about the perceived world, not truth.

Husserl (1900–1901), a student of Brentano, in taking from his teacher the notion of intentionality and criticism to the naturalistic method in human sciences, particularly in psychology, shows little interest for the metaphysical problem of establishing the reality of what we perceive. Recognising that the 'natural standpoint' is characterised by the belief that objects materially exist and exhibit properties that we see as emanating from them, Husserl (1931/1913) proposed a radical new phenomenological way of looking at objects by examining how people, in their many ways of being intentionally directed towards them, actually 'constitute' them. By rejecting both the assumption of an existence of objects outside thought (the objectivist view), and the assumption of an existence of objects within the psychological content of consciousness (the subjectivist view), Husserl sees in the relationship between subject and reality, between consciousness and its object, the possibility for the creation of a world. The notion of objects as real is not excluded by phenomenology, but 'bracketed' by means of phenomenological reduction, or 'epoché', consisting in questioning what appears to be obvious and given once and for all. This is how the domain of the pre-categorial, subjective operations is brought to light, and new realities are revealed to the person.

Heidegger is emphatic about the realism/idealism debate and the question of whether it is possible to know if something outside our subjective experience exists or not. 'The "scandal of philosophy" is not that this proof has yet to be given, but that *such proofs are expected and attempted again and again*' (1962/1927, p. 249, italics in the original). Heidegger extends Husserl's phenomenology by describing the primary mode of human experience as engaged activity rather than detached knowing, and emphasising the dimension of historicity and sociality. Being is always a being-there/here in its world (*Dasein*), and finds itself thrown into the world amidst things and with others. The person's way of being is that of possibilities, of a continuous overcoming of the present reality. Moreover, 'the world of Dasein is a *with-world [Mitwelt]*. Being-in is *Being-with* Others. Their Being-in-themselves within-the-world is *Dasein-with [Mitdasein]*' (ibid., p. 155, italics in original), in the sense that the world in which one happens to find oneself thrown is always that which one shares with others.

Based on the philosophical hermeneutics initiated by Heidegger, Gadamer (1960, 1989) develops his account of the nature of human understanding. His arguments can be grasped more easily if one refers to the process of interpreting a text. The text has no intrinsic meaning, independent of an interpretation. Interpretation arises from the interaction between the 'horizon' supplied by the text and the 'horizon' given to it by the interpreter. In the same way, each person in understanding the world, themselves and other people, is continuously involved in a process of interpretation. This, in turn, is bound and embedded in history because understanding deploys the knower's 'effective-history', that is, their personal experience and cultural traditions, to assimilate new experiences. In other words, the initial structure of an effective-history constrains the range of possible interpretations, excluding some possibilities and bringing forth others. Effective-history constitutes the 'prejudices' or 'pre-conceptions' brought to bear in understanding, and implies the historicity of any interpretation. The 'critical self-consciousness' of a rational agent who introspectively questions their prejudices may counter part of the consequences of effective-history, but their fact is inescapable.

Both Heidegger and Gadamer share the notion that language is the foundation of being: 'Language is the house of being, which is propriated by being and pervaded by being' (Heidegger, 1998/1976), 'being that can be understood is language' (Gadamer, 1989, p. 474), 'language is not only an object in our hands, it is the reservoir of tradition and the medium in and through which we exist and perceive our world' (Gadamer, 1976, p. 29). Though not directly influenced by them, Wittgenstein's account of language represents a further shift from a metaphysical level to everydayness. Language is inextricably woven into the fabric of life, and 'the speaking of language is part of an activity, or a form of life' (2001/1953, p. 23). Wittgenstein rejects the idea that ostensive definitions can provide us with the meaning of a word. Words are not defined by reference to the objects or things which they designate in the external world, nor by the thoughts, ideas, or mental representations that one might associate with them, but rather by how they are used in effective, daily communication.

Following a close analysis of the actual workings of everyday language, Wittgenstein believes it possible to avoid much of the confusion present in philosophical problems, so as to arrive at dissolving rather than solving them. The neopragmatist Rorty (1979) pursues a similar aim in relation to foundationalist epistemology that rests on the false view that the main function of the mind is to faithfully represent a mind-independent external reality.

Another criticism to the nature of traditional philosophy, following Heidegger and Husserl, comes from the controversial work of Derrida (1976/1967), whose name is usually associated with 'deconstruction', a notion difficult to define. Fundamentally, deconstruction is an attempt to open a text (literary, philosophical or other) to several meanings and interpretations by questioning the stability of meaning, deriving from the binary oppositions within a text. Such oppositions (i.e. speech/writing, presence/absence, meaning/meaninglessness, mastery/submission), far from being clear-cut and stable as believed by traditional metaphysics, are instead culturally and historically defined. Deconstruction – echoing the Greek sophists – attempts to compensate for the historical power imbalances that consist in conceiving the first term as original, authentic and superior, and the following as secondary, or derivative, and to develop concepts which do not fit in either terms of oppositions.

In turn, following the work of Husserl and Heidegger, Merleau-Ponty brings into the phenomenological inquiry the role of the body, questioning the Cartesian dualism. Starting from a view of perception as an active dimension in that it allows a primordial openness to the life world, Merleau-Ponty (1962/1945) suggests a distinction between the 'objective body', as treated by mechanistic physiology, and the 'phenomenal body', or body-subject. It is the latter that represents a permanent condition of experience in the form of embodied subjectivity.

Ricoeur also rejects the version of a substance dualism in the person that the Cartesian *cogito* or the Kantian transcendental subject would require, arguing that the self is essentially embodied. The self's identity is constituted by an inextricable tie between a selfsameness and a selfhood or ipseity: between the self's *idem*-identity – that which gives the self its spatiotemporal sameness – and the *ipse*-identity – which gives it the unique ability to initiate something new, imputable to him or herself. Personal identity, on the whole, is a narrative identity in that we make sense of our own identities by telling ourselves a story about our own life (Ricoeur, 1984/1983, 1985/1984,1988/1985). This is why identities are not fixed structures or substances; instead, they are mobile and, until the story is finished, the identity of each character or person is subject to revision. Ricoeur's analysis of personal narrative identity yields four conclusions that are basic to his anthropology (Dauenhauer, 2005).

1   Because my personal identity is a narrative identity, I can make sense of myself only in and through my involvement with others.
2   In my dealings with others, I do not simply enact a role or function that has been assigned to me. I can change myself through my own efforts and can reasonably encourage others to change as well.
3   Nonetheless, because I am bodily and hence have inherited both biological and psychological constraints, I cannot change everything about myself. And because others are similarly constrained, I cannot sensibly call for comprehensive changes in them.
4   Though I can be evaluated in a number of ways, e.g., physical dexterity, verbal fluency, technical skill, the ethical evaluation in the light of my responsiveness to others is, on the whole, the most important evaluation.

In *Oneself as Another* Ricoeur (1992/1990) develops his theory of narrative into full-blown ethics.

Before finishing this discussion on the contribution of phenomenology to the development of contemporary postmodern thought, we have to talk about Foucault. He focuses on the role of discursive practices in constituting subjectivity, particularly the historical discursive and practical means of truth and meaning production (Foucault, 1965/1961). To demonstrate the principles of this production in various discursive formations, he details how truth claims emerge during various periods on the basis of what was actually said and written during these times (Renaissance, the age of Enlightenment, the twentieth century). The above is related to Foucault's (1977/1975) analysis of the importance of power in human activities, and the link between power and knowledge.

Much of the above matter elaborated by philosophers representative of phenomenology and hermeneutics has had, and still has, a large influence on the development of psychotherapy. When applied to psychiatry and psychotherapy, the phenomenological vein derived from Husserl and the existentialist one attributed to Heidegger entwine each other in ways so that, any attempt to distinguish which psychotherapeutic approaches derives from one and which from the other, is rather difficult and possibly useless.

The variegated field of existential-phenomenological approaches to psychotherapy sees the psychiatrist and philosopher Karl Jaspers as the most acknowledged point of reference. His phenomenological approach to psychopathology (Jaspers, 1968/1912, 1997/1913), being mainly based upon the empathic understanding of personal worldviews, values and beliefs and the subsequent search for general principles transcending the individual case, still represents an alternative to traditional psychiatry.

While Jaspers' approach to mental disorders can be regarded as a method of investigation that can lead only to more accurate generalisation and classification, Binswanger's (1963) 'daseinanalyse', Frankl's (1962) 'logotherapy', and Minkowski's (1970) 'structural-phenomenological method' are designed to have therapeutic effects. Minkowski is quoted on the first page of *The Divided Self*, the most famous book of Ronald Laing (1960), which gives fresh contributions to the existential-phenomenological approach in psychiatry.

The connection between phenomenology and hermeneutics, and the most contemporary expressions of postmodern thought mostly related to the view of knowledge, concern the research program regarding the theory of **autopoiesis** which we shall look into further on (see section 2.4.4). Here, it is sufficient to hint at the close relationship between Heidegger and Gadamer's hermeneutics and Maturana's theory brought forward by Winograd and Flores (1986), and Varela's attempt to bring phenomenology to bear on a scientific theory of cognition (Petitot et al., 1999) and consciousness (Varela & Shear, 1999; Varela et al.,1991) within the field of contemporary cognitive science.

As to personal construct psychology, the links with phenomenology and hermeneutics are surprisingly rare (Chiari & Nuzzo, 2000). The language of personal construct theory – maybe together with the metaphor of the 'person-as-scientist' (Chiari, 2000) – invites a prevalently cognitive-rationalistic interpretation (Adams-Webber, 1990), in spite of Kelly's repeated claims that his theory is not a cognitive one. Nonetheless, there are outstanding exceptions within the Kellyan community. Warren (1985, 1989, 1990a, 1991) is an advocate of the phenomenologic rootedness of personal construct theory. Butt (2004) utilises Dilthey's (1924) distinction between understanding and explanation to clarify the personal construct project, in terms of an approach to an understanding of the complexity of the lived world. Furthermore, Butt (1998a, 1998b) has given important contributions to an understanding of the Kellyan notions of role and C-P-C cycle in the light of Merleau-Ponty's (1962/1945, 1963) phenomenology of embodiment. Lastly, Epting (1988) has declared his hermeneutic interpretation of personal construct psychotherapy, and has shown similarities and differences between personal construct theory and humanistic psychology (Epting & Leitner, 1992; Epting & Paris, 2006).

Beyond the philosophical roots of psychological constructivism, it is obviously within contemporary psychology that it is possible to find lines of thought which, rather than show affinities with psychological constructivism, represent many different expressions of it.

2.4 Contemporary expressions of psychological constructivism

2.4.1 The path opened by genetic epistemology

According to Piaget (1971/1967, p. 4), 'the essential starting point [. . .] is the fact that no form of knowledge, not even perceptual knowledge, constitutes a simple copy of reality, because it always includes a process of **assimilation** to previous structures'. Following this process of integration, previous structures can remain unchanged or undergo a more or less deep modification, but without discontinuity with the previous one, adapting to the new situation without being destroyed.

The notion of adaptation thus implies that the development of knowledge consists in a recursive process, founded on the person's previous knowledge, and therefore simultaneously constrained by it. For example, the early structures a child acquires at the sensory-motor level represent the basis of many further operational structures.

However, the Piagetian notion of adaptation is often misinterpreted in a way that the more traditional view of knowledge as a representation of reality is maintained (von Glasersfeld, 1982). That is, cognitive adaptation is commonly meant as the generation of knowledge that corresponds more and more closely to an external world.

In order to avoid such frequent misinterpretation, von Glasersfeld (1977, 1980, 1982) has repeatedly proposed to replace the misleading term 'adaptation' with 'viability'.

> From the organism's point of view, on the biological level as on the cognitive one, the environment is no more and no less than the sum of constraints within which the organism can operate. The organism's activities and operations are successful when they are not impeded or foiled by constraints, i.e., when they are viable. Hence it is only when actions or operations fail that one can speak of "contact" with the environment, but not when they succeed.
>
> (1982, p. 615)

Consequently, 'the "real" world manifests itself exclusively there where our constructions break down' (von Glasersfeld, 1984/1981, p. 39). It is not possible to know reality as it is, but only what it is not: knowledge has to be meant as a construction of possible realities.

In describing the notion of viability, Watzlawick offers the following metaphor:

> A captain who on a dark, stormy night has to sail through an uncharted channel, devoid of beacons and other navigational aids, will either wreck his ship on the cliffs or regain the safe, open sea beyond the strait. If he loses ship and life, his failure proves that the course he steered was not the right one. One may say that he discovered what the passage was *not*. If, on the other hand, he clears the strait, this success merely proves that he literally did not at any point come into collision with the (otherwise unknown) shape and nature of the waterway; it tells him nothing about how safe or how close to disaster he was at any given moment. He passed the strait like a blind man. His course fit the unknown topography, but this does not mean that it matched it – if we take matching in von Glasersfeld's sense, that is, that the course matched the real configuration of the channel. It would not be too difficult to imagine that the actual geographical shape of the strait might offer a number of safer and shorter passages.
>
> (1984/1981, pp. 14–15, italics in original)

In turn, von Glasersfeld makes clear the view of the relationship between knowledge and reality in terms of fitting rather than matching by resorting to other enlightening analogies. The simplest is the analogy between the key and the lock:

A key fits if it opens the lock. The fit describes a capacity of the key, not of the lock. Thanks to professional burglars we know only too well that there are many keys that are shaped quite differently from our own but which nevertheless unlock our doors.

(1984/1981, p. 21)

In other words, knowing the structure of the key does not say anything about that of the lock. Should it unlock, the only knowledge obtained is that it was a key suitable for that lock.

An even more clarifying analogy utilises the relation between the river and the landscape (von Glasersfeld, 1985). The river forms wherever the landscape allows the water to flow. There is a continuous and subtle interaction between the inner 'logic' of water – for instance, the fact that it must form a horizontal surface and cannot flow upward – and the topography of the territory. Both of them impose constraints to the water-course, and do it in inseparable way. Under no circumstances could one say, for example, that the river turns to the right 'because' there is a hill, without implicitly assuming the logic of water that prevents the river from flowing upward. Therefore the river does not 'represent' the landscape, but 'fits' into it, in that finding its course between the constraints imposed, not from the landscape nor from the logic of water, but always and necessarily from the interaction of both aspects.

This analogy, by highlighting the complementary relationship between knowledge and reality moves von Glasersfeld's radical constructivist view towards Maturana's view, even though, as we shall see further ahead (section 2.6), in the former we note an expression of what we define as epistemological constructivism and in the latter, the distinctive characteristics of hermeneutic constructivism.

Piaget's constructivism has been associated with Kelly's constructive theory (Rychlak, 1981, pp. 664–753), to be meant as a radical constructivist epistemology.

2.4.2 The path opened by social constructionism

Another important expression of postmodern thought in psychology is represented by the movement of social constructionism (Gergen, 1985).

The basis of this movement, headed by outstanding authors (Gergen, 1982; Gergen & Davis, 1985; Harré, 1979, 1983; Shotter, 1984; Shotter & Gergen, 1989), can be found in the recognition of the role played by language in the discourse about the world, following Berger and Luckmann's (1966) seminal volume *The Social Construction of Reality*. Notwithstanding the frequent references to the theses of von Glasersfeld, von Foerster, Maturana and Varela, the above authors prefer to emphasise the differences between the constructivist and the social constructionist approach.

Particularly relevant to this issue is the debate between Mancuso (1996a, 1996b), a supporter of the possible coalescence between personal construct psychology, social constructionism and narrative psychology, and Burkitt (1996) and Wortham (1996), who claim that the first demonstrates closeness to traditional cognitive psychology by focusing on individuals' cognitions and by ignoring the social and relational context in which meaning is constructed.

Indeed the main difference, according to Gergen and Gergen (1991), consists in the overcoming of the subject/object dichotomy. From the perspective of the social constructionist stance, in fact:

> it is not the cognitive processing of the single observer that absorbs the object into itself, but it is language that does so. Accounts of the world (in science and elsewhere) take place within shared systems of intelligibility — usually a spoken or written language. These accounts are not viewed as the external expression of the speaker's internal processes (such as cognition, intention), but as an expression of relationships among persons. From this viewpoint, it is within social interaction that language is generated, sustained, and abandoned. [. . .] The emphasis is thus not on the individual mind but on the meanings generated by people as they collectively generate descriptions and explanations in language.
>
> (p. 78)

Some developments of social constructionism closely intertwine with those of the narrative approach. Gergen, together with Sarbin and Bruner, has been one of the most important promoters of the 'narrative turn' in psychology in the early 1980s.

2.4.3 The path opened by the narrative framework

According to the narrative principle, 'human beings think, perceive, imagine, and make moral choices according to narrative structures' (Sarbin, 1986b, p. 8). Based on Gergen's (1973) argument that social psychology is history, Pepper's (1942) worldview of contextualism (reflected in the work of pragmatists), whose root metaphor is the historical event, and MacIntyre's (1981) consideration of narrative as central to an understanding of human conduct, Sarbin suggests regarding narrative as a root metaphor for psychology, an organising principle.

Also in the 1980s, Bruner maintains the richness of storytelling as a way of knowing. In his *Actual Minds, Possible Worlds* (1986), Bruner relates the logical-scientific language and the literary language to two types of thought, two different ways of constructing reality, complementary and irreducible to one another: the paradigmatic and the narrative thought.

The 'paradigmatic' or 'logical-scientific thought' (Bruner, 1986, 1990) follows the ideal of a formal and mathematical descriptive and explicative system, and to this end recurs to categorisation or conceptualisation. Synthetically, the paradigmatic thought deals with the causes of overall order and of the ways to single them out; using procedures that can ensure the referential verificability within a true/false criterion (see also Polkinghorne, 1988). Its language is regulated by the demands of coherence and non-contradiction, and its imaginative application leads to 'good theory, tight analysis, logical proof, sound argument and empirical discovery guided by reasoned hypothesis' (Bruner, 1986, p. 13).

As to the narrative mode, its imaginative application leads to 'good stories, gripping drama, believable (though not necessarily "true") historical accounts' (ibid., p. 13). While the arguments based on paradigmatic thought try to convince of their truth and are liable to verification, the narrative thought tries to convince of the verisimilitude through coherent stories, analogies and metaphors, that is, by interpretations that describe the human world in terms of intentionality (Feldman, 1994). 'It deals in human or human-like intention and action and the vicissitudes and consequences that mark their course' (Bruner, 1986, p. 13).

In reference to Iser's reflections in *The Act of Reading* (1978), Bruner maintains that the efficiency of the literary texts is linked to the fact that they, unlike scientific texts, 'initiate "performances" of meaning rather than actually formulating meanings themselves' (Iser, 1978, p. 21). To this end, according to Bruner, a narrative discourse must be made up of three essential characteristics: the triggering of *presupposition*, that is, the 'creation of implicit rather than explicit meanings'; *subjectification*, the 'depiction of reality not through an omniscient eye that views a timeless reality, but through the filter of the consciousness of protagonists in the story'; and *multiple perspective*, 'beholding the world not univocally but simultaneously through a set of prisms each of which catches some part of it'. Together, these three aspects succeed in *subjunctivising reality*, on the premise that the subjunctive mode denotes that we are 'trafficking in human possibilities rather than in settled certainties' (1986, pp. 25–26).

Whereas the paradigmatic explanation is deductive, demonstrative and quantitative, the narrative explanation is inductive, hermeneutic (interpretive) and qualitative. Those who rely upon paradigmatic explanations are usually affiliated to a realistic philosophical attitude, in assuming the existence of a world beyond the observer that can be objectively understood (Toukmanian & Rennie, 1992). On the contrary, an explanation of the narrative type would be more in line with an idealistic philosophical perspective (better still, according to us, with a constructivist one).

Bruner (1990), in the attempt at founding a cultural psychology able to steer cognitive psychology towards its early object – meaning and its construction rather than information and its elaboration – makes reference to Goodman's (1976, 1978, 1984) constructivist philosophy. According to which:

> contrary to common sense there is no unique 'real' world that preexists and is independent of human mental activity and human symbolic language; that what we call the world is a product of some mind whose symbolic procedures construct the world.
>
> (Bruner, 1986, p. 95)

The worlds we create may arise from the cognitive activity of the artist, or in the sciences or in ordinary life. Such worlds have been constructed, but always out of other worlds, created by others, which we have taken as given.

> We do not operate on some sort of aboriginal reality independent of our own minds or the minds of those who precede or accompany us. [. . .]
> On Goodman's view, then, no one 'world' is more 'real' than all others, none is ontologically privileged as the unique real world.
>
> (Ibid., p. 96)

What allows such a construction of worlds is an organisation of experience that assumes a narrative form, within a social context of negotiation of meanings (Bruner, 1990). It is the very creation of narrative realities by story-telling; historical (culturally and socially negotiated) selves.

2.4.4 The path opened by cybernetics and the theory of autopoiesis

A fourth contribution to the development of the constructivist thought comes from disciplines external to psychology: in particular, cybernetics and biology. We have decided to consider them together because of the close affinities they show.

In the late 1940s and 1950s, Heinz von Foerster together with Warren McCulloch, Margaret Mead, Gregory Bateson and a few others, became a founder of the discipline based on Wiener's cybernetics. Later, von Foerster distinguished a first-order cybernetics (of observed systems) from a second-order cybernetics (of observing systems); the latter being a cybernetics which deals with the pervasive role of self-reference in the second-order observation of the observer. The observer, in second-order cybernetics, or cybernetics of cybernetics, is understood to be both within the system being described and affected by it.

> Usually, developing a theory of the brain is very easy: I cut off the top and open up somebody else's skull, I put the electrodes into somebody

else, then I wiggle something in front of his eyes, and then I see what the brain is doing inside, and then I see and know how the brain reacts. Unfortunately, it is only the *other* brain that I watch. So, the problem is: how can a brain scientist develop a theory of the brain when the theory of the brain is written in such a fashion that *it writes itself*?

(von Foerster, 1981, p. 102, italics in original)

The constructivism of von Foerster can be regarded as 'concerned with the convergence of two central themes: (1) how we know what we know, and (2) an abiding concern for the present state of the world and its humanity' (Segal, 1986, p. 3). Nevertheless, it would be quite difficult to synthesise his work. When questioned about the origin of his thought, von Foerster replied that if he were to derive his central principle from anything, he could only do it from his personal life, his personal biography and his experiences of life (von Foerster & Bröcker, 2002). Parenthetically, it is interesting to see the affinities between von Foerster's and von Glasersfeld's biographies (von Foerster & von Glasersfeld, 1999). We have opted to illustrate his professional path by going through some of his incisive aphorisms.

The metaphysical activity, according to von Foerster, is that with which we decide in principle; undecidable questions; one of these being: 'Am I *apart from* the universe or am I *a part of* the universe?' (von Foerster & Bröcker, 2002, italics in original)

The first choice, the 'peep-hole position', underlies the idea of objectivity, predominant in the scientific worldview. The second position, which von Foerster adopted for himself, implies that, when I change, the universe changes with me because I am a part of it.

There is, in the latter choice, a reminder of Bateson's (1979) 'pattern which connects'. From this standpoint, 'objectivity is the delusion that observations could be made without an observer' (von Foerster, 1974), and 'truth is the invention of a liar' (von Foerster & Pörksen, 1998), because 'the environment as we perceive it is our invention' (von Foerster, 1984/1981, p. 42), the result of operations in the nervous system. Thus, the biblical metaphor 'Let there be light, and there was light' has to be translated into 'Let there be vision!, and there was light' (von Foerster, 1989, p. 225).

The complement to objectivity is not subjectivity, but ethics. Objectivity ('I am apart from the universe') implies 'monologic', where the essential condition for a sentence to make sense is that it be either true or else false. If we choose to regard ourselves as a part of the universe, we enter the realm of dialogue with its extended logic: 'dialogic'. Questions are part of dialogic. Here we ask: what is the intent of a proposition? 'Since intent is an internal state of the speaker, intent cannot be pointed at; it cannot be *denoted*. In dialogue, language takes up its *connotative* function, that is, an utterance invites interpretation' (von Foerster, 1989, p. 225, italics in the original). Denotation is monologic, and carries with it the notion of commitment. Connotation is dialogic, and carries the notion of responsibility. From here derives von Foerster's concern for ethics. Ethical precepts should not begin with 'Thou shalt. . .', but with 'I will. . .'. Von Foerster's *ethical imperative* is 'Act always so as to increase the number of choices' (1984/1981, p. 60), that is, so as to open new possibilities.

It is through the presence of the observer that the second-order cybernetics is seen to be related to the theory of autopoiesis. Actually, Maturana's work complements and expands von Foerster's ideas moving within the field of biology.

The ontological choice, according to Maturana, is between the transcendental ontology of 'objectivity' and the constitutive ontology of '(objectivity)', or 'objectivity in parenthesis' (1987). Putting **objectivity in parenthesis** implies that reality is 'a domain specified by the operations of the observer' (1978, p. 55), being an **observer**:

> a human being, a person, a living system who can make distinctions and specify that which he or she distinguishes as a **unity**, as an entity different from himself or herself that can be used for manipulations or descriptions in interactions with other observers. An observer can make distinctions in actions and thoughts, recursively, and is able to operate as if he or she were external to (distinct from) the circumstances in which the observer finds himself or herself. Everything said is said by an observer to another observer, who can be himself or herself.
>
> (1978, p. 31, bold our own)

The Chilean biologists Maturana and Varela arrive at this 'ontology of the observer', in which knowledge is regarded as a specification of domains of reality, through a conceptualisation of living systems as autonomous systems — that is, systems defined as unities by their own organisation.

The term *organisation* denotes 'those relations that must exist among the components of a system for it to be a member of a specific class', whereas '*structure* denotes the components and relations that actually constitute a particular entity and make its organization real' (Maturana & Varela, 1987/1984, p. 47, italics in original). Living systems differ from each other in their structure, but are alike in their organisation: the **autopoietic organisation**.

'Autopoiesis' is composed from the Greek words 'self' and 'to produce'. In fact, autopoietic systems are defined as:

> a class of dynamic systems that are realized, as unities, as networks of productions (and disintegrations) of components that: (a) recursively participate through their interactions in the realization of the network of productions (and disintegrations) of components that produce

them; and (b) by realizing its boundaries, constitute this network of productions (and disintegrations) of components as a unity in the space they specify and in which they exist.

(Maturana, 1978, p. 36)

The structure of the system realises this organisation and specifies the domains of **perturbations**, that is, what can interact with it. Maturana speaks of 'perturbation' – significantly a term borrowed from Piaget – because all systems we deal with are 'structurally determined', and the environmental 'stimuli' can only 'trigger' an effect, not 'determine' it. As long as a living system does not enter into an interaction destructive of its organisation, we as observers will necessarily see a compatibility or congruence between the structure of the environment and that of the living system. As long as this compatibility exists, environment and living system act as mutual sources of perturbation, triggering structural changes: that is, there is complementarity between them, a '**structural coupling**' allowing '**adaptation**'.

When a human being enters into structural coupling with other human beings, it is possible that their interactions acquire a recurrent nature in the course of their ontogeny. The co-drifting organisms give rise to a new phenomenological domain, and within this consensual domain linguistic behaviours and human consciousness (and therefore observers) can emerge as products of recursive consensual coordination of actions.

> Cognition is therefore a phenomenon that emerges as a kind of realisation of the autopoietic organisation of living systems, and is constitutive of their being.
>
> Every interaction of an organism, every behavior observed, can be assessed by an observer as a cognitive act. In the same way, the fact of living – of conserving structural coupling uninterruptedly as a living being – is to know in the realm of existence. In a nutshell: to live is to know (living is effective action in existence as a living being).
>
> (Maturana & Varela, 1987/1984, p. 174)

Besides his contribution to the development of the theory of autopoiesis, Varela (1979) described formal tools to represent autonomous systems, particularly the immune and nervous systems and their cognitive processes.

By working at the very edge of the mainstream cognitive science, Varela later on proposed an alternative, partly based on the autopoietic theory: the 'enactive cognitive science' (Varela, 1985; Varela et al., 1991). Blending epistemology and phenomenology, when elaborating the writings of Husserl and Merleau-Ponty in the light of the Buddhist tradition, Varela argues that human cognition and consciousness can only be understood in terms of the enactive structures in which they arise; namely the body and physical world with which it interacts. His analysis of experience culminated in the foundation of 'neurophenomenology' (Petitot *et al.*, 1999), and in the 'first person science' (Varela & Shear, 1999).

It is worth mentioning, as this section draws to a close, the contribution of a German zoologist of the early 1900s, Jacob von Uexküll, founder of semiotic biology, or biosemiotics. Though not widely known, von Uexküll influenced the work of Heidegger, Merleau-Ponty, Deleuze, Maturana and Varela.

In his discussion on animals' relationship with the environment, von Uexküll (von Uexküll & Kriszat, 1934) gives a description of the subjective spatio-temporal worlds (*Umwelt*) of some living beings: ticks, sea urchins, amoebae, jellyfish and sea worms. Such worlds are constituted by a series of elements called 'carriers of significance', or 'marks', which are easy to liken to the Piagetian notion of schemata, or Kelly's notion of construct. For example, the tick is supposed to live in a world reduced to only three carriers of significance:

1   the odor of butyric acid, which emanates from the sebaceous follicles of all mammals
2   the temperature of 37 degrees celsius, corresponding to the blood of all mammals
3   the hairy typology of mammals.

On the basis of the same reflections, von Uexküll argues that time can also be regarded as a personal construction. In fact, it can be defined as a succession of instants, where for 'instant' von Uexküll intends the briefest interval of time during which the environment does not change in any perceptible way. Such an interval therefore corresponds to indivisible elementary perceptions: for the duration of an instant the world remains motionless. Consequently, time varies from one subjective world to another according to the number of instants different subjects live during the same interval. Therefore, 'If till now we were saying: "Without time there cannot be any living subject", from now on we shall have to say: "Without subject there is no time"' (translation by the authors). Significantly, a similar conceptualisation of time can be found in Piaget (1946), von Glasersfeld (1996a), and Maturana (1995b) (see Chiari *et al.*, 2001).

The four paths outlined above, together with Kelly's personal construct theory (outlined in Chapter 1), represent in our opinion the most important contributions to the development of a postmodern thought in psychology. At the same time, given their derivation from different fields of enquiry, their diversity of languages, and their openness to a variety of interpretations, it would be inappropriate to say that they have concurred to give a shape to something like a psychological constructivism, as we shall discuss in the next section.

2.5 Constructions (and misconstructions) of psychological constructivism

Constructivism, as we know it today, has emerged in the field of psychology in the first half of the last century, thanks to the seminal work of few authors, and spread in the 1980s. In his foreword to the book *The Invented Reality: How Do We Know What We Believe We Know? (Contributions to Constructivism)*, Watzlawick (1984/1981) makes reference to the consideration of reality as an invention, and writes that 'a rather unfortunate term, constructivism, is gaining acceptance'. According to Watzlawick, the term is 'unfortunate because, first, the word already has an established but somewhat different meaning in traditional philosophy; second, it refers to a short-lived movement in the arts [. . .]; and, third, it is ugly' (p. 10).

Piaget's (1937) *La Construction du Réel Chez l'enfant* can be regarded as the first empirical elaboration of the idea of a constructive activity in the personal process of knowledge in terms of a developmental approach. Piaget presented a model of how the conceptual structures of objects, space, time and causality can be built up. Moreover, he was probably the first to use the term 'constructivism' in relation to a specific trend of contemporary scientific epistemology; contrasting it with reductionism and anti-reductionism (Piaget, 1967). In the same year he also uses the term 'dialectic constructionism' in contrast with atomism (Piaget, 1971/1967, p. 212).

Piaget wrote many books and papers throughout his life, possibly changing his mind about some complex epistemological issues during this long period. Furthermore, he came to be known in English-speaking countries mainly through a summary of his theory of development (Flavell, 1963), this being the main reason why Piaget's ideas are likely to be interpreted in significantly different ways. It is just one of the interpreters of Piaget, the previously mentioned von Glasersfeld (1974, 1980, 1982, 1985), who saw the work of the Swiss psychologist as informed by a constructivist epistemology meant in a radical sense.

According to von Glasersfeld, Piaget has often been misinterpreted, that is, understood in terms of a **trivial constructivism**. It is the distinction between 'trivial' and '**radical constructivism**' that allows us to introduce the question of the polysemy of the terms 'constructive' and 'constructivism'. For instance, Neisser (1967), whose *Cognitive Psychology* is regarded as the foundation of the homonymous school, states that the particular approach he is personally interested in has as a central point the belief that seeing, hearing and remembering are acts of construction. However, in his second, important contribution to cognitive psychology, meaningfully titled *Cognition and Reality*, Neisser (1976) specifies his 'constructive' approach, making clear its definitely realistic assumption. Neisser's epistemology is therefore an example of trivial constructivism, whereas radical constructivism:

is radical because it breaks with convention and develops a theory of knowledge in which knowledge does not reflect an 'objective' onto-logical reality, but exclusively an ordering and organization of a world consisted by our experience. The radical constructivist has relinquished 'metaphysical realism' once and for all.

(von Glasersfeld, 1984/1981, p. 24)

Von Glasersfeld makes clear the opposition between the trivial and the radical constructivist view of knowledge by pitting the words 'match' and 'fit' against one another. The metaphysical realist – such as the trivial constructivist – 'looks for knowledge that matches reality in the same sense as you might look for paint to match the color that is already on the wall you have to repair' (1984/1981, p. 20). But if we say that something fits, we have in mind a different relation (illustrated in section 2.4.1).

Von Glasersfeld's distinction between trivial and radical constructivism is just an example – even though probably the best known and quoted – of the attempts to discriminate, in the broad sense, different types of 'con-structivist' approaches (see Table 2.1). Actually, the lack of a clear defini-tion of the term 'constructivism' has led many authors to declare themselves constructivists, even though their approaches can be differentiated from each other at a metatheoretical level.

To give an idea of the complexity of the matters in question, it would be enough to refer to Mahoney's criticism to the above definition of radical constructivism. In fact, according to Mahoney, von Glasersfeld's radical constructivism is 'basically indistinguishable from "idealism"' (1988, p. 4) in that it would deny the existence of any reality. Consequently, Mahoney is the proponent of a 'critical constructivism' which does not deny the existence of a real physical world, although recognising our limitations to its knowledge. On the other hand, Mahoney's critical constructivism appears to us indistinguishable from critical realism. He himself, after all, says that 'critical constructivists [. . .] are essentially "realists", albeit "hypothetical, critical, or representational realists"' (1988, p. 4).

Mahoney's distinction, in our opinion, derives from a gross misunder-standing. When von Glasersfeld (1984/1981, p. 24) writes that 'radical constructivism [. . .] develops a theory of knowledge in which knowledge does not reflect an "objective" ontological reality', he refers to the impossibility of knowing reality objectively, not to the existence of an ontological reality. After all, the notion of 'fit' refers directly and clearly to some reality. Von Glasersfeld himself has subsequently made clear that 'constructivism deals with knowing not with being [. . .]. As a con-structivist I have never said (nor would I ever say) that there is no ontic world, but I keep saying that we cannot know it' (1991a, p. 17). On the other hand:

Table 2.1 Different forms of psychological constructivism

Proposer	Distinction	Criterion
von Glasersfeld (1974)	trivial vs. radical constructivism	representation of (*match*) vs. adaptation (*fit*) to reality (*viability*)
Moshman (1982)	exogenous vs. endogenous vs. dialectical constructivism	external structures (environment) vs. internal coordinations (previous knowledge) vs. interaction (subjective experience) as sources of knowledge
Armon-Jones (1986)	weak vs. strong constructionism	existence of a limited range of natural emotions vs. emotion as an irreducibly socio-cultural product
Mahoney (1988)	radical vs. critical constructivism	idealist vs. realist ontological assumption
Steier (1991)	naïve or first-order vs. second-order or social constructionism	non-self-reflexive vs. self-reflexive stance on other people's construction of reality
Chiari and Nuzzo (1993)	epistemological vs. hermeneutic constructivism	personal constructions of an external reality vs. subject–object complementarity
Soffer (1993)	weak vs. strong constructivism	lesser vs. greater 'belonging' to the subject of an object of construction
Greenberg and Pascual-Leone (1995)	categorical vs. dialectical constructivism	existence of certain a priori fundamental principles vs. relativisation of all categories
Lyddon (1995)	material vs. efficient vs. formal vs. final constructivism	Pepper's (1942) formistic vs. mechanistic vs. contextualist vs. organismic world hypothesis
Geelan (1997)	social-objectivist vs. social-relativist vs. personal-relativist vs. personal-objectivist	set of Cartesian coordinates, whose axes are represented by the personal vs. social and objectivist vs. relativist dimensions

Source: adapted from Chiari and Nuzzo 1996b.

> for believers in representation, the radical change of the concept of knowledge and its relation to reality, is a tremendous shock. They immediately assume that giving up the representational view is tantamount to denying reality, which would indeed be a foolish thing to do.
> (1995, p. 14)

Paradoxically, Mahoney's stand has been criticised for being anti-realistic according to Held's (1995) criticism of postmodern theory in psychotherapy.

A critique of constructivism as anti-realist, anti-determinist and anti-scientific was also expressed by N. Mackay (2003). The response to his arguments (Raskin & Neimeyer, 2003) helps to see clearly the differences between constructivism and foundational philosophical assumptions.

Turning to the different constructions of constructivism, Soffer (1993) suggested a distinction between a 'weak' and a 'strong constructivism'.

Again, Piaget's work is acknowledged as an example of strong constructivism because of the dominant role of the subject in the creation of meaning and the integral nature of knowledge organisation. On the other hand, weaker constructivism locates a property intrinsic to a construed entity that exists independently of the construing subject and forcing its meaning on the subject. Kelly's theory, according to Soffer, approaches Piaget's stronger position in certain aspects, particularly in its notion of construing (equivalent to Piaget's assimilation), and in its understanding of the inseparability of cognitions and emotions.

Just the reference to a different way of dealing with emotions is central to the distinction proposed by Armon-Jones (1986) between a 'weak' and a 'strong constructionism'. Weak constructionism concedes the existence of a limited range of natural emotions untouched by socio-cultural influences, whereas strong constructionism claims that emotion is an irreducibly socio-cultural product and locates the origin of affectivity in the dynamics of construing itself.

Steier (1991), a researcher focused on systemic and constructionist approaches, chooses reflexivity instead of emotion as a criterion of difference. In doing research on other people's constructions of reality, one can attempt to keep out of one's constructions, according to a 'naïve', or 'first-order constructivism' (or 'first-order constructionism'). On the contrary, one can recognise how one's research is co-produced, assuming a self-reflexive stance coherent with a 'second-order constructionism' (or 'social constructionism').

Greenberg and Pascual-Leone (1999) distinguish 'categorical' from 'dialectical constructivism'. The former – attributed to Chomsky, Kant, Newell and Simon, Kelly, and the early Piaget – 'emphasizes the existence of certain a priori fundamental principles, or categories, that [. . .] are not informed by, but rather inform, experience' (ibid., p. 175). The latter – recognised in Gibson (1979) and in the authors' approach – 'relativizes all categories and sees basic psychological principles [. . .] as being open to change as a result of experience' (p. 176).

Many authors working in the field of education, where constructivist approaches enjoy a wide diffusion, have proposed other distinctions.

Moshman (1982) bases his distinction among 'exogenous', 'endogenous' and 'dialectical constructivism' on Pepper's (1942) work about the different world hypotheses more or less explicitly held by philosophers and psychologists. Exogenous constructivism (rooted in the mechanistic worldview) emphasises the reconstruction of structures pre-formed in the environment. Endogenous constructivism (rooted in the organismic worldview) emphasises the coordination of previous organismic structures, as exemplified by Piagetian theory. Dialectical constructivism (rooted in the contextualistic worldview) emphasises the construction of new structures out of organism–environment interaction, exemplified by Vygotsky's (1962) theory.

Again on the basis of Pepper's (1942) philosophical framework of root metaphors, Lyddon (1995) outlines questionable contrasts among 'material constructivism' (formistic world hypothesis, exemplified by the radical approaches of von Glasersfeld, von Foerster, Maturana and Varela), 'efficient constructivism' (mechanistic world hypothesis, evident in cognitive theories based on information-processing and social learning conceptualisations), 'formal constructivism' (contextualist world hypothesis, including social constructionist theory and narrative approaches) and 'final constructivism' (organismic world hypothesis, exemplified by cognitive-developmental, dialectical, and living systems approaches).

Finally, Geelan (1997) draws out from the literature six forms of constructivism, and locates them within a set of Cartesian coordinates whose axes are represented by the personal/social and objectivist/relativist dimensions. The social-objectivist quadrant includes Vygotsky; the social-relativist, Gergen; the personal-relativist, von Glasersfeld and Kelly and the personal-objectivist, Piaget.

2.6 Epistemological and hermeneutic constructivism

The previously mentioned distinctions among different types of constructivism – and others that could be found in the psychological literature (Bodner et al., 2001; Good, 1993; Solomon, 1994; Taylor, 1998) – are made possible and maybe necessary by the lack of a clear definition of the subject.

Consider, for instance, one of the most authoritative attempts: 'Psychological constructivism refers to a family of theories that share the assertion that human knowledge and experience entail the (pro)active participation of the individual' (Mahoney, 1988, p. 2). This definition – based as it is on the mere dimension of (pro)activity/reactivity – is not at all helpful in making clear specifically what constructivism is and what it is not. Actually, the human organism is regarded as reactive and passive only in few schools of psychology, whereas many psychologies share a view of the human organism as intrinsically active and therefore in a certain sense, constructive. Surely, most cognitive psychologists would recognise themselves in the above definition, finding a feature of individual activity in the personal process of symbolic representation of reality. On the other hand, most constructivist psychologists reject the representational view of knowledge.

Following the lack of a clear definition, the specification of one's theoretical position or of one's psychotherapeutic approach as 'constructivist' or 'social constructionist' can hardly help to deny, by contrast, the acceptance of a 'realist' or 'objectivist' metatheoretical assumption, or of a 'rationalistic' perspective (see section 2.7). It is not adequate to specify anything, so much that it has been pointed out that 'there have been many who have adopted a constructivist label on a package whose contents are still defined by "objectivist" inquiry' (Steier, 1991, p. 3), and even that 'many of the constructivisms that arise every six months represent even attempts to safeguard the traditional realist position' (von Glasersfeld, 1993).

Much of the preceding discussion is concerned with the difficulty of abandoning the familiar realist view without falling into its traditional opposite, namely, the idealist view. We are inclined to swing between the idea of a reality demanding to be known as it is (exposing us to the danger of being wrong), and the idea that we can invent reality at our whim (and therefore that everything goes well). Science, obviously, embraces the first view and strives to discover what reality definitely is; looking with suspicion at the attempts to question such a premise.

Actually, in our opinion (Chiari & Nuzzo, 1996a, 1996b), constructivism can be regarded, above all, as an attempt to conceptually bridge realist and idealist approaches to knowledge, looking for a third way, or a 'middle way' in the Buddhist meaning (see Table 2.2). Where realism holds the view that material objects exist externally to us and independently of our sense experience, idealism (in its most radical interpretation, perhaps a caricature of what is meant by idealist philosophers) maintains that no such material objects or external realities exist apart from our knowledge or consciousness of them, the whole universe being dependent on the mind or, in some sense, mental.

Idealism and realism can be regarded, therefore, as antithetical answers to the question of whether an external reality exists. In the negative case, the knowledge we presume to have of an external reality is nothing but an *invention* without any foundation and the knowledge/reality relationship is consequently one of *coincidence*. In the affirmative case, the possibility arises of knowing such external reality as a *reflection*, and the knowledge/reality relationship can aim at being one of *correspondence*.

Since its beginning, cognitive psychology rejected the possibility of such an ultimate correspondence of knowledge with reality. In fact, both the approaches prevailing in cognitive psychology and science – the ecologically oriented approach that stresses the importance of the relationship between the person-as-knowing-being and the environment-as-known, and the human information processing model founded on computation as the dominant metaphor – share an ontological view definable as *limited realism*: that is, both of them claiming that our knowledge of the world is a little less than perfect, in the sense of incompleteness, not of veridicality.

Within the ecological approach, knowledge coincides with *direct perception*, which consists of the accumulation of accurate information provided by the environment. Evolution selected the perceptive systems to directly extract meaning from the propagation of structured energy, without the necessity of resorting to any mediation. Cognitive structures, at the most, prepare the perceptor to accept certain types of information rather than others, by means of anticipatory schemata (Neisser, 1976). The relationship between knowledge and reality is in terms of an *incomplete correspondence*,

Table 2.2 Views of knowledge and knowledge-reality relationship according to different philosophical assumptions

Philosophical assumption			Knowledge as	Knowledge–reality relationship
	Idealism		Invention	Identity
Hermeneutic	} Constructivism		Specification	Complementarity
Epistemological			Construction	Adaptation as viability
Limited	} Realism		Representation or incomplete correspondence	Adaptation as symmetry
Extreme			Reflection	Correspondence

Source: adapted from Chiari and Nuzzo 1996b.

that is, limited to the genetically pre-tuned perceptive invariances that represent the ecologically meaningful properties of the perceiver's world.

Within the computational model, the cognitive system is conceptualised and analysed as a flow chart, whose blocks represent the components and the successive stages of the elaboration of information contained in environmental stimuli: perception, attention, memory, decision making and production of responses able to reach an aim. Given the supposition that external stimuli cannot enter the organism directly, information consists of representation in the form of symbols: an inferential process precedes perception. Thus, within a cognitive system, symbols represent more or less adequately some aspects of the real world: that is, realise a *representation* of reality. The relationship between knowledge and reality is in terms of a greater or lesser *symmetry* between the representation of an object and the object itself, rather than in terms of correspondence.

Nevertheless, the theories and approaches that maintain the incomplete correspondence or the representation of an 'out there' reality keep sharing a realist, though 'limited', metatheory, and as a consequence should be excluded by the constructivist camp. In fact, they hold the idea that it is partly possible to know reality directly, and therefore they do not actually grapple to overcome the realism/idealism dichotomy.

Consequently, our suggestion is that:

> the label of psychological constructivism has to be limited to the set of theories and approaches that strive to transcend the traditional opposition between realism and idealism by adopting the metatheoretical assumption that the structure and organization of the known - the knower-as-known included - is inextricably linked to the structure of the knower.
>
> (Chiari & Nuzzo, 1996b, p. 178)

In turn, the link may be in the form of an ordering and organisation of a world constituted by the person's experience (*epistemological constructivism*), or in the sense of a mutual specification between knower and known which results in the overcoming of the subject/object dichotomy (**hermeneutic constructivism**). This distinction, based on the knowledge–reality relationship, has been described as 'a close account offered to facilitate the conversation about constructivist ideas' (Warren, 1998, p. 70). Let us try to make it a bit clearer by referring to the elaboration presented by Raskin (2002) for further details.

Epistemological constructivists espouse ontological realism in that they acknowledge a real world. Yet, from an epistemological viewpoint, they assert that it is not possible to know reality except through *personal constructions*, that is, 'heuristic fictions useful for understanding the world' (Raskin, 2002, p. 4).

Kelly's personal construct theory can be easily interpreted as an expression of epistemological constructivism. In fact, Kelly locates the impossibility to know reality as it is at an epistemological level:

> it is a real world we shall be talking about, not a world composed solely of the flitting shadows of people's thoughts. But we should like, furthermore, to make clear our conviction that people's thoughts also really exist, though the correspondence between what people really think exists and what really does exist is a continually changing one.
>
> (1991a/1955, p. 5)

Actually, according to Warren, 'an understanding of personal construct psychology as a *hermeneutic constructivism* appears as defensible as an understanding of it as an *epistemological constructivism*' (Warren, 1998, p. 169, italics in the original), given the great deal of similarities between some of the key topics and themes of hermeneutics and Kelly's theory.

Moreover, similarities have been observed between epistemological constructivism and von Glasersfeld's radical constructivism. Actually, both Kelly and von Glasersfeld indicate the existence of two 'realities': the extra-linguistic, and the constructed, experiential reality of the subject (Kenny & Gardner, 1988; Rasmussen, 1998). 'Life [. . .] involves an interesting relationship between parts of our universe wherein one part, the living creature, is able to bring himself around to represent another part, his environment' (Kelly, 1991a/1955, p. 6). In other words, Kelly and von Glasersfeld share a subject–object dualism (Domenici, 2004).

What we call hermeneutic constructivism represents a way out of any dualistic approach, a proper *tertium datur* between realism and idealism. The alternative to such an opposition/separation between subject and object derives from a consideration of what appears as an irreducible fact in our culture – we *and* the world – as just a personal construction embedded in a background of biological, social and cultural practices. Everything we claim to know (cognition and language included) is a phenomenon in a domain of experiences that emerges in our praxis of living. We can then regard ourselves as enmeshed in a world we cannot observe and describe from the outside – we are *in* the world. Our supposed knowledge of ourselves and the world cannot be other than a *specification* dependent on the history of our structure coupled with the environment, therefore based upon previous experiences and inseparable from our body, our language and our social (biological, cultural, personal) history. Expressed differently, hermeneutic constructivism views knowledge (and truth) as 'an interpretation historically founded rather than timeless, contextually verifiable rather than universally valid, and linguistically generated and socially negotiated rather than cognitively and individually produced' (Chiari & Nuzzo, 1996b, p. 174). It has been described as 'a position for identity as a reflexive third position located in the interactional, or the space between the individual and the social' (Thomas *et al.*, 2007, p. 875).

The following passage clearly illustrates the overcoming of the mind/ world opposition, distinctive of what we interpret as hermeneutic constructivism.

> Tradition would have it that experience is either a subjective or an objective affair, that the world is there and that we either see it as it is or we see it through our subjectivity. However [. . .] we may look at that quandary from a different perspective: that of *participation* and *interpretation*, where the subject and the object are inseparably meshed. This interdependence is revealed to the extent that nowhere can I start with a pure account of either one, and wherever I choose to start is like a fractal that only reflects back precisely what I do: to describe it. By this logic, we stand in relation to the world as in a mirror that does not tell us how the world is: neither does it tell us how it is not. It reveals that it is *possible* to be the way we are being, and to act the way we have acted. It reveals that our experience is *viable*.
>
> That the world should have this plastic texture, neither subjective nor objective, not one and separable, neither two and inseparable, is fascinating [. . .]. It shows that reality is not just constructed at our whim, for that would be to assume that there is a starting point we can choose from: inside first. It also shows that reality cannot be under- stood as given and that we are to perceive it and pick it up, as a recipient, for that would also be to assume a starting point: outside first. It shows, indeed, the fundamental *groundlessness* of our experi- ence, where we are given regularities and interpretations born out of our common history as biological beings and social entities. Within those consensual domains of common history we live in an apparently endless metamorphosis of interpretations following interpretations.
>
> (Varela, 1984, p. 322, italics in original)

The rejection of both an objectivist and a subjectivist position in favour of a consideration of the subject/object interdependence, of a mutual specifica- tion between knower and known, is the ontological premise of phenom- enology and hermeneutics. Philosophers like Brentano (1995/1874), Husserl (1931/1913, 1976/1936), Heidegger (1962), Merleau-Ponty (1962/1945, 1963), and Gadamer (1960, 1989) were among the very first to explore in depth the possibility of placing the meaning of being in the basic level of being-in-relation. To give up the idea of a reality 'out there', implies abandoning the idea of representation as a cognitive mediator between subject and object. Cognition and reality emerge from interaction: they are in a relation of *complementarity*, and an immediate experience of the world precedes any explanation and distinction, any construction of that experience.

Though many forms of hermeneutic constructivism can be distinguished, they all share some fundamental premises.

First of all, the primacy of experience, emerging from the encounter that happens in the space that connects subject and object; transcending both of them (Chiari & Nuzzo, 2006): a relationship happening in the 'sphere of between', borrowing the expression of Buber (1937/1923). Second, historicity, that is, the recursive, self-referential process of change resulting in the embodiment of the history of interactions (Chiari & Nuzzo, 2004). The interpersonal nature of existence and cognition has to be emphasised, since it results in the emergence of language. With language, self-consciousness and reality arise as constructions, as interpretations of the ongoing experience.

A similar view emerged in philosophy thanks to members of the generically definable 'hermeneutic family'. Kuhn's (1962) and Feyerabend's (1976) anti-foundationalist philosophies of science, Habermas' (1971) critique of the neutrality of social science knowledge, and Clifford's and Marcus' (1986) questioning of the objectivity of ethnographic reports, are among the developments of the so-called 'postmodern turn' in other areas. As to psychology, a hermeneutic constructivist assumption is witnessed by the recent emergence of several, largely intertwined and overlapping disciplinary approaches: narrative psychology (Sarbin, 1986a); storytelling psychology (Mair, 1989b); cultural psychology (Bruner, 1986, 1990); discursive psychology (Edwards & Potter, 1992; Harré & Gillett, 1994) and postmodern psychology (Kvale, 1992). Members of the social constructionist movement (Gergen, 1985), as well as Maturana (1978), who maintains an ontology of the observer in his theory of autopoiesis, share a similar attitude according to which there is no given reality independent of the observer. In commenting on our distinction in relation to the drawing of philosophical guidelines for practising psychotherapists, Downing (2000) suggests the addition of psychoanalytic intersubjectivity (Natterson & Friedman, 1995) to our list of hermeneutic constructivist approaches.

2.7 Effect of psychological constructivism on psychotherapy

The spreading of constructivist epistemology in psychology has had and is still having important repercussions on the theory and practice of psychotherapy.

Once more, in order to analyse the presence of a constructivist assumption in various psychotherapeutic approaches, it would be important to consider the type of constructivism such approaches more or less explicitly refer to. Being such a very difficult task, we shall in the following sections limit ourselves in most cases to rely upon the statements made by the various authors who claim the adoption of a constructivist epistemology in the elaboration of their approach.

Instead, it seems possible, as well as useful for an explanatory purpose, to distinguish, among the psychotherapies of 'constructivist matrix', between those already formalised some time ago and recently reinterpreted in a constructivist mode or that have shown significant developments towards it, and those that can be narrowly defined as constructivist in that originating as such or transformed to an extent unable be traced back to their originating theoretical matrix.

An exception to this framework is represented by personal construct psychotherapy which, already definable as constructivist at its origin, has been in recent years reconsidered and retrieved. It is in fact our revision of Kelly's therapeutic approach that we will deal with extensively in the following chapters.

2.7.1 Constructivist interpretation or developments of already well-established psychotherapies

We have previously mentioned Kelly's and Adler's common referral to Vaihinger's philosophy of 'as if'. By stressing this philosophical root and the social embeddedness of Adlerian theory, some authors argue that individual psychology can legitimately be included in the constructivist approaches (Carlson & Sperry, 1998; Jones, 1995; Jones & Lyddon, 1997; Shulman & Watts, 1997; Watts, 2003; Watts & Phillips, 2004).

A weak relation with constructivism has been acknowledged in regard to a main representative of humanistic psychology, Carl Rogers, who had been defined as an 'unwitting postmodernist pioneer' (O'Hara, 1995), whose educational writings would be in line with the constructivist theories on learning (Maharg, 2000). Furthermore, according to Tudor and Worrall (2006), apart from Rogers' (1961) borrowing the term 'personal constructs', person-centred therapy embodies those principles of constructivism particularly relevant to therapy.

In recent years a branch of Gestalt therapy is also taking a wink at constructivism. It seems significant that the editorials of two new journals, *Gestalt Review* (Melnick, 1997) and *Studies in Gestalt Therapy: Dialogical Bridges* (Bloom *et al.*, 2007), engage with constructivism.

Even though it is only recently that the spreading of psychotherapies explicitly following a narrative approach is in expansion, the recent definition of the features characterising such an approach allows us to trace back the precursors within the psychoanalytic universe.

Thanks to his elaboration of Freud's remark that 'the childhood memories did not, as people are accustomed to say, emerge; they were formed at that time', and that 'a number of motives, with no concern for historical accuracy, had a part in forming them, as well as in the selection of the memories themselves' (1899, p. 322), Schafer (1976, 1983, 1992) can be portrayed as a leading figure in the hermeneutic, and more recently narratologic, trend. Such an approach has been introduced as an alternative to Freudian metapsychology, based on physicalist metaphors such as forces, drives, and structures (Soldz, 1988).

> We are forever telling stories about ourselves. In telling these self-stories *to others* we may, for most purposes, be said to be performing straightforward narrative actions. [. . .] Additionally, we are forever telling stories about others. These others, too, may be viewed as figures or other selves constituted by narrative actions.
>
> (Schafer, 1980, p. 35, italics in original)

Patient and analyst describe various stories of the past exactly as they re-establish different versions of the present, and each one may be equally valid. The 'analytic attitude' is informed by the awareness of possible narrative lines potentially rich in new perspectives.

Spence (1982, 1990) follows the path opened by Schafer orienting the narrative approach towards a direction which has recently brought him to turn to the field of rhetorics, starting from a radicalisation of the diversity between the historical truth of the patient (what actually happened) and the narrative truth created by the therapeutic work. According to Spence (1982), in fact, Freud's most successful clinical cases also have an important literary quality. Facts alone are not sufficient; they have to be introduced in a context which allows the reader to appreciate fully their value, without necessarily having any further information on the case. Spence maintains that the very same definition should be adapted to interpretation: the presentation of the formulation is no less important than its content.

Also within Jungian analytic psychology, one can single out a narrative trend in the work of Hillman (1983), who asserts that all psychotherapies may be considered as narrative activities deriving from the 'poetic basis of mind'. In addition to the above, Jung's psychology, especially complex, archetype and transcendent function, has been regarded as consonant with constructivism (Young-Eisendrath, 1997).

An important non-metapsychological approach to psychoanalysis is represented by the theory of Atwood and Stolorow (1984) where, through the adoption of the Piagetian concepts of **accommodation** and assimilation, subjective experience is taken as the subject matter. 'The basic units of analysis [. . .] are *structures of experience* – the distinctive configurations of self and object that shape and organize a person's subjective world' (p. 33, italics in original). According to Soldz (1988, 1996), such a conceptualisation of personality structure bears striking resemblance to the basic tenet of personal construct psychology: that organised systems of personal constructs are the basic units of personality. Moreover, affinities can be envisioned in their emphasis on the importance of the person's experience of self and others in maintaining self stability, in their definition of psychological health in terms of 'optimal structuralisation' involving the possibility to assimilate many different types of experience, and in their revision of the concept of transference, viewed as a creation rather than a distortion.

Soldz (1988) envisions signs of constructivist developments also in the 'heuristic approach' of Peterfreund (1983). Therapy should involve a process of discovering personal meanings on behalf of both the patient and therapist, the latter being open to re-evaluating everything, including the heuristics (general strategies) used in conducting the therapy.

To remain within the analogies between psychoanalysis and personal construct theory, Warren (1990b) underlines the common concern with language and meaning arising from the French rereading of Freud, of Lacan and Ricoeur. According to them, 'psychoanalytic therapy originally was a process of enquiry into meaning, a mutual search rather than interpretation coming down from on high' (p. 461), and this would allow to place both Freud and Kelly within the broad perspective of phenomenology.

A particular case in the panorama of the relation between psychoanalysis and constructivism is represented by Ryle's (1975, 1979) work. Well versed in both personal construct and object relations theory, he attempted to operationalise a variety of psychodynamic concepts by means of the repertory grids (see section 4.4.1). He also searched for new measures to represent the repetitive patterns of interpersonal construal – such as dilemmas, traps and snags – supposed to form the basis of the patient's problems.

Certain developments in psychoanalysis moving towards a change of paradigm represented by the postmodern thought are worth mentioning. The constructivist view of Sullivan's (1953) interpersonal psychoanalysis elaborated by Stern (1985, 1997) on the basis of Gadamer's (1960) philosophical hermeneutics, and I. Hoffman's (1998) 'dialectic constructivism' that reconsiders the analyst's role and responsibility in the psychoanalytic situation, represent the most advanced expressions of this movement. They both have the merit, typical of psychoanalytic literature, of the profundity in the reflection about the relational aspects in the therapeutic situation, and the merit of allowing as never before a comparison with the non-psychoanalytic constructivist approaches, the latter of which we retain would obtain quite a bit in terms of knowledge of the complexity of the therapeutic process.

2.7.2 Contemporary psychotherapies arising from an epistemological constructivist matrix

Given the difficulty of arriving at a clear definition of what is meant by psychological constructivism, so too the attempts to specify epistemological, theoretical and practical contrasts between different forms of constructivist psychotherapies rest on distinctive features which are too comprehensive or, on the contrary, not likely to be shared by all the insiders (Mahoney, 1991; Mahoney & Lyddon, 1988; Neimeyer, 1993a, 1993b). Neimeyer appears aware of these 'variations on a constructivist theme' when he writes that 'constructivist psychotherapy is better viewed as a "fuzzy set" with indistinct boundaries, whose members manifest considerable diversity and even occasional contradiction' (1993a, p. 224).

An attempt at distinguishing, within the wide range of cognitive psychotherapies, the rationalistic and the constructivist approaches appears much easier.

Rationalist cognitive therapies, according to Mahoney and Lyddon (1988), are exemplified by Ellis' (1962) rational emotive behaviour therapy, despite his claims of being a constructivist (Ellis, 1998). In fact, his idea that human suffering has to do with the presence of 'irrational ideas' to be corrected, substituted or eliminated through logical reasoning, fits nicely the criteria to be included in this list. According to us, Beck (1976) also, given his concern with distorted cognitive processes, is an influential representative in this type of cognitive therapy. When he defines cognitive therapy as 'all the approaches that alleviate psychological distress' by correcting 'faulty conceptions', 'erroneous beliefs', 'distortions of reality', or 'illogical thinking' (ibid., pp. 214–219), he reveals the realist–rationalist matrix of his view of psychological problems and remedy.

Rationalist cognitive therapists, in synthesis, argue for 'the causal supremacy of explicit beliefs about self and world', and tend to emphasise realistic thinking, reality contact and rationality, regarding disorders and irrationality as synonymous. On the other hand, constructivist cognitive therapies – exemplified by Kelly's (1991a/1955, 1991b/1955) personal construct approach – 'challenge traditional concepts of reality, knowing, and rationality, as well as disorder, disease, and development' (Mahoney & Lyddon, 1988, p. 212).

Nevertheless, many psychotherapies that could deserve to be labelled 'constructivist', do not originate from cognitivism, but instead derive from other trends we previously examined.

In order to sort out the different lineages or traditions of the family of constructivist psychotherapies, we retain, as particularly useful, the referral to the four basic metaphors suggested by Neimeyer (1995):

1   therapy as personal science
2   therapy as selfhood development
3   therapy as narrative reconstruction
4   therapy as conversational elaboration.

Of course, the boundaries among these categories are vague, in that the individual psychotherapeutic approaches are not always univocally classifiable within them. However, these metaphors allow for a reordering of what otherwise would remain a chaotic rather than fuzzy set. We shall now outline them, adding new references to the ones reported by Neimeyer.

Therapy as personal science

The metaphor of the person-as-scientist suggested by Kelly (1991a/1955, 1991b/1955) has been adopted by the therapists applying personal construct theory to the psychological reconstruction of life. According to the metaphor, each person, as a scientist, actively formulates hypotheses about the world, themselves and the others, and refines, revises, and elaborates them in the course of their ongoing experience.

Within the Kellyan psychotherapeutic community, the metaphor has been applied to constructive change in slightly different ways (see Chapter 1), but on the whole maintaining a close orthodoxy with Kelly's original formulation. There are however some prominent exceptions, such as Mair (1989a), inspired by Kelly and other explorers of the mind, who stresses the importance of a poetic approach in psychology and psychotherapy, and the need to use an imaginative freedom of language. Viney (1993, 1996) too, has found it both possible and useful to insert personal construct psychotherapy in a narrative framework. Leitner (Faidley & Leitner, 1993; Leitner, 1988; Leitner et al., 2005) in addition, would like to emphasise what characterises his elaboration of Kelly's ideas by giving to his approach the name of 'experiential personal construct psychotherapy' (EPCP). EPCP underscores the relational, experiential and existential aspects of Kelly's theory, sharing similarities with Buber's (1937) notion of I–thou relationships and Yalom's (1980) existential approach to psychotherapy.

Therapy as selfhood development

Several constructivist therapies, particularly those arising within the cognitive field, have as a common denominator the importance ascribed to an individual's early and ongoing social interactions. Such importance – once a prerogative of the psychodynamic approaches – lies in the possibility that a consideration of such an aspect allows an understanding of the development and maintenance of the disorder, and is also reflected in the structuration of the client–therapist relationship for therapeutic purposes.

Nonetheless, Piaget's theory – even though considered a radical constructivist theory of personal development – has been seldom used for that end by cognitive therapists, maybe because the place of affect in it is ambiguous (Friedman, 1978). Rather paradoxically, it is in the psychoanalytic field that the dichotomy affect/cognitive has been criticised in order to attempt a rapprochement between the cognitive preoccupations of Piagetian psychology and the affective focus of Freudian psychoanalysis

(Aron, 1993; Weiner, 1975). Anyway, extra-psychoanalytic contributions to the analysis of the implications deriving from the use of Piaget's theory of cognitive development can also be found (Polkinghorne, 1995; Rosen, 1985, 1996). Actually, though the field of constructivist approaches to psychotherapy is variegated, it tends to refer mainly to Bowlby's attachment theory (1969, 1973, 1980).

This reference may appear odd, since Bowlby's theory can be regarded as a re-elaboration of the psychoanalytic theories of dependency in terms of a cognitive, information-processing model (Chiari *et al.*, 1994). On the other hand, the description of the patterns of attachment resulting from the early relationship between primary attachment figures and the child, and the observation of their relevance as to the making and breaking of affectional bonds in adults (Bowlby, 1979), have revealed to be fertile in suggesting clinical applications of the theory (Bowlby, 1988).

The model of therapy as an accelerated form of selfhood development is best represented by Guidano. His contribution is grounded in Bowlby's attachment theory in the description of 'cognitive organisations', to be meant as the suggestion of a developmental approach to psychopathology (Guidano, 1987), but also on Mead's (1934) distinction between the experiencing 'I' and the explaining 'me', in the formulation of a 'post-rationalist cognitive therapy' (Guidano, 1991).

A similar focus on an ongoing dialectic between explanation and direct experience and the related perception of contradictions as a source of emotional distress, as well as the search for new syntheses that can provide a greater sense of personal coherence, are the core of other constructivist therapies ascribable to the metaphor of therapy as selfhood development (Cionini, 1999; Greenberg & Safran, 1987; Safran & Segal, 1990).

Therapy as narrative reconstruction

The latest developments in the narrative approach are situated in the field of constructivist or social constructionist psychologies and psychotherapies, and appear as a natural evolution from an intra-individual to an inter-individual and dialectical constructivism. The latter identifies the 'seat' of personal knowledge in social processes mediated by language. In relation to this, we have already mentioned the role of authors like Bruner and Sarbin in the elaboration of the concept of narration (see section 2.4.3).

Narrative therapy is rapidly and extensively spreading, particularly in the field of family therapy (Freedman & Combs, 1996; Wedge, 1996), but also in the application to individual and couple settings (Angus & McLeod, 2004; Payne, 2000). We suspect that, at least partly, this is due to the ease with which the narrative metaphor may be applied to the idea that therapy consists 'solely' in encouraging the 'rebiographing' (Howard, 1990) of life stories that have become constraining or incoherent to the person.

Most of the narrative approaches to psychotherapy acknowledge their gratefulness to White's work (1995; White & Epston, 1990). On the basis of references to Bateson and social constructionism (which sometimes may appear to derive from a rather superficial understanding), White has elaborated a particularly pragmatic therapeutic strategy. The initial and crucial step in such a strategy consists in externalising the problem, that is, in anthropomorphising the symptom as something external to the client. Distanced from the problem in this way, the client is better prepared to perform an alternative story loaded with a greater sense of personal agency.

More elaborate, though less formalised, is the contribution to the narrative approach deriving from the personal construct psychology, which we mentioned in the section concerning the metaphor of therapy as personal science. It is particularly Mair who emphasises the ease with which Kelly's original formulation – based as it is on the epistemological assumption of constructive alternativism, centred on the notion of anticipation, and supplied with such instruments as self-characterisation and fixed-role therapy – may be paraphrased in a narrative key. Mair (1988, 1989b) dares to propose a story-telling psychology as a discipline of discourse rather than a natural or social science.

Therapy as conversational elaboration

Social constructionism also represents the main conceptual point of reference for the therapists (once again mainly family and relational) who have adopted the metaphor of therapy as an elaboration of conversation. The approaches that may be assigned to this metaphor show aspects that blend into the narrative metaphor we have just outlined.

Two of the most illustrative representatives of this kind of approach to therapy are Goolishian and Anderson (1981). Their narrative position leans on the following premises (Anderson and Goolishian, 1992, italics in the original).

1 Human systems are language-generating and, simultaneously, meaning-generating systems. '*The therapeutic system is such a linguistic system*'.
2 Meaning and understanding are socially constructed, and we do not arrive at, or have, meaning and understanding until we take communicative action. '*A therapeutic system is a system for which the communication has a relevance specific to its dialogical exchange*'.
3 Any system in therapy is one that has dialogically coalesced around some 'problem'. '*The therapeutic system is a problem-organizing, problem-dis-solving system*'.
4 Therapy is a linguistic event that takes place in a therapeutic conversation, that is, in a mutual search and exploration through dialogue

in which new meanings are continually evolving toward the 'dissolving' of problems, and thus, the dissolving of the therapy system.

5 The role of the therapist is that of a conversational artist – an architect of the dialogical process – whose expertise is in the arena of creating a space for and facilitating a dialogical conversation. *'The therapist is a participant-observer and a participant-facilitator of the therapeutic conversation'.*

6 The therapist exercises this therapeutic art through the use of conversational questions, that is, *'asking questions from a position of "not-knowing" rather than asking questions that are informed by method and that demand specific answers'.*

7 Problems we deal with in therapy are actions that express our human narratives in such a way that they diminish our sense of agency and personal liberation. In this sense, *'problems exist in language and problems are unique to the narrative context from which they derive their meaning'.*

8 Change in therapy is the dialogical creation of new narrative, and therefore the opening of opportunity for new agency. *'We live in and through the narrative identities that we develop in conversation with one another'.*

(pp. 27–28)

The skill of the therapist is the expertise to participate in this process. The means to achieve this goal is situated in a definitely hermeneutic context.

To the extent that the metaphor of therapy as a conversational elaboration is based on the acknowledgement that all which exists, exists in language in language: we may also include in this metaphor the therapeutic approaches that refer to the intertwined contributions of Bateson's epistemology, von Foerster's cybernetics of observing systems, and Maturana's and Varela's theory of autopoiesis (Boscolo *et al.*, 1987; Efran *et al.*, 1990; Keeney, 1983).

Chapter 3

A constructivist understanding of the person

3.1 The biological roots of human understanding

The conception of living systems as autonomous systems allows understanding of the hermeneutic constructivist view of personal knowledge as a specification of realities. It also explains how language and knowledge emerge as outcomes of the changes of a living system in its relationship with the environment. The reality which appears to exist external to us and independent from us emerges parallel to the emerging of knowledge, and is therefore closely tied to life: to live is to know (see section 2.4.4).

The 'rootedness' of knowledge in the biology of living systems makes the considerations of their relationship with the environment applicable both to the phylogenetic path, regarding the evolution of species, and to the ontogenetic one, related to individual development. Of course, as psychotherapists we are more interested in personal knowledge. In this regard, we consider that it is useful to illustrate its nature and development through Piaget's, Maturana's and Kelly's contributions, emphasising the affinities and the differences we see in their theorisations.

All three authors have had a particular professional history. Piaget, originally a zoologist, successively formulated one of the most accredited psychological theories of cognitive development; even though, according to us, it is underestimated, especially in Anglo-Saxon psychology. Maturana, a biologist, elaborated a biological theory of knowledge that suggests important implications for cognitive science and psychotherapy, but also (maybe mainly) for epistemology. Kelly began his education studying physics and mathematics before becoming a psychologist and formulating the first constructivist theory specifically applied to clinical psychology and psychotherapy. Moreover, all three have shown particular interest in the philosophical and epistemological grounds of their theorisation, as well as in the social and ethical implications.

In the following sections we shall describe the process of personal knowledge as it takes shape in the previously mentioned contributions. We shall discern, for explanatory purposes, the role that the distinctions have in the construction of experiential worlds, the change of personal knowledge in the continuous process of the person's adaptation to the environment, the anticipatory value of construction processes and the circularity of the relationship between knowledge and action. For each of these aspects, we shall consider the most relevant implications relative to the theory and practice of psychotherapy.

3.2 The making of distinctions: from the perception of reality to the construction of experiential realities

As observed in Chapter 2, the constructivist views on knowledge regard it as having an adaptive function instead of a representational one. They stress that knowledge does not arrive ready-made from the outside, it is not a matter of receiving impressions: knowledge is constructed over time, as a result of structural changes in a living system in its relationship with the environment.

The theory of autopoiesis offers the possibility to recognise the biological ground of knowledge without falling into the mind–body dualism of many psychologies; pointing out instead the necessary continuity between the autopoietic organisation regarded as the basis of life, and the structural changes encountered by the system throughout its ontogenesis as long as the organisation itself is conserved. It is following such structural change that, in human beings, language emerges and, together with it, the observer is able to make **distinctions** and specify what he or she distinguishes as unities, as entities different from, and external to, him or herself.

To the extent that the observer can distinguish in a unity a number of components through further operations of distinctions, he or she can distinguish a unity as simple (as a wholeness) or as composite. The components of a **composite unity** and the simple unity related to that are in a constitutive relation of reciprocal definition, and therefore their phenomenal domains do not intersect, being the domain of the **simple unity** 'meta' respect to that of the composite one. Parenthetically, the possibility envisioned by Maturana to treat a unity as simple or composite, corresponds in Kelly to treating anything as a construct or as an element (a subordinate construct) within the hierarchical structure of a person's construction system.

In Chapter 2 we dealt with Maturana's distinction between organisation and structure of a living system (see section 2.4.4). Now, with the above distinction between simple and composite unities, we can introduce the notion of '**structural intersection**' which we regard as a useful conceptual tool for a constructivist understanding of some issues central to psychotherapy. The starting point is that the organisation of a composite unity brought forth by an observer does not exhaust the relations and interactions in which the components that realise it may participate in their domain of existence. The components may thus participate in the realisation of the organisation of many other composite unities, which therefore structurally intersect with it. Furthermore, when the components of a composite unity are themselves composite unities, this may participate in structural intersections that take place through the components of its components. 'In any case, when an observer distinguishes two or more structurally intersecting systems, he or she distinguishes two or more different composite unities realized through the same body' (Maturana, 1987, p. 347), and also their ontogenic drifts intersect forming a network of co-ontogenic drifts. Maturana reports the example of the distinction, in the structural realisation of a human being as a living system, of a mammal, a person, a woman, a doctor and a mother. They are conceived as different composite unities defined by different organisations, conserved and realised in different domains of existence. Their structural intersections result in dependent domains of disintegrations and conservations, not necessarily reciprocal. For example, the disintegration of the organisation 'human being' would entail the disintegration of the other organisations, but the disintegration of the 'doctor' (e.g. following retirement) does not entail the disintegration of the 'mother'. A consideration of the structural intersections among the autopoietic organisation, the organisation of self, and other 'subordinate' organisations, can reveal itself of great importance in psychology and psychotherapy, as we shall see in the following chapters.

Coming back to the issue of continuity between biology and knowledge, Piaget also postulates that:

> intelligence does not by any means appear at once derived from mental development, like a higher mechanism, and radically distinct from those which have preceded it. Intelligence presents, on the contrary, a remarkable continuity with the acquired or even inborn processes on which it depends and at the same times makes use of.
>
> (1952/1936, p. 21)

And so, according to Piaget, the biological processes of morphogenesis, intelligence and language show an inevitable continuity, given that 'le dépassé est toujours intégré dans le dépassant' (Piaget and Garcia, 1983, p. 303), that is, one **structure** is surpassed by another in such a way that the structure surpassed is integrated in the structure that surpasses it.

Following his choice of dealing only with the realm of psychology, Kelly does not dwell on exploring the biological bases of knowledge, restricting himself to emphasise that 'life [. . .] involves an interesting relationship between parts of our universe wherein one part, the living creature, is able to bring himself around to represent another part, his environment', where 'representation' is made clear soon later as 'construction of reality' (Kelly, 1991a/1955, p. 6). Anyway, Kelly appears to adhere to what Maturana will call, more than twenty years later, 'ontology of the observer' when, expounding the fundamental postulate of personal construct theory, he chooses to use the adverb 'psychologically' instead of the adjective 'psychological' with reference to the processes 'channelised' by the anticipation (see section 1.1.1).

As to the central issue of this section, how does a human being, once becoming an observer (that is, a person), create realities?

Despite the differences in language, several authors, broadly definable as constructivists, seem to give similar answers. Their views are characterised by an understanding of the relationship between any entity and its environment in terms of complementarity rather than interaction, what we consider a feature of hermeneutic constructivism (Chiari & Nuzzo, 2006).

'A universe comes into being when a space is severed or taken apart. The skin of a living organism cuts off an outside from an inside. So does the circumference of a circle in a plane', writes the mathematician Spencer-Brown (1969, p. xxix). Adding, 'The act is itself already remembered, even if unconsciously, as our first attempt to distinguish different things in a world where, in the first place, the boundaries can be drawn anywhere we please' (ibid., p. xxix). Kelly uses a similar phrasing, but casts the process into the dimension of time rather than space: 'The separation of events is what man produces for himself when he decides to chop up time into manageable lengths' (Kelly, 1991a/1955, p. 36).

Bateson holds a similar view of knowledge. Objects are our creations: our experience of them is based on 'information', defined as 'any difference that makes a difference' (1979, p. 246). In order to produce information, two entities (real or imaginary) are needed, such that the difference between them can be immanent to their reciprocal relationship:

> There is a profound and unanswerable question about the nature of those 'at least two' things that between them generate the difference which becomes information by making a difference. Clearly each alone is – for the mind and perception – a non-entity, a non-being. Not different from being, and not different from non-being. An unknowable, a *Ding an sich*, a sound of one hand clapping.
>
> (Ibid., 1979, p. 72)

Thus, we receive information in terms of events that correspond to 'outlines' of the world. We draw distinctions, that is, we draw them out. The distinctions that are not drawn out do not exist.

Again a similar view, in modern cognitive science, is sustained by Maturana and Varela in their understanding of cognition as a biological phenomenon. 'A distinction splits the world into two parts, "that" and "this," or "environment" and "system," or "us" and "them," etc. One of the most fundamental of all human activities is the making of distinctions'

(Varela, 1979, p. 84). 'The act of indicating any being, object, thing or unity involves making an act of distinction which distinguishes what has been indicated as separate from its background' (Maturana & Varela, 1987, p. 40). The operation of 'distinction' performed by an observer in his or her praxis of living brings forth a unity as well as the **medium** in which it is distinguished. Between the two terms of an act of distinction, a constitutive, metaphysical complementarity can be recognised. Varela (1976, 1979) elaborates further on the notion of complementarity, envisioning in it the possibility of a transition from dualities to 'trinities' (Chiari & Nuzzo, 1987).

In psychology, James had already stressed that knowledge derives from 'acts of discrimination and comparison' (1890, p. 311), that 'experience is trained by both association and dissociation' (ibid., p. 314), and that 'the perception of likeness is practically very much bound up with that of difference' (ibid., p. 336).

Piaget uses the notion of 'schema', definable as what in a single action may be applicable to the same situations or generalisable to similar situations. Starting from innate reflex, children organise in action schemata their experience and reorganise them through the processes of assimilation and accommodation, through to the constitution of objects and the emergence of conceptual structures (see next section).

The social psychologist Rokeach (1960) suggests a distinction between 'open' and 'closed mind' based on the organisation of 'belief–disbelief systems' that shows astonishing analogies with Kelly's theory, even though achieved independently. But it was only Kelly who offered the most articulate, consistent and sophisticated contribution to this issue. His notion of 'construct' is formulated in terms clearly referable to a metaphysical complementarity.

Kelly departs from the notion of 'concept' and from conventional logic by assuming that the differences expressed by a construct are just as relevant as the likenesses:

> We see relevant similarity and contrast as essential and *complementary* features of the same construct and both of them as existing within the range of convenience of the construct. That which is outside the range of convenience of the construct is not considered part of the contrasting field but simply an area of irrelevancy.
>
> (1991a/1955, p. 49, italics ours)

Interested in rejecting the epistemological assumption that leads to an understanding of speech as a way of denoting entities, Kelly argues that:

> a person never makes his choice merely between an entity and a nonentity. When he says that "A is B" it seems that he is also asserting

that "A is not C". The choice he makes is not, therefore, between "B" and "not-B", but between "B" and "C" – between two entities.

(1969/1961, p. 98)

Kelly called his choice the 'double entity choice' to distinguish it from the 'single entity choice' envisioned by classical logic.

It is in order to save this premise that Kelly describes a construct as dichotomous or bipolar in nature, but 'it must be understood that the personal construct *abstracts* similarity and difference *simultaneously*. One cannot be abstracted without implying the other' (1969/1961, p. 103, italics ours).

> Both the similarity and the contrast are inherent in the same construct. A construct which implied similarity without contrast would represent just as much of a chaotic undifferentiated homogeneity as a construct which implied contrast without similarity would represent a chaotic particularized heterogeneity.
>
> (Kelly, 1991a/1955, p. 35)

The implications of the constructivist view of knowledge are numerous and profound for psychotherapeutic practice.

Assuming the system's **organisational closure** and knowledge as a personal construction, the therapist's search for understanding the client's experiential reality becomes an essential condition. The empathic understanding of the client (to be discussed in Chapter 4) becomes an ineluctable starting point for the co-participation in an effective psychotherapeutic process. It implies substituting the traditional descriptive approach to the client in terms of categorical or dimensional diagnosis, with a phenomenological approach.

The difference between the two approaches may be clarified by resorting to the distinction between a third-person and a first-person perspective. Third-person descriptions are about brain processes, behaviour, interactions with the environment and such like; that is, they concern the descriptive experiences associated with the study of natural phenomena. First-person events – also referred to as 'phenomenal consciousness', 'qualia', 'conscious experience' or simply 'experience' – concern the person's lived experience associated with cognitive and mental events (Varela & Shear, 1999). The first-person data are assumed to be irreducible to third-person data, even though it could be useful to bridge them. An account of the source of first-person knowledge is essential for anyone who takes seriously the apparent evidence that the processes being studied appear as relevant and manifest for a 'self' or 'subject' that can provide an account; that we each have a distinctive access to knowing what we experience (Thomasson, 2005).

In both cases, the previous discussion mainly relates to the study of consciousness. For constructivist psychotherapists, the issue is simpler. We are not interested in assessing the presence (and the amount) in the client of categories such as ego strength, self-esteem, self-efficacy or the 'big five' personality traits, and such like. If people live in personal experiential realities made up of the distinctions they operate, we have to understand them – the clients' categories – if we hope to understand their possibilities and their constraints, and to help them overcome their disorder.

3.3 The changing of knowledge: from instructive interactions to structure-determined changes

Piaget, Maturana and Kelly also agree in describing knowledge as the result of variations triggered by disturbances to the system so as to maintain the organism's equilibrium in its adaptation with the environment. For them, living systems are autoregulatory, self-organising, or autonomous systems.

In Piaget, the process of adaptation (see Figure 3.1) is realised through an equilibrium (**'equilibration'**) between 'assimilation', or 'integration of external elements into evolving or completed structures' (1970a, p. 706) and 'accommodation', 'any modification of an assimilatory scheme or structure by the elements it assimilates' (ibid., p. 708).

> Assimilation and accommodation are not two separate functions but the two functional poles, set in opposition to each other, of any adaptation. [. . .] it must always be remembered that there can be no assimilation of anything into the organism or its functioning without a corresponding accommodation and without such assimilation's becoming part of an adaptation context.
>
> (Piaget, 1971/1967, p. 173)

Figure 3.1 can be explained in the following way:

The living systems (S_1) conserve their organisation as long as they maintain an adaptation with the environment (E) through structural changes triggered at every instant by environmental perturbations (a) and through the perturbations represented by the presence of other living systems (b). A history of reciprocal, recurrent interactions between a living system and its environment, and between a living system and other living systems can in time lead to a structural congruence between them (structural coupling). The person (P_1) conserves his or her existence as long as he/she maintains an adaptation with the environment (E) through his/her core constructs (a), and conserves his/her identity as long as he/she maintains an adaptation with other people through his/her core role constructs (b), being his/her identity (core role) the result of reciprocal, recurrent interactions between

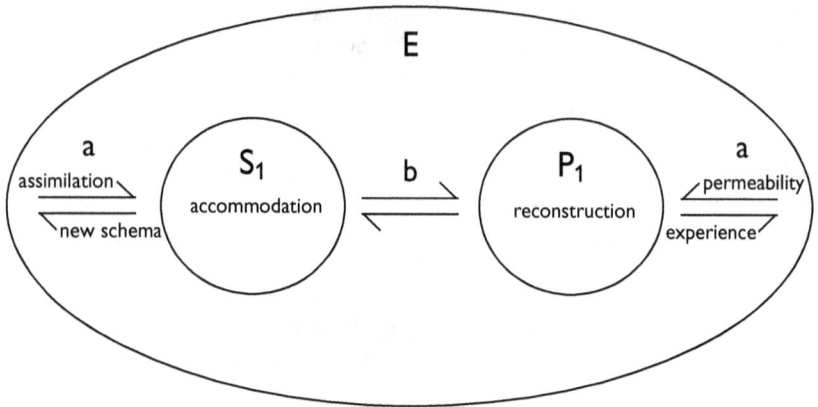

Figure 3.1 On the left: relationship between living system and environment in the biological domain (according to Piaget and Maturana); on the right: relationship between the person and environment in the psychological domain (according to Kelly).

the person and other people in terms of his/her understanding of their processes.

The basic functions of adaptation, embodied in the most diverse structures, are to be found at every hierarchical level, from the genome up to the cognitive mechanisms of higher order (Piaget, 1971/1967). Therefore, adaptation is at the basis both of phylogenesis (where it corresponds to what is called 'evolution') and of ontogenesis (corresponding to 'learning'), and their result has been conceptualised in terms of viability through the constraints of environment (von Glasersfeld, 1980).

In Maturana, notwithstanding the diversity of the disciplinary fields, we find a similar view of adaptation. At the end, Piaget and Maturana share a conception of knowledge as self-organising, as well as the cybernetic character of their models (Dooley, 1993; Varela, 1979).

Maturana defines adaptation or 'structural coupling' as 'the relation of dynamic structural correspondence with the medium in which a unity conserves its class identity [. . .] and which is entailed in its distinction as it is brought forth by the observer in his or her praxis of living' (1987, p. 338). Living systems exist as long as their organisation and their adaptation are conserved through the flow of their structural changes in structural coupling. A person remains alive as long as the flow of their continuous structural changes and the continuous structural changes of the medium occur; following the path in which the organisation and the adaptation (adequate operation in its domain of existence) of the person involved are conserved through their recursive interactions.

It is the structure of the system to realise the organisation and to specify the domains of perturbations (see section 2.4.4). They are 'perturbations' since, if the system is regarded as 'structure-determined', the environmental 'stimuli' can only 'trigger' an effect, not 'determine' it. As long as a congruence is preserved between environment and living system, they act as mutual sources of perturbation; triggering structural changes.

Since conception, every living being undergoes modifications that are determined at every instant by its structure in interaction with the environment, and that follow one another throughout its ontogenesis (seen as an '**ontogenic structural drift**') until such modifications allow for the conservation of life, that is, the autopoietic organisation. Loss of adaptation entails the destruction of the organisation of the living system, that is, death. The presence of a nervous system expands the domain of states of the living system, reaching the possible emergence of language and knowledge (see following).

In Kelly a similar notion of adaptation is dealt with in relation to the variation of a person's construction system. The experience corollary states that a person's construction system varies as he or she successively revises his or her construction of events in the light of the validation or invalidations of his or her anticipations (see Figure 3.2). This progressive variation, however, must itself take place within a system. In Kelly's words, 'one does not learn certain things merely from the nature of the stimuli which play upon one; one learns only what one's framework is designed to permit one to see in the stimuli' (1991a/1955, p. 55). Actually, such a variation is limited by the permeability of the system's superordinate constructs (modulation corollary). 'A construct [. . .] can be called permeable if it is so constituted that new experience and new events can be discriminatively added to those which it already embraces'. Permeability represents therefore a referent for novel events, allowing both continuity and change. In this way, 'the more subordinate aspects of a person's construction system can be systematically varied without making his whole psychological house does fall down' (ibid., p. 57).

We regard the Piagetian notion of assimilation as analogous to the Kellyan notion of permeability. In either cases, the result is a reorganisation of the structure (the scheme, the construct), which in turn modifies circularly what the structure may successively specify about environment.

Also the feature of **structural determinism** can be easily found in Kelly's writings. The following quotes appear particularly illustrative:

This personal construct system provides [man] both with freedom of decision and limitation of action–freedom, because it permits him to deal with the meanings of events rather than being helplessly pushed about by them, and limitation, because *he can never make choices outside the world of alternatives he has erected for himself.*

(1969a/1958, p. 88, italics added)

Within the realm of relevance his personal construct system defines for him, each man initiates what he says and does. Thus his words and his acts are not mere events consequent upon previous occurrences, but are expressions of what is relevantly affirmed and denied within his system.

(1969/1966, p. 35)

The theory of autopoiesis is particularly clear in defining what the structure of a unity specifies at every instant.

- *Domain of changes of state:* viz., all those structural changes that a unity can undergo without a change in its organization, i.e., with conservation of class identity.
- *Domain of destructive changes:* all those structural changes that a unity can undergo with loss of organization and therefore with loss of class identity.
- *Domain of perturbations:* all those interactions that trigger changes of state.
- *Domain of destructive interactions:* all those perturbations that result in a destructive change.

(Maturana & Varela, 1987/1984, pp. 97–98, italics in original)

The previous discussion has to do with another important aspect of the constructivist view of knowledge, that of anticipation, which we shall deal with in the following section.

Many therapists may consider obvious and trivial the implications that derive from a conceptualisation of the person as a structure-determined system. Essentially, they could say, it would be enough to consider the client's point of view as able to carry out a more efficient role in the psychotherapeutic relationship. Actually, the implications go well beyond this generic common sense.

First, all the directive psychotherapies (behaviour therapy, cognitive-behaviour therapy, rationalistic cognitive therapies, structural and strategic family therapies and so on), meant as therapies where the therapist has an active and often authoritative role consisting in advising, suggesting or requiring the client or family to follow detailed prescriptions, evidently do not share the perspective of structural determinism.

Nevertheless, even certain psychotherapies defined as non-directive, are apparently based on instructive interactions. Such is the case of psycho-analytic psychotherapies when the therapists try to impose their interpretations on the client. Starting implicitly from a structural determinist perspective, Kelly observes that:

all interpretations understood by the client are perceived in terms of his own system. Another way of expressing the same thing is to say that it is always the client who interprets, not the therapist. If the therapist is to be effective, he must take into account what the interpretation will mean to the client and not depend solely on the natural 'correctness' of the interpretation he offers.

(1991b/1955, p. 371, italics in the original)

Both the psychoanalyst and the constructivist psychotherapist, give the client's material a second meaning. The difference is that the psychoanalytic interpretation is likely to be rejected (or faithfully accepted) by the client because it is seen as meaningless, if not disqualifying, whereas the constructivist interpretation is offered on the basis of the therapist's anticipation that it fits the client's construction system, thus appearing plausible to him or her.

It was such an assumption that brought the formerly 'Freudian' Kelly to lay the foundation of personal construct psychotherapy:

I began fabricating 'insights.' I deliberately offered 'preposterous interpretations' to my clients. [. . .] My only criteria were that the explanation account for the crucial facts as the client saw them and that it carry implications for approaching the future in a different way. [. . .]

What happened? Well, many of my preposterous explanations worked, some of them surprisingly well.

(1969/1963, p. 52)

Many cases of 'resistance' – 'to most therapists [. . .] a kind of perverse stubbornness in the client' (Kelly, 1969a/1958, p. 83) – can be understood as deriving from the therapists' choice to act according to the belief in instructive interactions. From a constructivist perspective, which acknowledges that people are structure-determined systems, the clients are doing what their structures allow them to. Invoking the concept of resistance 'bespoke more of the therapist's perplexity than of the client's rebellion. [. . .] It was possible to see resistance in terms of the therapist's naivete' (ibid., p. 83).

The idea that it is possible to instruct other people goes against acceptance of others and contributes to make them feel wrong. Consequently, the statement of postmodern family therapists that 'directive therapy models [are] pathologizing' (L. Hoffman, 1993, p. 127) acquires a precise meaning.

The view of human beings as structure-determined systems goes beyond the modalities of interpretation. It informs the whole psychotherapeutic process given that any action by the constructivist therapists is based on their anticipation of the meaning it will acquire for the clients, and is guided by their professional construction of them. It is such a construction to suggest which kinds of perturbations are more likely to result in therapeutic structural changes.

3.4 Anticipation: the cause lies in the future

At any given instant, the structure of a living system, as stated in the preceding section, defines its possible ensuing transformations, in that it specifies what can interact with it. Consequently, autonomous systems are anticipatory systems.

The anticipation deriving from the structure of the system has to be distinguished from prediction. The latter has been termed by Dubois (2000) 'weak anticipation', being based on a predictive model of the system itself and its environment. 'Strong anticipation', on the contrary, is embedded in the system, being 'a consequence of *canalization* caused by the organization of the structural building-blocks of which the system in question consists' (Riegler, 2001, p. 534, italics ours).

In biology, the idea of canalisation can be traced back to the work of Waddington (1957). His dialectical view of the interaction between organism and environment is defined by Piaget (1971/1967, p. 120) as a 'tertium quid', able to bypass the more traditional antithetic views represented by Lamarckism and neo-Darwinism. Waddington's synthesis is depicted through the metaphor of 'epigenetic landscape', where sequential processes, such as embryogenesis, are seen as balls rolling downhill following a certain course (a 'chreod', a necessary path) through a continuously ramifying system of valleys. In other terms, the embryonic development is canalised according to certain attractors, represented by control genes. Influences exerted by the environment may eventually lead to lasting deviations in the chreod, but usually the process, deviating from its course under outside influence, is brought back on course by the interplay of coercive compensations. Developmental processes therefore show an equilibrium better described, as far as dynamical systems are concerned, in terms of 'homeorhesis' ('similar flow') rather than in terms of homeostasis as in static systems.

Piaget will return to Waddington's concepts, applying them to the development of schemata or ideas, to the conservation of information acquired previously (that is, 'memory'), and to anticipation. According to Piaget, the function of anticipation, as an extension of all forms of conserved information, is common to organic as well as cognitive processes at all levels, from the most elementary habits like perception and conditioned reflex, to the scientific thought based on experiments designed to verify hypotheses (Piaget, 1971/1967, pp. 191–201). 'One of the essential functions of knowing is to bring about foresight' (ibid., p. 191). On the other hand, the function of anticipation is implied by the assumption that cognitive structures are tied to action (see the following section). Therefore, a conceptual structure fails because it does not lead to the expected results, and is likely to be modified just because it clashes with an environmental constraint. 'If, instead, a scheme is successful [. . .], no inference about a "real" world can be drawn from this viability, because a countless number of other schemes might have worked as well' (von Glasersfeld, 1995, p. 73).

A similar view of anticipation can be found in Maturana, even though its role in the theory of autopoiesis is less emphasised:

> A living system, due to its circular organization, is an inductive system and functions always in a predictive manner; what occurred once will occur again. Its organization (both genetic and otherwise) is conservative and repeats only that which works.
>
> (1970, pp. 15–16)

Alternatively, anticipation occupies a central role in Kelly's personal construct theory.

We have seen in Chapter 1 that the formal structure of the theory derives from a fundamental postulate centred around the notion of anticipation. 'A person's processes are psychologically channelized by the ways in which he anticipates events' (Kelly 1991a/1955, p. 32). This kind of anticipation can be interpreted as 'strong' according to Dubois' (2000) distinction, in that Kelly considers anticipation as inherent to any personal construction. Here is how Kelly explains such an association between construction and anticipation:

> Consider a day. Concretely, today is not yesterday, nor is tomorrow today. Time does not double back on itself. But after a succession of time man is able to detect a recurrent theme in its ever flowing process. It is possible to abstract the recurrent theme in terms of the rising and the setting of the sun. Moreover, the same theme does not recur when time is segmented in other ways. Thus, the concept of a day is erected along the incessant stream of time – a day which is, in its own way, like other days and yet clearly distinguishable from the moments and the years.
>
> Once events have been given their beginnings and endings, and their similarities and contrasts construed, it becomes feasible to try to predict them, just as one predicts that a tomorrow will follow today. What is predicted is not that tomorrow will be a duplicate of today but that there are replicative aspects of tomorrow's event which may be safely predicted. Thus man anticipates events by construing their replications.
>
> (1991a/1955, p. 37)

As a consequence, 'it is the future which tantalizes man, not the past. Always he reaches out to the future through the window of the present' (1991a/1955, p. 34). Von Foerster (2003, p. 230) arrives to a similar consideration using one of his aphorisms: 'the cause lies in the future'.

To the extent that it is the future, rather than the past, that torments people, the costructivist psychotherapist will be more interested in the clients' anticipations than in their biographies.

The collection of the client's life story, which occupies a large part in many psychotherapeutic approaches beginning with psychoanalysis, holds a minor role (if any) in constructivist psychotherapy as we intend it.

There are numerous reasons for that, all ascribable ultimately to the anticipatory posture deriving from the fundamental postulate of Kelly's theory.

First, the person is not determined by her or his past experience. Behaviour is an experiment, aimed at verifying the validity of personal constructions (see the following section). Therefore, the therapists should ask themselves; 'what is that person verifying in this behaviour?', rather than 'what has brought this person to behave in such a way?'

Second, given the **recursion** of the persons' processes, their past is, so to say, included in their present. In fact, it is a concept nowadays common to other psychotherapeutic approaches, particularly cognitive, that memories of the past are inevitably a reconstruction of the present, and not a retrieval of events exempt from actual interpretations.

From the previous section it may be said that the way in which the clients relate to other people (including the therapist) in their present life 'recapitulates' the history of their construction of preceding relational experiences, beginning from the early relational experiences with their parents. The analysis of the role the clients tend to play in their relationship with others, together with the analysis of transference processes, will suffice to make the therapist understand the core role of the clients and to formulate a professional hypothesis on their disorder.

In certain cases, it may be useful to underline the 'historical coherence' between the clients' present role and their construction of early relational experiences. The utility of such an intervention, however, is tied to the possibility that clients interpret such coherence as an outcome of their attempts to give a meaning to their relational experiences, so as to encourage the search for alternatives. The choice would show itself to be therapeutically unfortunate should clients view such coherence in a deterministic way ('having had such an experience with my parents, it is inevitable that I encounter these difficulties today'). Such a risk would be even greater should one choose to 'dig' into the clients' past history as a first step to a reconstructive work.

3.5 The circularity between knowledge and action

Once again, the possibility of reversing the traditional viewpoint derives from a consideration of living systems as autonomous systems, implying in

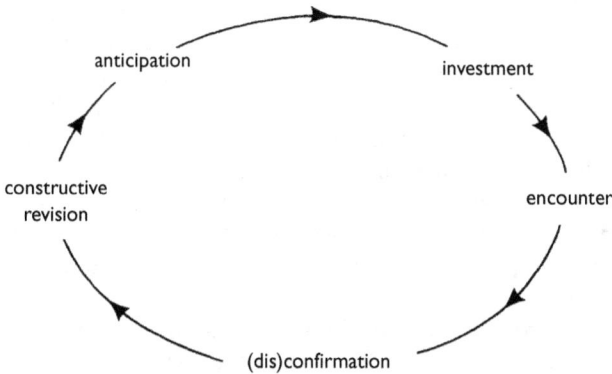

Figure 3.2 The experience cycle.

its turn a closed circular causality. For the same reason, knowledge and action are also circularly related.

According to Piaget, knowledge is doing: 'the fundamental fact [is] that any piece of knowledge is connected with an action and that to know an object or a happening is to make use of it by assimilation into an action schema' (1971/1967, p. 6). As a consequence, actions repeat themselves whenever similar situations arise, or, better still, 'if there is the same interest in a similar situation, but they are differentiated or else form a new combination if the need or the situation alters' (ibid., p. 7).

Maturana sees knowledge as an effective action in maintaining the equilibrium of the living system. The theory of autopoiesis envisions a circularity such that 'all doing is knowing, and all knowing is doing' (Maturana & Varela, 1987/1984, p. 26), in the bringing forth of a world that manifests itself in all our actions and all our being.

Personal construct theory shares a similar view. Kelly's latest writings (1970a/1966, 1977/1963, 1980/1967) deal with the aspects implied in the process of change in a personal construct system by regarding them as parts of a cycle, the '**experience cycle**'.

The full cycle which leads to a personal reconstruction of experience can be divided into five phases: anticipation, investment, encounter, confirmation or disconfirmation and constructive revision (Figure 3.2). On the basis of any construction, people anticipate some event, invest themselves in this anticipation, actively encounter the event, verify whether anticipation has been validated or invalidated and revise their construction accordingly. The fulfilment of the whole process is followed by a new anticipation giving rise to a subsequent experiential cycle (see also Epting & Amerikaner, 1980). In this circularity between knowledge and action, considered by Kelly as characteristic of high-level, optimally functioning people, it appears evident that behaviour is not seen as a reaction, as in behaviourism, or as a consequence, as in cognitivism. In personal construct theory, 'behaviour is an experiment' (Kelly, 1970b/1966, p. 255), 'a question posed in such a way as to commit man to the role and obligations of an experimenter' (ibid., p. 261), 'the method of man the scientist' (ibid., p. 269).

The circularity between knowledge and action is basic to the whole psychotherapeutic process. As a consequence of this circularity, the person may be seen as a form of movement, and a halt at a certain point of the experience cycle takes the form of a psychological disorder.

From the preceding considerations derives an important orienting question for the therapist: 'At what stage of the experience cycle has the client become "stuck", so that constructive revision of her system has become impossible?' (Neimeyer, 1987, p. 7). The answer to this question will orientate the therapeutic strategy, aimed at restoring the client's psychological movement.

3.6 The emergence of consciousness

As we mentioned previously the child, starting from innate reflexes, according to Piaget, organises experience in action schemata and reorganises them through the processes of assimilation and accommodation, up to the constitution of objects, the construction of their permanence and the emergence of conceptual structures.

This is the outcome of new schemata arising by differentiation from an earlier schema and by incorporating new elements into it, according to a process which results in the emergence of progressive levels of organisation. These levels correspond to four main developmental stages.

1   The *sensorimotor stage*, from birth to 2 years in which children experience the world through movement and senses and acquire object permanence. During this stage comes to fruition the transition (a 'Copernican revolution' according to Piaget) from an initial, complete undifferentiation between subject and object – between the I and the surrounding world – to a progressive and stable constitution of the subject and the objects.
2   The *preoperational stage*, from ages 2 to 6/7 years, in which children gain access to the first representative activity, that is, to the semiotic function. This latter gives the children the possibility to differentiate between signifier and signified, even if a situation of egocentrism appears again in relation to the subjective characteristics of the children's actions rather than in relation to the body as in the preceding stage.

3   The *concrete operational stage*, from ages 7/8 years to 11/12 years, in which the representative actions become connected with each other, as to form a network of relations capable of assuring their reversibility.

4   The *formal operational stage*, after age 11/12 years, in which operations constructed on the basis of concrete operations become possible, thus giving rise to a logic and to a knowledge of hypothetic-deductive type.

Within these stages Piaget places the subject's increasing awareness of their own functioning, whether in relation to the self or in relation to the object of knowledge (Piaget, 1937, 1952/1936, 1954, 1974a, 1974b).

According to the hypothesis of the 'three levels of consciousness' (Ferrari *et al.*, 2001), the emergence of consciousness already started in the sensori-motor stage with what may be called 'practical consciousness'. At this first level, consciousness consists of an unreflective awareness of the results of the child's sensory-motor functioning.

The second level, that of 'conceptual consciousness', emerges in the concrete operational stage. This kind of consciousness consists of an effort by the child to understand his or her organisation, contributing to comprehension through awareness of the organisation of a group of actions, and to its eventual reorganisation.

Finally, the third level during the stage of formal operations, represents a fully 'reflective consciousness', consisting of a reflection by the child on his or her functioning at the concrete operational level. 'Reflective consciousness is to be differentiated from conceptual consciousness by the fact that the subject [. . .] explicitly takes his or her own functioning as an object of consciousness. This effectively means that the subject is conscious of being conscious' (Pons & Harris, 2001, p. 222).

The process described by Piaget takes a dialectical form, in which each new stage, or level, is created through the further differentiation, integration and synthesis of new structures out of the old, according to a recursive process which implies:

- that the order of succession of the acquisitions is constant
- that the structures constructed at a given age become an integral part of the structures of the subsequent age, according to a vertical 'décalage'
- that each stage is characterised by a structured whole ('structure d'ensemble')
- that each stage implies a level of preparation on one hand and a level of fulfillment on the other hand, according to a horizontal 'décalage'
- that stages are characterised as forms of 'equilibrium', of adaptation between the organism and the environment, complementary to the 'equilibration' which governs the process of transition from one stage to the following stage.

(Bocchi & Ceruti, 1981)

A succession of levels structurally similar to Piaget's is described by Maturana in relation to the generative path-linking consensual behaviour to self-consciousness.

Language, better still, 'languaging' (an activity rather than a symbolic schema), according to Maturana (1978, 1987), is a biological phenomenon. It 'takes place in our relational domain as a manner of living in recurrent interactions in what an observer sees as recursive consensual coordinations of consensual coordinations of behavior' (1995a, p. 154). In other words, two structure-determined systems are sources (and targets) of perturbations each with respect to the other, and, as a consequence of recurrent interactions, there is a 'structural coupling' between them as long as they conserve their organisation.

One instance of this 'linguistic behaviour' is the consensual coordination of a cat scratching a door to be let out of the house by its owner.

A first recursion in the flow of consensual coordinations of behaviour, described by an observer as consensual coordinations of consensual coordinations of behaviour, constitutes language and languaging.

> If one observes the mother child relation in early childhood, one can see that the growing baby becomes a languaging being in the flow of its living in the intimate relation of care and play with his or her mother in the consensual co-ordinations of emotions and doings that such relation entails. One can see that the flow of doings that an observer may recognise as languaging begins to appear when there are consensual co-ordinations of doings that become recursive in the play of the mother and child much earlier than the appearance of vocal sounds. As an observer sees that the mother/child interactions of co-ordinations of doings become recursive consensual co-ordinations of doings, he or she sees language arising as a domain of living together in consensual distinction of objects that soon becomes an expanding domain of recursive co-ordination of consensual distinctions of objects and relations between objects. When this happens, the observer sees that the child begins to live with his or her mother and other people around him or her, in an ever growing domain of inter-objectivity.
>
> (Maturana, 2005, p. 67)

By 'inter-objectivity' Maturana means the domain of manipulable or thinkable entities, which we treat as if they existed independently of our doings.

In fact, with the emergence of language, objects arise. Such as in Heidegger's (1998/1976, p. 250) saying 'language is the house of being', so in Maturana 'objects arise with language and do not preexist to it' (1995a, p. 154). From here on, different kinds of objects will arise in language at every new recursion:

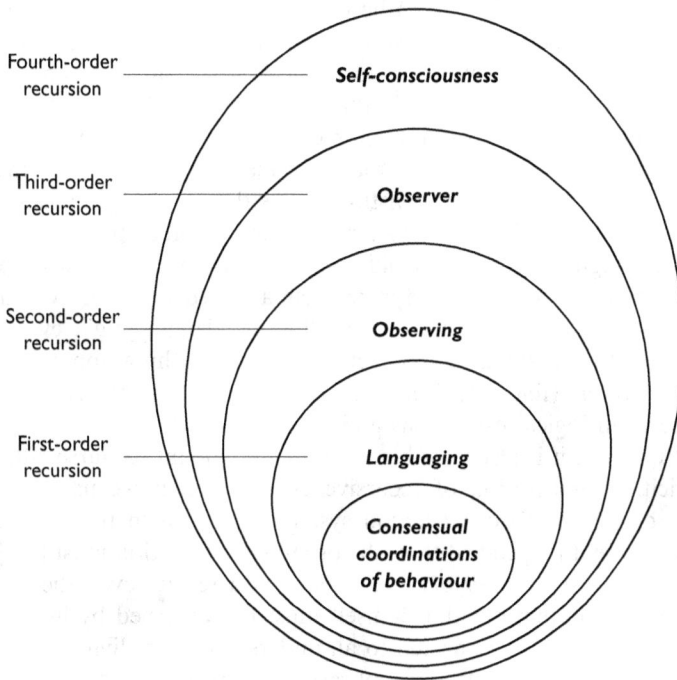

Figure 3.3 The emergence of consciousness through levels of recursion (according to Maturana).

In this dynamics, as an object arises in the first recursion in the consensual coordinations of behavior, the distinction of an object arises in the second recursion. As objects are distinguished, another recursion in the flow of consensual coordinations of behavior (a third recursion) distinguishes relations between objects, and the possibility is open for the constitution of a domain of relations as relations of relations are distinguished in a next recursion. In more general terms, since at any level of recursion the consensual behaviors coordinated become objects, and thus a fundament for further recursive distinctions, any level of recursion may recursively become a domain of objects that operates as a ground level for further recursions.

(Maturana, 1995a, p. 155)

In particular, 'observing' arises as an operation in a second recursion that distinguishes a distinction; the 'observer' appears in a third-order recursion that distinguishes distinguishing, that is, in the distinction of observing; and 'self-consciousness' arises in a fourth-order recursion in which observing the observer takes place (see Figure 3.3).

Maturana goes as far as hypothesising that a fifth order of recursion gives rise to the experience of 'responsibility' as self-awareness, and that a sixth order of recursion gives rise to the experience of 'freedom' as self-awareness of self-awareness (Maturana *et al.*, 1995, p. 22).

In addition the origin of human mental functions are explained by Maturana in terms of phenomena that take place in the relational manner of living that human language constitutes. 'As the circular processes of the brain become coupled to the linear flow of "languaging", that brain becomes a "languaging" brain' (ibid., p. 22). Consequently, 'it will operate giving rise through its internal dynamics as a closed network, to sensory/effector correlations that pertain to the flow of "languaging", even when the organism that it integrates is alone, or doing nothing apparent to an external observer' (ibid., p. 22). That is, a person can reflect, meditate, dream, perform logical operations and poetic abstractions and so forth.

In Kelly's work it is also possible to find an abundant recourse, although not explicit, to the notion of recursiveness. The recursive nature of the evolution of a person's construction system is implicit in the modulation corollary, where it is specified that 'the progressive variation must [. . .] take place within a system' (1991a/1955, p. 54). As a result, 'even the changes which a person attempts within himself must be construed by him' (ibid., p. 55). Recursiveness is connected to an understanding of living systems in terms of their **autonomy**. When rephrasing the preceding notion in contemporary terms, we can say that Kelly considers a person's construction system as an autonomous system and, as such, organisationally closed: that is, a system whose processes are related as a network so that they recursively depend on each other in the generation of the processes themselves (Chiari & Nuzzo, 2004). These very processes constitute the system as a unity recognisable in the domain in which the processes exist.

Coming to the analogy between Maturana's description of progressive levels of recursion and personal construct theory, consider how Kelly describes how we can 'talk' to one another with our behaviour:

> Two people, say a mother and a newborn child, may not have a full intellectual meeting of minds the first time they try to enter into a discourse with each other in the maternity ward. But by sharing their encounter with events — including their own behaviour — some mothers and daughters do develop a fair understanding, each of what the other is talking about.
>
> (1969/1966, p. 28)

One can recognise in the above sketch an instance of consensual coordination of behaviour. Here is how Kelly describes the psychologically crucial event of the emergence of self as the basis for the personal construction of one's role:

the *self* is [. . .] a proper concept or construct. It refers to a group of events which are alike in a certain way and, in that same way, necessarily different from other events. The way in which the events are alike is the self. [. . .] The self, having been thus conceptualized, can now be used as a thing, a datum, or an item in the context of a superordinate construct. [. . .]

When the person begins to use himself as a datum in forming constructs, exciting things begin to happen.

(1991a/1955, p. 91, italics in original)

In the process described in the previous section it is possible to recognise three distinct orders of recursion. As in Maturana's account, the order of recursion constituted by 'a group of events' (distinctions in observing, according to Maturana) operates as a ground level for a further recursion leading to the construct 'self' (the observer in the terminology of Maturana), in turn liable to be used as an element, a datum, a ground level for another recursion: the 'personal construction of one's role', that is, self-consciousness. Hereafter, 'much of his social life', Kelly writes, 'is controlled by the comparisons he has come to see between himself and others' (ibid, p. 91).

When referring to the self, it is important to be clear as to the order of recursion connected with different levels of consciousness. Most psychologists, phenomenologists and philosophers have described a duality of the self (see Lewis & Brooks-Gunn, 1979). Maturana's distinction between the 'observer' and 'self-consciousness' is equivalent to Kelly's distinction between 'self' and the 'personal construction of one's role', that is, between 'self as a construct' and 'self as an element'. Similar distinctions can be found in James (1890), between a 'pure Ego' or 'I' (self as knower) and an 'empirical self' or 'Me' (self as known); in Mead (1934), between 'I' and 'Me', the latter being similar to Cooley's (1912) 'social self'; in Wylie (1961), between the 'self as subject' and the 'self as object'; in Lewis and Brooks-Gunn (1979), between an 'existential self' and a 'categorical self'. All the above distinctions can be referred to different levels of recursion, the second term of each pair being at a 'meta-level' with respect to the first.

3.7 The development of self

The importance of early relational experiences for the development of child's personality, successively the adult's is underlined by various schools of psychology, particularly psychoanalysis and cognitivism.

The psychoanalytic literature on the child's tie to the mother is extremely rich and varied (Bowlby, 1958). Such interest is due not only to the role that early relational experiences are supposed to have for the successive development of personality, but also to the influences they exert on the transference relationship with the analyst. Freud's notion of transference shows that he viewed the clinical situation as structured in interpersonal terms according to the patient's early relational experiences. The object relations theorists, in particular, consider the social relations of primary importance for the development of personality, and have extensively explored their clinical significance (J.R. Greenberg & Mitchell, 1983).

As cognitive therapists have begun to recognise the importance of inter-personal processes, some of them found in Bowlby's (1969, 1973, 1980) attachment theory an understanding of the role of early relational experiences suitable for an integration with the epistemological and theoretical assumptions of cognitivism. In fact, even though attachment theory has its historical references in the psychoanalytic model, particularly in the previously mentioned object relations theories, it is characterised by its combining of the ethological study of child's behaviour with system control theory. The specific clinical applications of attachment theory (Bowlby, 1988) derive from an understanding of emotional disorders in terms of particular patterns of attachment, and from the consideration of the role these patterns have in the patient–therapist relationship (Guidano & Liotti, 1983).

As shown in section 3.7, starting from a constructivist perspective the 'self' is understood as a process rather than as an entity. It is regarded as a construction, a distinction which emerges in a human being as the result of a series of recursive processes beginning from its conception. In Maturana's words:

> the self is not an independent entity that some how can be expected to exist by itself and must be localised some where in the body or in the medium. The self is a relational dynamic that arises as an entity in the domain of inter-objectivity proper to living in languaging: the self occurs in the domain of inter-objectivity generated by the family or the community to which the persons that make such distinction belongs. That is, as a child grows in self-distinction, its self arises as the reflexive distinction that he or she makes of his or her bodyhood as the operational intercrossing of all the possible relational behaviours in which he or she participates in the domain of inter-objectivity to which he or she belongs in the realisation of his or her living.
>
> (2005, p. 68)

Maturana emphasises that the self occurs in the social domain represented by the family or the community to which the person belongs. In this connection, it seems worthwhile quoting Bateson:

> conventional epistemology, which we call 'sanity', boggles at the realization that 'Properties' are only differences and exist only in a context, only in relationship. We abstract from relationship and from the experiences of interaction to create 'objects' and endow them with

characteristics. We likewise boggle at the proposition that our own character is only real in relationship. We abstract from the experience of interaction and difference to create a 'self' which shall be 'real' or thingish, even without relationship.

(1976, pp. xi–xvi)

Also Buber's (1937/1923) 'I–Thou philosophy' appears extremely relevant in regard to the social embeddedness of self. According to him, personality is neither simply an individual matter nor simply a social product, but a function of relationship happening in the 'sphere of between' (Chiari & Nuzzo, 2006).

Piaget expresses a very similar view looking for a 'third alternative' in the field of sociology. In this case, the alternative consists of his commitment to relationalism in which the primary fact is 'neither the individual nor the set of individuals but the relationships among individuals, a relationship constantly modifying individual consciousnesses themselves' (1995, p. 136). Neither the individual nor society has priority over the other, since both are implicated in relationships whose terms may be either individuals or social groups. This position is presupposed by Piaget's model of social exchange (Mays & Smith, 2001).

However, both Piaget, interested in the origin of intelligence in the child, and Maturana, involved in the emergence of language and knowledge as biological phenomena, have little more to add about self-consciousness, that is, about the personal–social construction of ourselves that we human beings usually experience as a permanent entity.

We owe to von Glasersfeld (1995), who borrowed from Piaget, a clear first-person description of the steps supposed to be essential to arrive at 'seeing' our self. The process is likely to begin with the infant's discovery that there is a way to distinguish some of the moving shapes in its visual field. For example, the hands the mother move across the infant's visual field are experienced as purely visual, whereas the visual experience of the infant's own hand is associated to a kinaesthetic experience. Later on, the difference between the two experiences is increased by the realisation that its hand's movement can be initiated at will, whereas the movement of the mother's cannot. Moreover, when the infant touches some parts of its body, tactual signals are generated on both sides of the point of contact, in contrast with touching or being touched by other things. 'Once children have coordinated tactual and proprioceptive elements to form some notion of their own body [. . .], this sets the stage for a considerably more complex experience of the physical self: the recognition of [. . .] one's image in a looking glass' (von Glasersfeld, 1995, p. 126).

However, von Glasersfeld too, when arriving at the phase of the construction of the 'social self', limits himself to observe that in this connection there is 'a fundamental theoretical complication', consisting in the consideration that 'if it is others from whose reactions I derive some indication as to the properties I can ascribe to myself, and if my knowledge of these others is the result of my own construction, there is an inherent circularity in that procedure' (1995, p. 127). Von Glasersfeld does not regard circularity as a vicious circle, because we are not free to construct others in any way we like but only in terms of viability. Notwithstanding this, he prefers to turn to the ethical implications of this intersubjective corroboration of our own ways of thinking and acting.

It is at this point that personal construct theory can offer its contribution to the question.

The self as a construction has a peculiarity in respect to other personal constructions, given that it refers reflexively to the very (human) system which operates this kind of distinction.

Bannister (1983) explores its particular nature in terms of the fundamental postulate and the eleven corollaries of personal construct theory. We believe it is worthwhile to briefly outline his elaboration.

Among the events that the person anticipates (fundamental postulate), the self holds a crucial position. 'To anticipate the events of our own behavior, we use core role constructs – those constructs in terms of which we centrally define ourselves, constructs that govern the maintenance of self' (ibid., p. 381). When successful, our anticipation enables us to guide our behaviour. When our anticipation of ourselves is invalidated in a very central way, we may experience guilt, that is, we become aware of the dislodgment of self from core role structure (see section 5.3.4).

Construing replications of the event 'self' (construction corollary) means to interpret our lives following a continuous elaboration and a higher level of abstraction. 'As children we may say "I play football and cricket," and this identifying of self may later become "I love sports," and this in turn may have its essence abstracted into the later notion "I am competitive"' (ibid., p. 381).

People interpret 'self' in many different ways (individuality corollary): they show 'differences in their notions of responsibility; their views of self as causal; contrasting senses of being historical or concerned with the here and now; varying styles of articulation and strategies for monitoring self' (ibid., p. 381).

Moreover, we may differ significantly in where the self is located within the hierarchical organisation of our construction system (organisation corollary). 'For some, self versus not-self may be the most superordinate, the most overarching of constructs, in terms of which all other constructions are organized' (ibid., pp. 381–382). Alternatively, 'for many, the construction of self may have a position subordinate to constructions of God or Country or Nature or whatever' (ibid., p. 382).

As for all constructs, the meaning of 'self' arises when considering its contrasting pole (dichotomy corollary). We may contrast our self with other people, our self with not-self, our present self with our past self, our manifest self with self as we would like it to be, our true self with a socially acted out self. According to Bannister, 'the failure of orthodox "self-psychology" has been largely its failure to attend to the issue of what self is contrasted with' (ibid., p. 382).

Construing our self as having a particular nature, we behave accordingly with it (choice corollary). The choices we make in terms of our anticipation of the greatest possibility of elaboration of our system may be experienced in a variety of forms. 'We most often choose that which, to us, "makes most sense" in a particular context', as well as 'we make a multiplicity of choices that have been so often validated as necessary for maintenance of self [. . .] that we do not experience them as "choices"' (ibid., p. 382).

Also the construct of 'self' has a limited range of convenience varying from person to person (range corollary). 'For some "self" refers only to their lives as they are reflected in personal relationships and chosen recreations', whereas for others it 'incorporates aspects of work, region, political cause, religious belief, artistic taste, and so forth' (ibid., p. 383).

The variation possible for the construction of self (experience corollary) largely depends on the mode of the construct. A pre-emptive self construction ('If I am a nice person, I am *nothing but* a nice person') 'limits the person to choices of behaviors that can be exactly specified as *nice*'. A constellatory view of the self ('If I am nice then I am *necessarily* polite, hygienic, soft-spoken, generous, and kind to children') 'opens up a range of constellated possibilities but does not allow the person to explore beyond the constellation'. Only a propositional view of the self of the type '"I may look on myself *as if* I were (among many other things) nice" allows thematic replications to be seen and responded to but does not demand that the person repeat a circumscribed set of behaviors' (ibid., p. 383).

The elaboration of self also presents limits and possibilities connected with its permeability (modulation corollary). 'Moving from being single to being married, being student to being teacher, being employed to being unemployed, and so forth, all require extensions of self, and such extensions require an initially permeable construct of self' (ibid., p. 383).

We can maintain a consistent view of ourselves in terms of the super-ordinate constructs that govern the construct 'self' (fragmentation corollary). 'I may, on different occasions, be the life and soul of the party, or the reserved wallflower, or even the person who did not come to the party' (ibid., p. 384). Viewed by others, my behaviour can appear inconsistent. Yet, in terms of my own superordinate construing, I can be consistently adhering to the role of experimenter and explorer of 'what suits me best', and in this case the integrity of my self is maintained.

A further boundary in the elaboration of our sense of self is represented by the similarity of our construction of experience with those of other people (commonality corollary). To the extent that we elaborate our notion of self in contrast to others, we need differences to identify self. 'If we live within a relatively rigid and conformist society or subgroup, wherein constructions of work, morality, nature, and so forth, are shared and identical, then our construction of self may be attenuated' (ibid., p. 384). Such a society may devalue 'self', and condemn individuality connoting it in terms of immorality, heresy, or transgression.

We develop our construction of ourselves mainly by construing others' construction of us (sociality corollary). In other terms, we interpret other people's view of us through our view of them, and therefore the view of others becomes primary evidence of what we are. As a result, the elaboration of 'self' can be encouraged or constricted by our construction of others. 'The parent who says "Those are not your ideas, that's just your fancy friends talking," [. . .] or the psychologist who declares that your intelligence is "too low for job X or Y," and so forth, can be effective constrictors'. Moreover, 'such implanted identities tend to be self-fulfilling truths in that their acceptance discourages the active exploration of alternatives' (ibid., p. 384).

The constructs central to self (core role constructs) can be used with varying levels of awareness (see section 5.2.5). Some people can develop very consciously a notion of what they are like, and their conversation with themselves can be very clear. Others can have constructs relative to self prevalently non-verbal or preverbal, and consequently they can see their actions as responses to elements construed as external.

> Very different senses of self may be experienced by persons who see themselves as interpreting and reinterpreting an intrinsically mysterious world and who see their interpretations as central to their existence and by persons who see themselves as reacting realistically to a known and thereby determining universe.
>
> (Bannister, 1983, p. 385)

But let us try to outline the process which, starting with the emergence of self in the infant develops throughout the person's life span.

3.7.1 Early relationships and dependency

The appearance of the self and other people in the child's experiential reality, corresponds, in the language of personal construct theory, to the emergence of a construct that can be verbalised in terms of *self vs. other-than-self*, being the self, as reported above, 'a group of events which are alike in a certain way and, in that same way, necessarily different from other events', both animate and inanimate.

The self is supposed to develop in some form since the early months, insomuch as it has been proven that three and four-month-old infants are able to differentiate between mother and female stranger. After the emergence of the self/other differentiation, the self and other – being *other selves* is particularly important in connection with the question at issue – can be treated as elements, as objects, susceptible to be construed as all the other objects populating the child's environment. The construction of one's role, or construction of self, develops throughout the person's life and is subject to changes as a function of personal experiences in social relationships.

Actually, in the first phase of the process leading to the social construction of self, other people are construed as objects, figures, rather than as people. In fact, once the mother, and a few other people close to their social environment, have been distinguished, the children begin to associate them with nutrition and physical protection. In other words, the fact of having food is associated with the fact of having mother. The two are collected by means of a construct, a *dependency construct* (see section 1.1.12). Parenthetically, one could, according to us, abandon the use in personal construct theory of such a unique professional construct, by simply hypothesising that, in the child's construction, the mother is nothing but an object implying the anticipation of receiving food and other things relative to survival.

To the extent that the children's experiential reality includes other people connected to their maintenance processes, the conservation of their adaptation and organisation becomes linked to the conservation of such relations. This is why children, as well as adults, depend on other people: they realise and conserve their existence and identity in a network of social relations.

It is the very distribution of one person's dependencies in a social network to define the professional dimension *undispersed vs. dispersed dependency* with which Kelly (1966, 1969/1962) replaces the more traditional one, that is, *dependency vs. autonomy* (or *independence*). People show an undispersed dependency to the extent that they concentrate their dependencies, so that those they depend on are each expected to provide the satisfaction of everything they construe as indispensable for survival. This is the case of an infant, or child, who locates all their dependencies on the figure of a caregiver. People show dispersed dependency to the extent that they view their support network in more differentiated ways, so that some resources meet some, while others satisfy different dependencies (Walker, 2003). A person's maturity consists, as Kelly points out, in 'seeing the dimensional lines of his dependency extending through others' (1991b/1955, p. 79), not in a sort of autistic and unrealistic independence from others. Actually, in some sense, 'adults are more dependent than children':

> To be sure, a child cannot take care of himself, but then, when you come right down to it, neither can an adult.

An adult appears to be self-reliant merely because he is often better able to distribute his dependencies in proper relation to his potential resources.

But how many adults can survive on what is sufficient for a child? Indeed, in some cases, children are more adept in placing their dependencies than are their parents.

(1969/1962, p. 192)

The process of dispersion of dependency, together with the subsequent, related emergence of role constructs which come to join the dependency constructs, is closely tied to the type of relationship established between the child and the figures of attachment.

The personal construct understanding of the role of early relational experiences lies therefore in Kelly's ingenious elaboration of the notion of dependency. However, his invitation 'to look at psychology in a new way, more particularly at counselling in a new way, and especially at interpersonal dependency' (1966, p. 171) has not been satisfactorily followed. The role of early relational experiences has been almost ignored by personal construct psychologists, maybe as a consequence of the abandonment of a consideration of clinical disorders in terms of disease entities, and of the emphasis on anticipation rather than on the past determinants of personal disorders. It is only recently that we are taking part in a renewed interest for an understanding of people dependence on others and, to a more limited extent, for the appreciation of its role in the clinical setting (Walker, 1993, 1997, 2003).

A piece of our research (Chiari et al., 1994) was aimed at verifying the hypothesis that the process of dispersion of dependency is related to differences in early relationships between the child and the parents. Those relationships which permitted a transition of aggressiveness in the child were supposed to encourage a progressive dispersion of dependency, whereas the relationships which entailed transitions of threat or guilt were supposed to be unfavourable to the elaboration of role constructs, and more likely to result in personal disorders in the adult. Actually, our experience has shown that a high percentage of people referred to psychotherapy present personal disorders involving a low dispersion of dependency (see section 5.4).

3.7.2 Core role as organisation of self

An optimal development for people may be described in relation to the possibility of maintaining adaptation, thus conserving their organisation. This possibility, in terms of the theory of autopoiesis, is relative to the system's changes in structural coupling with the environment. In turn, in personal construct theory, such structural changes relate to the permeability of the superordinate structures (constructs); that is to their availability in accepting new experiences in their context.

During optimal conditions of development, such as those described in relation to the dependency path traced by aggressiveness, a progressive increase of permeability favours the entering of new resource-people in the context of the dependency constructs, thus giving way to a greater dispersion of dependency. The other preconditions are represented by a progressive differentiation of the needs perceived, and by a less pre-emptive mode of construing the people associated with them.

What the infant and young children construe as something they need is not only unverbalised, but also poorly differentiated. 'Young children, Kelly argued, depend on very few people to meet all their needs', such as 'food, shelter, physical comfort, love, protection' (Walker, 1993, p. 66). That infants come very early to discriminate among some of such needs is shown by the observation that what they anticipate by crying, for example when hungry, can be experienced as validated only if they receive food, while other supplies make them keep crying or cry even more strongly. As children mature, their needs become more differentiated, as well as the means of satisfying them. A tantrum can be more successful than a quiet request in order to obtain an ice cream instead of cream cheese from the parents.

At the same time, the dependency constructs allow a less pre-emptive construction of the people comprised in their context. 'Caregivers come to be viewed in terms of other dimensions, and others can substitute for their functions. The development of role constructs is integral to this process'. Role relationships are developed in order to distribute dependencies, since 'our construing of others' construing enables us to attune our demands on others to what they wish to give us as well as what they are able to provide' (Walker, 1993, p. 67).

Not all adults, however, adequately accomplish this process of dispersion of dependency. Some continue to employ a relatively undifferentiated way of making sense of their dependencies, appearing to 'go around looking for a replica of "mama"', conducting a 'search for more whole "mamas"' (Kelly, 1991b/1955, p. 250).

As children, and later on adolescents, construe other people in terms of objects who are also subjects of knowledge, that is, construers, they begin to construe their own personal role. The construct dimensions are the same (even though the elements can be under one pole or the other), given that they represent abstractions from the comparisons they have come to see between themselves and others. This is why the personal construction of one's role may be inferred from the construction the person places upon other people.

Some of the constructs constituting the personal construction of one's role are 'core constructs', that is, constructs 'which govern a person's maintenance processes', 'those by which he maintains his identity and existence'. Thanks to 'comprehensive but not too permeable' core structures, the person 'can see himself as a complex but organized person' (Kelly, 1991a/1955, p. 356). Those frames within one's core structure which 'enable one to predict and control the essential interactions of himself with other persons and with societal groups of persons [. . .] constitute his conceptualization of *core role*' (ibid., p 370).

To the extent that the notion of *core role* refers to the most invariant aspects of one's construction of oneself, it can be considered the personal constructivist conceptualisation of the more traditional, multifaceted notion of 'personal identity', most commonly regarded as composed of a sense of continuity of self in time, and of the sense of being distinct from other entities. To this regard, personal construct psychology emphasises the essential importance of social constructions. 'We are dependent for life itself upon an understanding of the thoughts of certain other people' (ibid., p. 370).

One of the main tasks of the constructivist psychotherapist consists in the effort to understand the client's core role. Usually, a personal disorder has a connection with jeopardy to the integrity of the person's core role. To this end, it is useful to recognise indications of the transitions of guilt or threat of guilt (the awareness of an imminent and comprehensive change in one's core role structures), in that 'it is the loss of status within the core role constructions which is experienced as guilt' (ibid., p. 371).

Here is how Kelly describes two examples of core role:

> A child construes himself as belonging to his family. He interprets his mother's behaviour. He interprets his father's behaviour. He enacts his presumed part in relation to this interpretation. Who is he? Who is he really? He is a child belonging to Mother and Father and he therefore does this and this and this. Some of the things he does are merely incidental or peripheral. He may mention them because they are easier to put into words. The more basic features of his role may exist for him in terms of preverbal constructs. When asked who he is he may be unable to put them into words.
>
> Now let us suppose that the child discovers that he has not been acting as his parent's child. Let us suppose that the discovery goes deep. His identity is affected. He really is not cast in the core role. The maintenance of his identity rests, he finds, not upon the filial part he thought he was playing, but upon some other, possibly more obscure, ground. It is at this point that he feels guilt!
>
> Another child construes her identity in terms of becoming a nourishing mother. When she grows up she is a fertile being and lives primarily 'for her children'. Her household is her queenly realm. Then the children get married and leave home. She becomes infertile. She

cannot even nourish her husband's sexual appetites. They move to a smaller apartment. Her realm has shrunk. Her core role construction of herself seems no longer applicable. She starts talking about her sins. She feels guilty about the most trivial things. Her doctor calls it 'involutional melancholia'.

(1991a/1955, p. 371)

Interesting enough, it is easier to describe the core role of people presenting a disorder. In fact, their understanding of others is more fixed and clear-cut, based as it is on prevailing dimensions of dependency. People with more complex, flexible, and articulated construction systems are more likely to maintain their adaptation and their organisation by assimilating and accommodating new experiences when confronted with changes in their social life.

3.7.3 The narrative organisation of experience

The various theories (biological, cybernetic, psychological, philosophical) which, in their own languages, regard knowledge as a personal construction made possible and constrained by the biology of the observers as well as by the culture of the community to which they are part, rather than as the revelation of a given and objectively describable world, agree in distinguishing such knowledge from the experience to which it refers. Following Heidegger, even though we are inherently a part of the world, to a certain degree, we separate ourselves from the wholeness of the world when we start to describe it. Such a duality is expressed by different authors in terms of rather overlapping distinctions: between experience and organisation of experience (Piaget, 1970b), praxis (or happening, or experience) of living and its explanation (Maturana, 1987), reality and construction of reality (von Foerster, 1981), experience and construction of experience (Kelly, 1991a/1955, 1991b/1955) or stories that are lived and stories that are told (Mair, 1988). In other words, the experience of our relation with the world becomes tellable (to ourselves and others) only after that the person has organised it.

Personal construct theory is the background for a clinical psychology and psychotherapy in which such organisation of experience is highly formalised in terms of a person's construction system. A more recent and widely accredited formalisation which is in terms of personal narratives (see section 2.4.3), we owe particularly to Bruner.

Nevertheless, Kelly's metaphor of the person-as-scientist and Bruner's metaphor of the person-as-storyteller show an epistemological more than a functional difference. Kelly does not utilise a specific theory of knowledge to describe the process of personal construction. What he means by his metaphor is that people construe their personal knowledge like scientists construe their scientific knowledge, starting from specific gnoseological theories (Chiari & Nuzzo, 1998). While Bruner refers to the narrative thought in opposition to the paradigmatic one, Kelly's intention is to emphasise that knowledge is a constructive process, and not that it has a specific form, i.e. narrative rather than logical-scientific (cf. Fransella, 1983).

For the preceding reason, personal construct theory is particularly suitable for interpretation and application in terms of a narrative metaphor. It is not accidental that early followers of Kelly's theory have suggested and elaborated such a possibility. Mancuso (1986) contributed to one of the first book on narrative psychology (Sarbin, 1986a). Mair argued that in personal construct psychology, dominated as it is by 'the more traditional, analytic, computational, statistical mapping of structures' employed by most who have followed Kelly's teaching, 'little attention has been paid to the much less familiar *narrative* or *story-telling* approach to psychology that Kelly also employs and [. . .] reaches toward advocating' (1989b, p. 4, italics in the original).

On the basis of supposed linking of 'story' and 'anticipation', Mair 'playfully' rewords the fundamental postulate 'to see where it might lead': 'Person's processes are psychologically channelized by the *stories that they live* and the *stories that they tell*'. And so with the corollaries: 'Individuals differ in the stories they live and the stories they tell', 'A story is convenient for the anticipation of a finite range of events only', 'A person's story varies as he successively construes the replications of events', 'A person may successively employ a variety of stories that are inferentially incompatible with each other', 'To the extent that one person construes the stories of another, he may play a role in a social process involving the other person' (Mair, 1989b, p. 5). But the most obvious involvement with story telling is in Kelly's use of 'self-characterisation' (a way of telling the story of a life) and 'fixed-role therapy' (an invitation to live a different story).

From such a narrative interpretation of personal construct theory derives a number of contributions to narrative psychology and psychotherapy on behalf of members of the Kellyan community (Botella *et al.*, 2004, 2005; Feixas, 1995; Mair, 1989a; Neimeyer, 1994, 2000, 2001; Neimeyer & Stewart, 2000; Viney, 1993).

Chapter 4

The therapist's understanding of the client

4.1 The credulous approach

The basic assumption of **epistemological constructivism** – that knowledge does not consist in the discovery of a given reality but in the construction of our own experience – has several implications which were discussed in Chapter 2. In the clinical domain the most important implication is relative to the therapist's absolute necessity, in order to act in therapeutically effective ways, to understand how the clients organise their experience of themselves, other people and the world. It is the clients' organisation of experience, their lived world, which represents the inescapable starting point of the psychotherapy process.

The analogies already described (see section 2.3.2) between contemporary psychological constructivism and the philosophical tradition of phenomenology also extend to the issue of how to arrive at such an understanding.

In phenomenology, Husserl (1931/1913) contrasts the natural attitude with the phenomenological. The former, in which we spend our day to day lives, makes us know a world that 'is there', not just for us, but independently of our experience. This 'positing' of the world as extending beyond our field of spatial and temporal experience is supposed to derive from the intersubjective (empathic) experience of it, and represents the foundation upon which the natural sciences are built. The phenomenological attitude, on the contrary, reveals our own experience of the world. It is described variously as the 'suspension of the natural attitude', the 'turning of regard', the 'exclusion of transcendencies', the 'bracketing of existence', the 'refraining from positing', the 'parenthesising of the positing' and the 'placing of objects in inverted commas'.

The transition from the natural to the phenomenological attitude, according to Husserl, is possible, and facilitated by the method of phenomenological reduction, or *epoché*. Ihde (1986) outlines the phenomenological reduction as shown in the following points:

- bracketing: the analyst attempts to bracket off their preconceptions in understanding phenomena

- phenomenological description: phenomena are described, but causal explanation is avoided
- horizontalisation: no assumptions about relative importance of phenomena are made.

A very similar attitude in relation to the clients, regarded as the experts of their own experience, is present and central in the narrative-hermeneutic family therapy approach proposed by Anderson and Goolishian (1992). Their recommendation to ask questions from a 'not-knowing' position brings to mind Husserl's method. The not-knowing position entails a general attitude, or stance, in which the therapist's actions communicate a genuine curiosity to know more about what has been said, without conveying preconceived opinions and expectations about the client. The therapist relies on the narrative made by the client. 'By learning, by curiosity, and by taking the client's story seriously, the therapist joins with the client in a mutual exploration of the client's understanding and experience' (Anderson & Goolishian, 1992, p. 30). Such a position allows the therapist to maintain continuity with the clients, and to grant primary importance to the client's own organisation of experience.

As to personal construct psychology and psychotherapy, a similar position is made possible by the assumption of a 'credulous approach'. According to Butt, 'the credulous approach is the phenomenological attitude' (2004, p. 25), as clearly emerges from the description given by Kelly:

> The clinician should maintain a kind of credulous attitude towards whatever the client says. He never discards information given by the client merely because it does not conform to what appear to be the facts! From a phenomenological point of view, the client–like the proverbial customer–is always right. This is to say that his words and his symbolic behaviour possess an intrinsic truth which the clinician should not ignore. But this is not to say that the client always describes events in the way other people would describe them or in the way it is commonly agreed that they did happen. It is not to say that he always describes events in the presence of one person in the way he would describe them in the presence of another. He may use one level of description in talking to the clinician, yet use another level of description in construing events for his own purposes. He may even describe events in a way that is intended to lead the clinician to make false inferences.
>
> But this does not mean that the phenomena of the client's speech, and what he says, are nonexistent, and therefore to be disregarded. The perceptive clinician always respects the content of his client's 'lies', although he is equally careful not to be misled by them. When he discovers that what a client has said does not agree with what has

actually happened, he is careful to lay out both versions side by side and not erase the client's version in order to replace it with the 'true' version. He is even inclined to ponder over the client's version more than he is to derive conclusions from the 'true' version. Indeed, the perceptive clinician may be quite as much concerned with the client's version of an event which happens to be 'incorrect' as he is with the event itself or with the fact that the client has not told the 'truth'.

(1991a/1955, p. 241)

Kelly exemplifies his approach by suggesting a golden rule for clinical psychologists, '*If you don't know what's wrong with a client, ask him; he may tell you!*' (1991a/1955, p. 140, italics in the original). Given that the clients are the experts in their own experiential worlds the therapist takes the client's perspective seriously, respecting it and takes a 'credulous' stance. It has been observed (Green, 2005) that Kelly was not one to choose words lightly. The dictionary definition of 'credulous' does not just indicate a willingness to believe, but an over-readiness to believe. 'Gullible' is a synonym, though 'unsuspecting' is probably a closer meaning to Kelly's use of the term.

Actually, Kelly's logic of respect substitutes that logic of suspicion which, according to the Gestalt psychologist Metzger (1941), is deeply rooted in many psychologies. In fact, most psychologists try to trace the clients' narratives to meanings deriving from their theoretical knowledge, supposedly able to reveal the underlying truth of the clients' naïve accounts (see also Armezzani, 2002). Contrariwise, the credulous approach is a way of understanding that demands the assumption that literally everything a client says is true, because the therapist is interested precisely in the felt reality of the client's experience. The credulous approach has a central role in a 'psychology of understanding', primarily aimed at the understanding of personal outlooks rather than at that 'manipulation' of behaviours pursued by other psychologies (Kelly, 1969/1962).

4.2 Acceptance and understanding

The credulous approach rests on the notion of *acceptance*. The constructivist psychotherapist is interested in understanding the constructs the clients apply to other people, to themselves and to the very therapist. In fact, by only relating to the clients on the basis of an understanding of them as people (as personal construct systems) the therapist has the possibility to act in therapeutically effective ways. Here is what Kelly means by 'acceptance':

Acceptance has been defined as the willingness to see the world through the client's eyes. It might be more precisely defined as the therapist's

> attempt to employ the client's own personal-construct system. In terms of our Commonality Corollary, acceptance is the movement of the therapist's mental processes in the construed direction of commonality with the client's construct system.
>
> (1991b/1955, p. 342)

But acceptance, in allowing an understanding of the clients as people, is also the precondition for the therapist's professional construction of them. Remember that personal construct theory is a psychological theory about personal theories, a metatheory. Thus, acceptance can be meant as a twofold process (see Figure 4.1):

> The accepting therapist tries earnestly to put himself in the client's shoes, but at the same time seeks to maintain a professional overview of the client's problems. This means that in accepting the client the therapist makes an effort to understand him in his – the client's – own terms, and that, also, he subsumes a major portion of the client's construction under his – the therapist's – own professional constructs.
>
> (Ibid., pp. 65–66)

Kelly goes as far as asserting that 'one might even say that the psychology of personal constructs is, among other things, a psychology of acceptance'. In fact:

> since the psychology of personal constructs lays great stress upon the interpretation of the regnancy of the constructs under which acts may be performed, rather than upon the mere acts themselves, and since it lays great stress upon *personal* constructs rather than *formalistic* constructs, it does demand of the psychologist that he have an acceptance of other persons.
>
> (1991a/1955, p. 277, italics in original)

Personal construct psychotherapy has, in common with Rogers' (1951) person-centred therapy, this underpinning of acceptance (positive regard) and empathic understanding (Tudor & Worrall, 2006). At the same time, acceptance distinguishes personal construct psychotherapy from other therapeutic approaches which seek to analyse, interpret or explain; even from those cognitive therapies defined as constructivist as opposed to the rationalistic cognitive approaches (Mahoney & Lyddon, 1988).

Acceptance does not imply a distancing from the other, nor a fusional empathy with the other: it is something transcending both of them. Once again, Kelly would agree with Rogers (1959, p. 210), who says that empathic understanding means 'to perceive the internal frame of reference

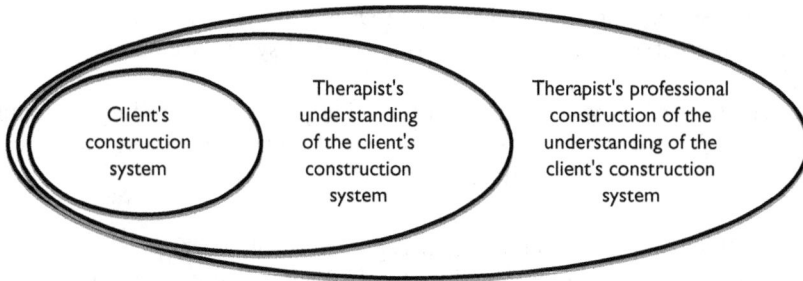

Figure 4.1 The relationship between the therapist's personal understanding and professional construction of the client.

of another with accuracy, and with the emotional components and meanings which pertain thereto, as if one were the other person, but without ever losing the "as if" condition'. It is 'a precondition to the intentional adoption of role relationships' as implied by the sociality corollary, and hence a precondition to a personal change. Acceptance is an attitude which characterises the role of the constructivist psychotherapists and consists in their striving to understand the construction processes of another person, and in using them to see how the world appears from that point of observation. This is the only possible access to the otherwise unconstruable experience of the other.

It is interesting to note that, in other authors who stress the importance of empathic understanding the dimension of acceptance takes the connotation of love (Chiari & Nuzzo, 2006).

Mead (1934) regards the biblical commandment 'love thy neighbour as thyself' as not simply a command, but rather as a 'law' of our very nature. It derives from the process of role-taking: having put ourselves in the other people's shoes we are in a position to see their points of view, know their troubles and limitations, understand why they act as they do and make their interests our own. Thus, the more roles we assume the more loving our attitudes will be (see Pfuetze, 1954, p. 86).

According to Buber (1937/1923), love is the central fact of life, the total direction of one's life and will, toward the being and the need of the other. *I* and *Thou* are two poles of an interpersonal relation: love is between *I* and *Thou* (see Pfuetze, 1954, p. 140).

Bateson (1979) offers a definition of love from a systemic point of view. The interpersonal relation has a crucial value in and of itself, as something that has a life of its own. Just as Mind, so love is immanent in the larger system as patterns of self-organisation, neither determined by individuals nor by the medium in which these 'love systems' live. Human loving corresponds to our capacity to become a part of something larger than our individual selves, and this something larger is a system that, in turn, is part of an even greater system. Bateson's is a vision of systemic embeddedness of 'loving'.

Love, defined as the acceptance of the other people surrounding us in our daily life, is, according to Maturana and Varela (1987), the biological foundation of social phenomena:

> Anything that undermines the acceptance of others, from competency to the possession of truth and on to ideologic certainty, undermines the social process because it undermines the biological process that generates it. Let us not deceive ourselves: we are not moralizing, we are not preaching love. We are only revealing the fact that, biologically, without love, without acceptance of others, there is no social phenomenon.
>
> (pp. 246–247)

Maturana maintains that, from a biological (not moral, religious or philosophical) point of view, we humans are loving animals, so much that our species should be named *Homo sapiens amans*. Love is the central emotion in the history of human evolution: one in which love – meant as 'the acceptance of the other as a legitimate other with whom to coexist' – is a necessary condition for the normal physical, behavioural, psychic, social and spiritual development of the child as well as of the adult (Maturana, 2001). 'The only emotion that expands intelligence is love, and this is so because intelligence has to do with the acceptance of the legitimacy of the other and the expansion of the possibility for consensuality that such acceptance entails'. According to Maturana, 'if we look at our individual human existence we can still see that what we search for in life is love, and all that we do in life, we do it to obtain love'. Echoing Bateson, Maturana sustains that 'in the blindness that the negation of love creates in our living, we stop seeing ourselves as part of the harmonious interconnectedness of all existence in the unending dynamics of life and death' (Maturana & Verden-Zöller, 1996).

4.3 The therapeutic conversation

The credulous approach and acceptance, prerequisites for the understanding of the clients' narratives and for their professional construction, are assumed by the therapist during the conversation with the client.

Conversation does not solely consist in a verbal exchange. It also includes all those aspects traditionally defined in psychology as 'non-verbal communication', made up of acts which, when interpreted, contribute to the construction of the other. The expression of one's face, the posture, the paralinguistic features (volume, pitch and voice qualifiers) and so on, therefore have a very important role in the structuration of the psycho-therapeutic relationship, starting from the first encounter with the client.

The therapist's acceptance of the clients also depends on these aspects from the very first interaction with them, and on the importance the therapist attributes to the spontaneous narrative the clients choose to expose (see section 6.6.1).

From a hermeneutic point of view, the process of personal narration does not consist in the account of elements of knowledge put in a stable and definite organisation. Personal narration is a social process which varies to a greater or lesser extent according to the structural and interpersonal contexts in which it is situated. Within a psychotherapeutic setting, where the clients are in relation with an accepting therapist interested in what they choose to tell about themselves and their problem, the narrative is not the same that would emerge in the relation with a directive therapist or during a psychiatric interview. It would be meaningless to declare that the former is more reliable or 'true' than the others, if only because 'unconditioned' by external interferences. One can only affirm that different kinds of relation aim at pursuing different purposes. A relational context of 'accepting listening' may be more favourable than other settings.

- The therapist's understanding of the elements the clients consider more directly connected to the complaint and more pertinent to the psycho-therapeutic situation as initially construed by them.
- A sense of legitimisation and intrinsic value of their narratives in the clients, in that not disputed by the therapist and attentively listened to.
- The construction of a collaboration in the psychotherapeutic task, through a definition of the respective roles as both necessary to achieve the therapeutic aim.

The techniques the constructivist psychotherapist will use throughout the psychotherapy process do not significantly differ from the more traditional techniques of interview used in psychology and psychiatry. Instead, the meaning given to their utilisation is significantly different. They are chosen and used according to the anticipation of the processes they can encourage rather than represent means for the gathering of information. Again, the reason lies in the assumption of the interactional nature of personal knowledge, viewed as a continuous process of narrative organisation of experience, where social experience represents the most significative element. This is what makes a psychotherapeutic relationship a particular one: the therapist's professional construction of the clients' personal knowledge allows him or her to act in therapeutically effective ways in conversing with them. That is why we like to refer to the techniques as 'conversational acts' (see section 6.4).

4.4 The exploration of personal knowledge

We consider the first interview as the very beginning of the psychotherapy process. That is, we prefer not to precede the beginning of the therapy with a series, more or less lengthy, of interviews aimed at having a picture of the client as a person and of his or her problems, to use successively in the therapeutic phase. Every choice made by the therapist, every act in relation with the client, encourages a certain process. The choice to subject the client to an initial assessment is likely to stabilise their personal constructions, the very same which successively we should help them to change. Furthermore, this choice could contribute to the client's construction of the therapist as the expert of the situation, the one who, based on the information gathered, shall be able to find a solution to his or her problems.

The psychology of personal constructs has developed a certain number of techniques or methods specifically directed to the exploration of personal knowledge. Some of them, in particular the repertory grid, are also frequently used outside the theoretical framework of personal construct theory. Even though we recur only rarely to these techniques, with the exception of self-characterisation, we feel it is useful to review them briefly by referring to the most recent texts specifically dedicated to an in-depth examination of them (Fransella *et al.*, 2003, Fromm, 2004; Jankowicz, 2003).

4.4.1 The repertory grid

Initially designed by Kelly (1991a/1955, Chapters 5 and 6), with the name of *Role Construct Repertory Test* (or *reptest*), as a means of assessing the content of an individual's repertory of role constructs, nowadays *repertory grids* (or *repgrids*) represent a widely used set of techniques for studying personal and interpersonal systems of meaning. They have been used in approximately 3,000 studies of a broad variety of topics.

Apart from a number of recently developed computer programs for their elicitation and analysis, the repgrid was originally devised as an interview-based or paper-and-pencil method, aimed at filling a grid composed of rows and columns.

The grid allows understanding of how people construe a part of their experiential reality. After having selected a number (usually 12–20) of elements (usually significant people in a clinical setting) to be written at the top of the columns, the respondent is asked to compare and contrast successive sets of triads (for example, myself, my mother, my father) and formulate 'some important way in which two of the figures are alike, and different from the third'. The three elements represent the basis for the elicitation of a personal construct consisting in an abstraction of a similarity between two elements, and a difference between them and the third element. For example, the person might respond, 'Well, my father and I rely upon ourselves, whereas my mother has always been dependent on someone'. The construct is now written in the first row according to the verbal labels used by the person ('relies upon himself or herself vs. depends on others'), and a convention is used to record the application of the construct to all the elements in the columns. Depending on the convention chosen, it is customary to distinguish 'binary', 'ranking' and 'rating grids' (Fransella *et al.*, 2003).

The procedure is repeated up to the elicitation of a number of constructs at least equal to the number of elements.

The grid is amenable to a wide range of analyses, nowadays facilitated by a number of computer programs (reviewed in Scheer, 2008), many of which available via the Internet. Analyses include:

- *correlations between constructs*, suggesting that two or more constructs tend to be applied together, forming a sort of semantic space
- *correlations between elements*, showing the perceived distances between them, allowing a number of 'thematic analyses': for example, the distance between 'self' and 'ideal self', that is, 'I as I am' and 'I as I would like to be' (used as an index of self-esteem); the distance between 'self' and 'social self', that is, 'I as seen by others' (index of comprehension); the distance between 'ideal self' and 'future self', that is, 'I as I expect to be' in a given future (index of expectancy of change); the distance between 'self' and 'others', that is, the average distance between the element self and each of the other not-self elements (index of social isolation)
- a number of more or less complex statistical analyses aimed at calculating several cognitive measures, such as:

  - *intensity*, regarded by Bannister and Fransella (1965) as related to a dimension of tightness–looseness, and therefore able to discriminate between thought disordered schizophrenics and other psychiatric and normal groups according to Bannister's (1960) hypothesis of serial invalidation (see section 5.4.3)
  - *cognitive complexity*, a measure defined as 'the capacity to construe social behaviour in a multidimensional way' (Bieri *et al.*, 1966, p. 185), and therefore relative to the number of independent discriminations available to the person
  - *extremity ratings*, the extent to which people tend to use the extreme points in bipolar scales as opposed to the more central points, indicating, depending on the authors, maladjustment or personal meaningfulness
  - *ordination* and *superordinacy*, measures aimed at assessing a dimension of subordinacy/superordinacy between constructs

- *articulation*, a measure described by Makhlouf-Norris, Jones and Norris (1970), aimed at judging the structure of personal construct systems in terms of their being articulated (the normal conceptual structure), or non-articulated (the obsessional conceptual structure), that is, monolithic or segmented

principal components analysis, factor analysis, cluster analysis, correspondence analysis, all aimed at somehow mapping the structure of personal construct systems in terms of their components (elements, constructs, groups of constructs) and the distances between them.

Particular types of repertory grids have been invented for specific purposes. The *Grid Test of Thought Disorder* (Bannister & Fransella, 1966) is designed to discriminate people diagnosed as thought-disordered schizophrenics on the basis of their grossly loosened construing. Ryle and Breen (1972), in order to explore the role relations in couples, suggest using a *double dyad grid* in which elements are represented by the relationship between the members of a couple and between each of them and their parents.

4.4.2 The implications grid

Developed by Hinkle (1965), a student of Kelly, on the basis of a theory of construct implications, the *Implications* and the *Resistance-to-Change* grids allow assessment of the level of superordination and nuclearity of a set of personal constructs relevant to the person.

The *Implications grid* (*impgrid*), in contrast to the repertory grid, has no elements; it is aimed at understanding what meaning each construct has for the person in terms of other constructs by asking to indicate which goes with which. The basic instructions are:

Consider this construct for a moment (Construct 1). Now, if you were to be changed back and forth from one side to the other – that is, if you woke up one morning and realized that you were best described by one side of this construct while the day before you had been best described by the opposite side – if you realized that you were changed in this *one* respect – what other constructs of these nineteen remaining ones would be *likely* to be changed by a change in yourself on this one construct alone?

(Hinkle, 1965, p. 37, italics in original)

The number of implications of each construct is indicative of its level of superordination, whereas the overall number of implications in the grid gives some information on the structure of that part of the person's construction system pertinent to the constructs under consideration.

4.4.3 The resistance-to-change grid

Along with the Implications grid, Hinkle (1965) developed the *Resistance-to-Change grid* to test the hypothesis that superordinate constructs are more resistant to change than subordinate ones.

Having first found out which pole of each construct the person preferred to see themselves on, the basic instructions are:

> Look at these two constructs. The check marks indicate the sides you said you would prefer to be on. Now, let's assume for the moment that you had to change from the preferred side to the unpreferred side on one of these constructs, but would remain the same on the other. Which of these two constructs would you prefer to remain the same on? Remember, you will have to change on the other. What we are trying to find out here is if you had to change, which of these two changes would be the more undesirable, as you see it?
>
> (Ibid., p. 36)

A simple count allows calculate the score for resistance of each construct and the ranking of the constructs from the more resistant to the less resistant to change.

To the extent that the more resistant to change constructs are those that cannot be modified without the person's perception of a significant change in their core structures, in our opinion the Resistance-to-Change grid supplies information for the nuclearity rather than the ordination of the constructs under consideration.

4.4.4 The dependency grid

Developed by Kelly (1991a/1955, Chapter 6) as the *Situational Resources Repertory Test*, the usually referred to as *Dependency grid* (*depgrid*) is aimed at assessing the dimension 'dispersion of dependency' (see section 3.7.1).

The grid contains a list of 23 problem situations which are likely to be relevant for most people. The person selects from a list of role titles the people they believe have or have had an important part in their life. The person is allowed to indicate more than one individual for each role, and to include people who are dead or not geographically close. The indication of a minimum of ten resources is encouraged. Sometimes, the element 'myself' is introduced by the administrator as the last resource in the grid.

The following instructions are then supplied: 'Think of a time when you had the most problem with "x". If these people had been around at that time, to whom would you have gone for help?' A variant of these instructions has been suggested: '"If" such a situation happened, to whom would you turn amongst those around you at the moment?' (Walker *et al.*, 1988, p. 68).

Participants note with a tick which people they would have turned to for help. It is specified that for each problem situation more choices are possible, and that the self category can be filled in addition to going to others or as a choice between either themselves or others.

Face inspection (see Figure 4.2) yields information as to whether the person tends to call on everyone for every kind of help or to turn pre-vailingly to one or two people (both strategies would indicate a relatively 'undispersed dependency'), or the ticks are almost distributed among the resources ('dispersed dependency').

Walker, Ramsey and Bell (1988) have presented a statistical way to determine relative dispersion of dependency other than by inspection, and named it 'Dispersion of Dependency Index' (DDI).

The previously mentioned type of dependency grid is also named *Being-Helped grid*. Hinkle (1965) suggested reversing the grid by asking, 'Who turns to you for help or leans on you in what sorts of situation?' This *Helping grid* can be particularly useful to explore the propensity to play helpful roles with other people.

4.4.5 The laddering procedure

This is a procedure described by Hinkle (1965) to elicit increasingly superordinate constructs starting from constructs elicited from triads.

The person is asked to indicate by which pole of the construct they would prefer to be described. Hinkle's instructions are:

> Now on this construct you preferred this side to that side. What I want to understand now is why you would prefer to be here rather than there. . . What are the advantages of this side in contrast to the disadvantages of that side as you see it?
>
> (1965, pp. 32–33)

The answer will be a construct superordinate to the first, which also has a preferred side. The question 'why' is asked again and again, until the person is unable or unwilling to produce more.

Usually, the procedure ends when the person begins to repeat the same answer. Sometimes the person shows signs of knowing the answer, being unable to articulate it by means of verbal labels. In this case, the clinical psychologist or the psychotherapist can try to help the person to symbolise the construct.

Consistently with the organisation corollary, one is likely to arrive at the same superordinate construct even though starting from different sub-ordinate constructs of a person's construction system.

	R1	R2	R3	R4	R5	R6	R7	Rn
S1		X						
S2		X						
S3		X						
S4		X						
S5		X						
S6		X						
S7		X						
Sn		X						

(a)

	R1	R2	R3	R4	R5	R6	R7	Rn
S1	X	X	X	X	X	X	X	X
S2	X	X	X	X	X	X	X	X
S3	X	X	X	X	X	X	X	X
S4	X	X	X	X	X	X	X	X
S5	X	X	X	X	X	X	X	X
S6	X	X	X	X	X	X	X	X
S7	X	X	X	X	X	X	X	X
Sn	X	X	X	X	X	X	X	X

(b)

	R1	R2	R3	R4	R5	R6	R7	Rn
S1				X				
S2		X						
S3								X
S4						X		
S5	X							
S6			X					
S7							X	
Sn					X			

(c)

Figure 4.2 Dependency grids showing two kinds of highest possible undispersed dependency (*a* and *b*) and the highest possible dispersed dependency (c).

S = Situation
R = Resource

The preceding procedure can be termed 'laddering upwards' when contrasted with the 'laddering downwards', which consists of asking such questions as, 'How do you know when a person is X?' This procedure leads to more and more subordinate and incidental constructs.

Though laddering looks simple, it requires, like many other tools, the ability to be a credulous listener, to suspend one's own value system, and, thereby, to be able to subsume the client's construing (Fransella, 2003b).

4.4.6 The pyramid procedure

In this procedure, suggested by Landfield (1971), people are asked to think of someone they know, with whom they feel most comfortable, and whose company they most enjoy.

They are then invited to focus on one aspect of the acquaintance. When people have named the characteristic, they are asked to state what kind of person would represent the opposite of that characteristic. When the two construct poles have been elicited, the psychologist returns to the first pole and asks what kind of person X is.

In Landfield's example, the psychologist elicits a construct which is exemplified by 'open guy'. The contrast 'closed guy' then is elicited. The psychologist records this construct at the top of the pyramid. Next, 'listens to you' is associated with 'open guy', and 'somebody not interested in you' is contrasted with 'listens to you'. Returning to the pole 'closed guy', 'people don't like' is associated with it. Finally, 'doesn't like me' is contrasted with 'people don't like'. There can be a third and final level which is elicited by asking about each construct pole at the second level.

Also this procedure takes the person 'down' a ladder. Both Hinkle's laddering procedure and Landfield's pyramid procedure can become parts of a psychotherapeutic conversation.

4.4.7 The ABC model

This technique was introduced by Tschudi (1977) to be used with clients who seemed unable to change or were dissatisfied with the results of change.

Tschudi, influenced by Greenwald (1973), starts from the assumption that there was an incentive to remain unchanged, as the consequences of change could be perceived as worse than the client's current state of affairs. In other words, it is assumed that 'the symptom always has its *payoffs*, that there are *advantages of the symptom* here and now' (Tschudi, 1977, p. 323, italics in the original). All in all, this assumption, we may add, is in line with Kelly's notion of 'elaborative choice' (see section 1.1.8). Tschudi then elaborated Hinkle's (1965) idea of 'implicative dilemma': a1 has not only negative (b1), but also positive (c2) implications; likewise a2 has not only positive (b2), but also negative (c1) implications.

The ABC model enables the client and therapist to elicit underlying theories concerning behaviours resistant to change. The client is asked to describe the actual state and then the desired state (a1 and a2); the disadvantages of the actual state and the advantages of the desired state (b1 and b2); and the advantages of the actual state and the disadvantages of the desired state (c1 and c2).

For example, 'being depressed' (a1) can have as desired state 'not being depressed' (a2). 'Being depressed' has the disadvantage 'I can't do things I'd like to' (b1), whereas 'not being depressed' would have the advantage 'I could do things I like to' (b2). But 'being depressed' has also the advantage 'avoid doing unwanted things' (c1), whereas 'not being depressed' would have the disadvantage 'must do unwanted things' (c2).

Fransella and Dalton (1990) consider the ABC model to be an assessment tool that can play a part in the reconstruction of personal constructs. However, the authors warn, this technique must be used with care and with appropriate timing. To expose the client to the idea that they may find their actual state advantageous, can be threatening and potentially damaging.

4.4.8 The self-characterisation

Although much less used than the 'computational' grid method, *self-characterisation* (Kelly, 1991a/1955, Chapter 7) is the technique that better fits the basic assumptions of personal construct theory, or, at least, its interpretation in terms of a narrative or story-telling approach to psychology (Mair, 1989b).

It comprises a narrative produced by people when they are asked to characterise themselves. According to Kelly, a psychological test is useful primarily because it yields likely *clinical hypotheses* – in contrast with 'cut-and-dried *findings*' (1991a/1955, p. 240, italics in original) – which, during the course of the client's treatment, can become the bases of inquiry and exploration. Self-characterisation, as an application of the credulous approach, allows such a tentative understanding of the client.

After a great number of revisions, Kelly arrived to formulate the request in the following way:

> I want you to write a character sketch of Harry Brown, just as if he were the principal character in a play. Write it as it might be written by a friend who knew him very *intimately* and very *sympathetically*, perhaps better than anyone ever really could know him. Be sure to write it in the third person. For example, start out by saying, 'Harry Brown is. . .'
>
> (1991a/1955, p. 242, italics in original)

The term 'character sketch' permits the client more latitude than terms such as 'self-description', 'self-analysis' and such like. The term 'sketch', as well as the invitation to use the third person, conveys the idea that the wholeness of the characterisation is important, rather than detailed elements or a catalogue of faults. Also the suggestion to write as if in the role of a friend encourages a construction of the client from an 'external' point of view, while the phrase 'perhaps better than anyone ever really could know him' tends to free certain clients from writing the sketch as some actual, known person would write it. 'Intimately' indicates that something more than superficial appearances is to be covered by the client, and 'sympathetically' is likely to encourage an acceptance of themselves and thus a narrative of what they are, rather than of what they are not, or ought to be. An overall purpose of such instructions is that of minimising threat, placing the client 'in a protected spot within a loosely construed system which has the given dimensions of first, second, and third persons, friendship, intimacy, and sympathy' (ibid., p. 243).

Kelly suggests various *techniques in the analysis of self-characterisations*, 'not to "score" the protocol in a conventional sense, but to bring it into focus' (ibid., p. 247). They are qualitative techniques of text analysis, in a contemporary language, consisting of the following.

- *Observation of sequence and transition*, starting from the assumption that the protocol represents a true continuity, as far as the client is concerned, and that the apparent 'breaks' are either unexpected elaborations of personally similar content or contrast elaborations.
- *Observation of organisation*, seeking the topic sentences, both in terms of first sentences of paragraphs and in terms of sentences which seem to carry the greatest generality. Particular attention is paid to the opening sentence of the protocol, intended as a statement either having the greatest level of generality, or representing the safest ground to use as a point of departure.
- *Reflection against context*, consisting in taking each statement not only for its meaning as an independent declaration, but for its meaning in the context of the protocol as a whole, like saying to oneself 'If all the rest of the protocol might be considered an explanation or an elaboration of this one statement, what would the statement mean?'
- *Collation of terms*, observing the terms which are repeated as such or through their personal equivalents, and the linkages between terms. They can represent the attempt at communicating some construct having no clear-cut symbolism.
- *Shifting emphasis*, so as to experiment with alternative emphases and inflections in reading each sentence and paragraph.
- *Restatement of the argument*, with the psychologist or psychotherapist trying, from time to time, to express the same theme in their own

words, in the attempt to subsume the client's point of view rather than to memorise or categorise it.

Having used the above techniques, the psychologist then proceeds to the *analysis of contextual areas invoked by the protocol*.

It consists of paying attention to the topical areas selected by the clients, within which they identify themselves: personal appearance, family, friendships, interests, work and so on. The sequence of the areas discussed usually represents a progression either from the well-structured to the more problematical or from general to specific.

The *thematic analysis* is relative to the cause–effect relationships, that is, the client's reasons and explanations. The client may reveal a reliance upon chance, personal influence, historical explanations and his or her own actions in the attempt to understand what has happened. As a consequence, this analysis will allow the therapist to understand how the client will insist upon approaching therapeutic change.

Even more meaningful to the therapist's understanding of the client's constructions is the *dimensional analysis*. Here the emphasis is placed upon similarities and contrasts, so as to understand the dichotomised alternatives the client continually has to choose from. The therapist will not only look for the principal dimensions and their subjective equivalences but also for the constellations of dimensions, and not only for the manifestly contrasting poles, but also for the poles which are implicit but not stated and for how the clients characterise themselves with respect to these poles.

The final step consists of the *professional subsuming of personal constructs*. As in the therapeutic conversations, the therapist will try to reach a professional construction of their understanding of the client's construction system by means of the professional constructs we have described in Chapter 1.

Chapter 5

The therapist's construction of the client's narrative

The therapist's understanding of the constructs with which the clients organise their experience of the world runs parallel to its inclusion in a set of professional constructs.

Having already defined (see section 1.1.6) what Kelly means by 'professional' or 'diagnostic constructs', we may add they deal inevitably (and coherently with the theory's epistemological assumption) with constructs, whose peculiarity is to have as elements other constructs, that is, the personal constructs. They 'are designed to help the clinician assume professionally useful role relations with his clients' (Kelly, 1991a/1955, p. 335), in the same way as the person's construction of other people's construction processes by means of 'role constructs' is the primary basis of role relationships. We have also reviewed the most important professional constructs, limiting ourselves to Kelly's definitions. Now we shall reconsider them, by integrating them in our theoretical framework. There, they appear as interacting processes, directed at maintaining an adaptation between the person and the environment (particularly the social environment), and at conserving the organisation of self.

5.1 Processes relative to structural changes

The person is a form of movement, changing at every instant. These changes are usually relative to 'peripheral' rather than 'core' constructs. Based on his theorisation, Kelly's (1969b/1958, p. 231) hypothesis is that, as a result of therapeutic strategies but also during their daily life, people can undergo eight possible types of changes:

1 a 'slot change', or 'contrast reconstruction': the person construes people, events, or him/herself on the opposite pole of an existing construct
2 the selection of an alternative construct and its application to matters at hand
3 the higher explicitness of some preverbal constructs (or 'dredging the unconscious')

4   the elaboration of one's personal construct system to test its internal consistency
5   the testing of a construct's predictive validity
6   the increasing of the range of convenience of certain constructs so as to apply them more generally or, on the contrary, the decreasing of the range of convenience of certain constructs so as to reduce them to a kind of obsolescence
7   the alteration of the meaning of certain constructs ('rotation of the reference axes')
8   the emergence of new personal constructs ('erection of new reference axes').

According to Kelly, the 'alteration or replacement of constructs' – the last two methods mentioned – 'is essentially a creative kind of effort' (ibid., p. 231). In reference to the theory of autopoiesis, we suggest that the first six types of changes be viewed as structural changes allowing the conservation of organisation, whereas the last two be considered as structural changes destructive of the organisation, which can be substituted by another (see also Kenny, 1988).

When speaking of organisation and structure (see section 2.4.4), Maturana refers, respectively, to those relations that must exist among the components of a system for it to be a member of a specific class (organisation), and to the effective components and relations that constitute a particular unity and realise its organisation (structure). We consider that it is useful to substitute Kelly's distinction between core and peripheral constructs with Maturana's distinction between organisation and structure. Both distinctions regard the differential importance of components of the system in order to conserve life and identity. However, it is Maturana's distinction that appears more precise. Kelly, in fact, defines peripheral constructs by negation of the criterion used to define core constructs.

Anyway, there is a continuous movement towards the anticipation of events as stated by the fundamental postulate, and 'this movement is the essence of human life itself' (Kelly, 1991a/1955, p. 48). The experience cycle (see section 3.5) describes how people, behaving on the basis of their anticipations, test their constructions which, according to their validation or invalidation, will eventually be revised.

5.1.1 Loosening/tightening

An important diagnostic construct in personal construct psychology and psychotherapy is that of *tight vs. loose* construct (see also section 1.3).

'Tight constructs are those which lead to unvarying predictions' (Kelly, 1991a/1955, p. 357). The elements included in the range of convenience of a tight construct are clearly constructed as belonging to the likeness end or the contrast end.

On the contrary, 'loose constructs are those which lead to varying predictions but which, for practical purposes, may be said to retain their identity' (Kelly, 1991a/1955, p. 357). A loose construction is like a rough sketch subjected to flexible interpretations.

A tight construct may be considered similar to a falsifiable hypothesis according to Popper (1959/1934): in fact, it leads to anticipations that may be easily verified (validated or not). Instead, the anticipations related to a grossly loosened construct may not be clearly verified: the person cannot be wrong, but it is equally true that he or she cannot be right either.

Kelly describes the alternation between tightening and loosening as a 'creativity cycle' (see section 3.5). 'The Creativity Cycle is one which starts with loosened construction and terminates with tightened and validated construction' (Kelly, 1991a/1955, p. 388). In encouraging reconstructions, the creativity cycle has an important role in the psychotherapy process.

5.1.2 Constriction/dilation

Another fundamental process in personal construct psychology and psychotherapy is relative to the diagnostic dimension of *constriction vs. dilation* (see also section 1.3). Both are applicable to the person's perceptual field, not to personal constructs. The perceptual field has been defined as 'all those aspects of the external world to which at a given time an animal makes a discriminating response [. . .] It consists of what the animal perceives, not what is there' (English & English, 1958, p. 379).

'When one minimizes the apparent incompatibility of one's construction systems by drawing in the outer boundaries of one's perceptual field, the relatively repetitive mental process that ensues is designated as "constriction"'. On the contrary, 'when, following a series of alternating uses of incompatible systems, a person broadens his perceptual field in order to reorganize it on a more comprehensive level, the adjustment may be called "dilation"' (ibid., p. 352).

> When a person moves in the direction of dilation he jumps around more from topic to topic, he lumps his childhood with his future, he sees vast ranges of events as possibly related, he participates in a wider variety of activities, and, if he is a client undergoing psychotherapy, he tends to see everything that happens to him as potentially related to his problem.
>
> When a person moves in the direction of constriction he tends to limit his interests, he deals with one issue at a time, he does not accept potential relationships between widely varying events, he beats out the

path of his daily routine in smaller and smaller circles, and he insists that his therapist stick to a sharply delimited version of his problem.

(Kelly, 1991a/1955, p. 352)

5.2 A constructivist understanding of the unconscious

Starting from the epistemological assumption, according to which all we know is a construction of personal experience to be considered as the outcome of the history of our relation with the environment, psychological constructivism excludes any possibility to formulate theories about the world that may be labelled as discoveries on the real structure of nature and living beings, including humans. Coherently, personal construct theory may be better considered as a metatheory, that is, a theory of personal theories. Consequently, in order to be applied to people, particularly to help them overcome their complaints, the theory must be based on the clients' personal constructions. It requires, in other words, an understanding of the clients and the possibility of construing their construction processes.

Often, psychotherapists who have experience in various 'clinical cases', that is, have had the possibility of construing the construction processes of many clients, have the feeling of knowing the people in front of them more or better than the people know themselves. This experience may serve as an introduction to the constructivist understanding of that theoretical construct which in psychoanalytic tradition and contemporary cognitive psychology is given the name of 'the unconscious'.

A possible explanation of the previously mentioned phenomenon consists of the consideration that the aspects we 'see' in the clients and that they do not 'recognise' lie in their unconscious. Consequently, as the clients approach the construction the therapist has of them, the therapist may think this movement is due to the increasing awareness of material formerly unconscious.

If we move within a constructivist perspective, we can turn to another explanation:

> If a client does not construe things in the way we do, we assume that he construes them in some other way, not that he really must construe them the way we do but is unaware of it. If later he comes to construe them the way we do, that is a new construction for him, not a revelation of a subconscious construction which we have helped him bring to the fore. Our constructs are our own. There is no need to reify them in the client's "unconscious".

(Kelly, 1991a/1955, p. 345)

The 'unconscious', therefore, can be conceptualised as 'delimited' by those elements that an external observer has included in the construction of other people's construction, and are not taken into consideration in the construction people have of themselves. In a certain sense, the unconscious of a person is 'present' in the construction that another person has of him or her, rather than in the person him or herself (Chiari & Nuzzo, 1983).

Following the preceding description one can wonder what the difference is between the construction the therapist has of the clients and the latter of themselves. We are not talking about a difference of contents, in which case the therapist would regard it as an alternative construction with respect to the client's one. We are talking about a difference the therapist construes in terms of an awareness of the construction of the clients greater than that of the clients themselves. The difference therefore derives from the processes, not the contents.

The processes that may justify such a difference, and therefore represent a constructivist alternative to the traditional notion of unconscious, are relative, according to Kelly, to three professional constructs: *preverbal constructs*, **submergence** and **suspension**. All three, together with the **level of cognitive awareness**, account for a person's 'covert constructions'.

5.2.1 Preverbal constructs

'A preverbal construct is one which continues to be used even though it has no consistent word symbol' (Kelly, 1991a/1955, p. 340).

In Kelly's conceptualisation, constructs are usually symbolised by invoking one of their elements. The element stands not only for itself, but also for the whole construct. The introduction of a word in the construct context – usually as one of the 'like' elements – allows the person to use it as a symbol. This 'trick' makes the revision of constructs relatively feasible. 'We can sit on our rocking chair and twiddle our constructs to our endless amusement. We may even test out some of our convictions without rising from our comfortable position' (ibid., p. 341).

The lack of word symbols makes it difficult for people to communicate their constructs or their elements, and for the therapists to understand their clients. The clients can act out their constructions, or just sit and have feelings they cannot describe. The therapist will have to infer the client's constructions, and eventually make recourse to role playing and other 'non-intellectual' approaches.

Ordinarily, a preverbal construct 'was originally designed to construe those elements of which an infant could be aware. [. . .] The therapist has before him an infant who is speaking with the voice of an adult' (ibid., p. 341). Consequently, the utilisation of preverbal constructs in an adult client is often found together with undispersed dependency, and it is likely that such a client tries to structure a dependency transference with the therapist.

5.2.2 Submergence

When one of the two ends of a construct is markedly less available than the other, it can be termed the 'submerged' end. Commonly it is the contrast end of the construct to be submerged.

Submergence may be a way of keeping a construct from being tested. This is particularly the case when the self is a potential element for inclusion in the context of the construct at the submerged end. The clients may fear that, if the submerged end of the construct is uncovered the construct may be invalidated, and they will have to reconstrue themselves with far-reaching results. The therapists then should be sure that their clients are able to deal with the results before helping them to uncover the submerged ends of their constructs.

5.2.3 Suspension

As a result of the revision of one's personal construct system, some of the elements previously included in the old structure tend to drop out. Simultaneously, the new structure can allow the inclusion of elements previously outside the range of convenience of the old one. 'A suspended element is one which is omitted from the context of a construct as the result of revision of the person's construct system' (Kelly, 1991a/1955, p. 390).

The above movement accounts for the phenomena traditionally identified as 'forgetting', 'dissociation' and 'repression'. Moreover, it accounts for the reappearance of 'memories' which formerly appeared forgotten. This latter phenomenon also accounts for the changes in dream content in clients undergoing psychotherapy; considered as incipient signs of new constructions.

5.2.4 Other professional constructs accounting for 'unconscious'

Preverbalism, submergence and suspension do not fully cover the notion of the unconscious. The professional constructs of subordination, impermeability and loosening too can have a role. The following quote is particularly illustrative in this regard.

> A client may fail to construe his behaviour in the meaningful way the therapist construes it because he is organizing it under minor, subordinate, and nonregnant constructs. His elements are personally arrayed in little collections only, whereas the therapist may be seeing them arrayed in larger collections to which the little collections are subordinate. Again, a client may have "closed out" a construct – that is, made it impermeable – whereas the therapist may see it as capable of embracing many new elements. It is easy for the therapist to accuse the

client of "unconscious resistance" in such a case. Finally, the therapist may observe the apparent shifting that goes on under loose conceptualization, and, because he cannot follow it, hypothesize that some stable unconscious conceptualization is taking place.

(Kelly, 1991a/1955, p. 345)

5.2.5 Level of cognitive awareness

To identify the direction of certain movements during the course of the psychotherapy process, Kelly suggests the use of a scalar type of diagnostic construct: the construct of *level of cognitive awareness*, ranging from high to low.

A construct at a high level of cognitive awareness 'is one which is readily expressed in socially effective symbols; whose alternatives are both readily accessible; which falls well within the range of convenience of the client's major constructions; and which is not suspended by its superordinating constructs' (ibid., pp. 390–391).

5.3 Processes relative to organisational transitions

The topic of emotion is central for any school of psychology, and even more for any psychotherapeutic approach. Human suffering is, ultimately, an emotional suffering, so much so that the notion of psychological disorder practically coincides with that of emotional disorder.

Most traditional psychologies consider emotion an association between mental and physiological states, according to a dualistic, interactionist view of the mind–body problem (Popper & Eccles, 1977). Such a view is held in particular by the cognitive theories of emotion where, for example, the cognitive process of appraisal leads to autonomic arousal (Lazarus, 1991) or to action tendencies (Frijda, 1986).

Among the approaches which refer to a constructivist epistemology, the panorama of the theories on emotion is particularly varied.

Piaget substantially remains within a dualistic conception in his rare references to affectivity (Piaget, 1962, 1981/1954), understood as the energetic (motivational) and regulatory function of behaviour, interdependent with, and indissociable from cognition. The two are different, but complementary, aspects of any act of behaviour.

Far from the preceding and other similar approaches, the social constructionist view of emotion emphasises the overlay of cultural and linguistic factors on biology, and relegates the physiological aspect of some emotional states to a secondary status (Harré, 1986). By giving priority to a proper understanding of how various emotion vocabularies are used the emotive event unfolds, revealing itself as a part of its social strategies and practices linked to cultural differences.

Maturana sees 'emotioning' as the background of 'languaging'. The recurrent interactions between two or more human beings through which languaging takes place occur in a particular flow of body dispositions ('emotional flow') that allows them to remain in recurrent interactions. In the words of Maturana (1988, p. 49), 'languaging flows in the co-ordinations of actions of human beings in a background of emotioning that constitutes the operational possibility of its occurrence, and specifies at any instant the consensual domains in which it takes place'. The peculiarity of human beings is represented by their living in language in the constitutive braiding of languaging and emotioning.

Regarding the topic of emotion, the stance of personal construct theory is particularly original; an originality deriving from a rigorous respect of the constructivist assumption, as already mentioned in the first chapter. This makes the Kellyan treatment of emotion difficult to understand, justifying the misunderstanding of some authors (Bruner, 1956; Mackay, 1975; Peck & Whitlow, 1975; Rogers, 1956) who considered personal construct theory too mentalist, intellectual, cognitivist, and in any case incapable of adequately handling the topic of emotion. Also Kelly 'realized that he had not succeeded in putting over his point about emotions being related to our awareness of our own construing' (Fransella, 1995, p. 114).

On the other hand, personal construct theory as a whole eludes being framed in the pigeonholes of the more traditional schools of psychology, as witnessed by the following story:

> I have been so puzzled over the early labeling of personal construct theory as "cognitive" that several years ago I set out to write another short book to make it clear that I wanted no part of cognitive theory. The manuscript was about a third completed when I gave a lecture at Harvard University with the title, "Personal Construct Theory as a Line of Inference." Following the lecture, Professor Gordon Allport explained to the students that my theory was not a "cognitive" theory but an "emotional" theory. Later the same afternoon, Dr. Henry Murray called me aside and said, "You know, don't you, that you are really an existentialist."
>
> Since that time I stepped into almost all the open manholes that psychological theorists can possibly fall into. For example, in Warsaw, where I thought my lecture on personal construct theory would be an open challenge to dialectical materialism, the Poles, who had been conducting some seminars on personal construct theory before my arrival, explained to me that "personal construct theory was just exactly what dialectical materialism stood for." Along the way also I have found myself classified in a volume on personality theories as one of the "learning theorists," a classification that seems to me so patently ridiculous that I have gotten no end of amusement out of it.

A few years ago an orthodox psychoanalyst insisted, after hearing me talk about psychotherapy, that, regardless of what I might say about Freud, and regardless even of my failure to fall in the apostolic succession to which a personal psychoanalysis entitled one, I was really "a psychoanalyst." This charge was repeated by a couple of psycho-analytically sophisticated psychiatrists in London last fall, and nothing I could say would shake their conviction.

I have, of course, been called a Zen Buddhist, and last fall one of our former students, now a distinguished psychologist, who was invited back to give a lecture, spent an hour and a half in a seminar corrupting my students with the idea that I was really a "behaviorist."

(Kelly, 1969/1965, pp. 216–17)

The book Kelly would have liked to write but did not have time to finish would have been titled *The Human Feeling*.

The absence of the construct 'emotion' in personal construct theory – similar to the absence of other theoretical constructs which occupy a central role in other psychologies, such as 'cognition', 'learning', motivation' – derives, as mentioned, by the choice of considering knowledge as a personal construction. This makes Kelly's a metatheory; one of the personal theories that cannot recur to the same constructs which are included as elements in its field of pertinence. In other words, 'emotion', 'cognition', 'motivation' and such like are not considered as entities, but constructs, that a constructivist psychology must deal with as such if wanting to avoid contradiction.

The notion of 'construct' goes beyond the cognitive/emotive dichotomy, as well as many other dichotomies which correspond to personal constructs used as if referring to given entities and traditionally used to explain the human functioning:

The difficulty in understanding personal construct theory as a non-cognitive theory arises out of our assumption that all discrimination, as well as all of our sense of identity, is essentially cognitive. But human discrimination may take place also at levels which have been called "physiological" or "emotional." Nor is discrimination necessarily a verbalized process. Man discriminates even at a very primitive and behavioral level.

(Kelly, 1969/1965, p. 219)

Kelly specifies in another passage that:

in order to make the point, I have had to talk about constructs in such an explicit manner that I have probably given the impression that a construct is as highly articulate and cognitive as my discussion has had to be. If I had been able to say what I have said in metaphor or hyperbole I might have left the impression that a construct had something to do with feeling or with formless urges too fluid to be pinned down by labels. But personal construct theory is no more a cognitive theory than it is an affective or a conative one. There are grounds for distinction that operate in one's life that seem to elude verbal expression. We see them in infants, as well as in our own spontaneous aversions and infatuations. These discriminative bases are no less constructs than those the reader may have been imagining during the reading of the preceding paragraphs.

(1970a/1966, p. 15)

Returning to the main theme of this section, we could ask the question: in which way therefore does Kelly propose giving reason to this set of processes labelled and distinguished as emotions by the traditional psychologies?

Personal construct theory is a constructivist theory, therefore one relating to the personal organisation of experience. This organisation shows continuous structural changes, allowed and constrained by the permeability of the superordinate constructs, as described in the modulation corollary. Even the changes which take place in one's construction system must themselves be construed. One's construction of transitions, or of the prospect of a transition, is part of one's construction of experience. Some of them can be usefully differentiated by means of professional constructs.

Kelly regards, as particularly important in clinical application, four experiential phenomena labelled by him as threat, **fear**, anxiety and guilt. Though widely used in traditional psychologies, these terms have in personal construct theory a specific meaning: they refer to one's awareness of transitions in one's construction system.

5.3.1 Threat

Thus, '*threat is the awareness of imminent comprehensive change in one's core structures*' (Kelly, 1991a/1955, p. 361, italics in the original).

For example, death is threatening for most people, to the extent that it is construed both as likely to happen in a short time and as likely to require drastic changes in core constructs. Such changes may not necessarily entail a worse outcome. People who expect an improvement in their life may be threatened by psychotherapy if they sense that this must be preceded by a significant change in personality.

Even people who have already experienced a change may feel threatened 'by the prospect of relapse under certain precipitating conditions. The old ways of looking at things are still so clear, so easily structured, so palpably available' (ibid., p. 362). In relation to this, Landfield (1951), one of Kelly's former students, proposed two threat hypotheses. Some people can be seen as threatening if they appear to exemplify what the perceiver once was, but no longer is (*exemplification hypothesis*) or even if they appear to expect the perceiver to behave in the old ways (*expectancy hypothesis*). In both the cases, it would be too easy for the perceiver to regress.

In the psychotherapy process there can be many other situations in which the client may feel threatened. The therapists can be seen as threatening not only, according to Landfield's expectancy hypothesis, if they appear to expect the clients to behave in a way in which they no longer wish to behave, but also if they appear to expect the clients to behave in other ways which are different from the clients' more personal ones. Furthermore, the clients can be threatened by the progressive plausibility of an alternative interpretation of themselves, as a result of the work being done in the psychotherapy process. Frequently, threat and defenses from threat occur just before the clients make major shifts in their core structures.

5.3.2 Fear

'*Fear is like threat, except that, in this case, it is a new incidental construct, rather than a comprehensive construct, that seems about to take over*' (Kelly, 1991a/1955, p. 364, italics in the original).

The person's core structures are at stake here, as in the case of threat, and therefore the maintenance processes are involved. However, the core construct is an incidental construct, and consequently it subsumes a narrower variety of events.

In our experience, even if the theoretical propriety of such a distinction between threat and fear is understood, it is neither particularly easy nor useful to discriminate between them in a clinical setting.

5.3.3 Anxiety

'*Anxiety is the recognition that the events with which one is confronted lie outside the range of convenience of one's construct system*' (Kelly, 1991a/ 1955, p. 365, italics in the original).

To be precise, the events with which one is confronted lie *mostly* outside the range of convenience, otherwise one could not even perceive them. Anxiety, in other terms, consists in 'the recognition that one is inescapably confronted with events to which one's constructs do not adequately apply' (ibid., p. 366), that is, in the recognition of a relative lack of structure.

This is especially the case when the person's superordinate constructs are insufficiently permeable to admit the impending variants into their ranges of convenience. The person is confronted with new experiences which he or she cannot adequately organise.

Given its definition, anxiety may be considered a precondition for making revisions. Still, it is not always so. Actually, in order to protect themselves from anxiety, people resort to various adaptive processes which replace the search of a construction wholly applicable to the events. The observation of such devices allows the therapist to appraise the presence of anxiety in the client.

People can loosen their constructs, in particular their superordinate ones, so as to increase their permeability and permit greater variety in their application while retaining their essential identity. In this way, the person can approximately anticipate events, even though the confusion of anxiety is substituted by the vagueness of loosening. This kind of 'defense' against anxiety reaches the highest point in people labelled as schizophrenic, as described in the research by Bannister (see section 5.4.3).

They can also choose the opposite process, that is, tighten their constructs, in particular the subordinate ones, so as to maintain a greater organisation at the lower levels of the system. In doing so the person works out the little routine of living in a highly structured manner, yet renouncing the achievement of a more comprehensive adaptation.

They can try to lay their whole dependency on one resource. In such cases, weeping, as a childish expression of dependency, is frequently present, and can even represent a request of appeasement if the client is hostile. The way the therapist deals with the client's weeping can be a crucial point in the making of the psychotherapeutic relationship.

People can show impulsivity in their eagerness to substitute confusion with structure. The person seeks quick solutions by shortening the circumspection phase of the C-P-C cycle, but the choice may confront them with unexpected and undesirable outcomes later on.

People can also frantically search for structure by means of dilation, that is, by looking for additional elements in the hope that they enable them to regain structure. In this case, this may give the impression of distractibility. On the contrary, they can make recourse to constriction in the areas of confusion, showing lack of versatility and an inability to take into account more than a few features of the situation at a time.

5.3.4 Guilt

The 'perception of one's apparent dislodgment from one's core role structure constitutes the experience of guilt' (Kelly, 1991a/1955, p. 370, italics in the original).

The sociality corollary defines a role as a course of activity which is based upon one's interpretation of the thinking of other people in relation to whom the role is enacted. Therefore, a role is based upon a construction whose elements are the presumed constructs of other people. 'A core role involves that part of a person's role structure by which he maintains himself as an integral being' (ibid., p. 370).

This is where personal construct theory reveals the basic importance it attributes to the social constructions. 'We are dependent for life itself upon an understanding of the thoughts of certain other people' (ibid., p. 370), and it is precisely the loss of one's core role structure which is experienced as guilt.

Given that guilt implies core structure – that is, constructs which govern the person's maintenance processes implied in the conservation of life and identity – it is often related to 'physical' health. In works of ours (Chiari & Nuzzo, 1992; Nuzzo & Chiari, 1987, 1992) we theorised the relation between the experience of guilt and the onset of cancer, seen as an 'oncopoietic process'.

If people experience guilt, and they consider no alternatives, it is likely they will become hostile (see section 5.3.6). Rather than revise their core role structure – an enterprise implying too many subordinate changes – they demand reinstatement of it and look for appeasement.

In addition to threat, fear, anxiety and guilt, other professional constructs, having to do with transitions in a person's construction system, appear particularly useful in the clinical practice. These are the constructs of aggressiveness and hostility.

5.3.5 Aggressiveness

'*Aggressiveness is the active elaboration of one's perceptual field*' (Kelly, 1991a/1955, p. 374, italics in the original).

In personal construct theory, the term 'aggressiveness' does not apply to antisocial, essentially destructive, impulses. On the contrary, according to the principle of the elaborative choice, all people show the tendency to choose that alternative which allows the greater possibility of extending their predictive systems. However, some are particularly active in precipitating themselves and others into situations which require decision and action. Usually, this aggressiveness is shown by the person in some areas more than in others. In these 'interest areas' the person shows initiative and freedom.

To the extent that aggressiveness can be shown in the person's areas of anxiety, thus allowing them to find a structure applicable to relatively unstructured events, 'one might say that the areas of one's aggression are those in which there are anxieties he can face' (ibid., p. 375).

5.3.6 Hostility

'*Hostility is the continued effort to extort validational evidence in favour of a type of social prediction which has already proved itself a failure*' (Kelly, 1991a/1955, p. 375, italics in the original).

Like aggressiveness, even hostility loses its ordinary meaning in personal construct theory. When understood from the viewpoint of the person's experience hostility is not a disposition to harm someone. This eventuality can be an incidental outcome of something more vital for the person. On the contrary, hostility is an attempt to protect oneself from the anxiety; the threat or guilt which can arise from an invalidation demanding a major revision of the person's construction system. In other words, hostile people try to alter the events in an effort to make them conform to their own original expectations.

The relation between hostility and guilt has a particular importance in the clinical arena. In fact, 'hostility arises when one cannot live with the results of one's social experimentation' (ibid., p. 376). As a consequence, the person, instead of revising the construction which has proven to be misleading, strives for altering the data to fit their hypotheses:

> Yet, as much as he insists that people must be made into what he has already construed them to be, he continually keeps stumbling over bits of evidence that he is wrong, that his core role is on shaky ground – in short, that perhaps he is guilty after all.
>
> (Ibid., 1991a/1955, p. 377)

The greater the revision required by the invalidation, the greater the hostility, and greater the number of people to which it is directed.

The therapist, who defies the clients' hostility leading them to recognise the invalidation they strive to deny would precipitate them into guilt with devastating implications at the level of the maintenance processes. It would be appropriate for the therapists to respect the clients' hostility until the construction of a new core role able to gradually substitute the old, invalidated role. By 'respect', we mean to assume an attitude that does not make the clients feel contradicted nor that satisfies their search for appeasement. Practically, the therapist should demonstrate acceptance of the client, as defined in personal construct psychology (see section 4.2).

5.3.7 Other professional constructs relative to transitions

Playing with the permutations of the variables implied in the transitions – Kelly already used (validation/invalidation, core/non-core structure, fit/dislodgement) – McCoy (1977) managed to expand the list of professional constructs relative to transitions. In her attempt, McCoy strove to provide definitions for all the basic emotion categories described by the psychological literature and supposed to be biologically based (Ekman *et al.*, 1972; Izard, 1971; Tomkins, 1970). Though doubtful about this kind of operation reproposing a traditional view of emotion, we find some of McCoy's definitions useful for the clinician and the constructivist psychotherapist.

The transitions have been categorised according to the following headings:

- change in core structure: comprehensive (*threat*), or incidental (*fear*)
- change in non-core structure: comprehensive (*bewilderment*), or incidental (*doubt*)
- validation of core structure: comprehensive (*love*), or partial (*happiness*)
- validation of non-core structure: comprehensive (*satisfaction*), or partial (*complacency*)
- invalidation of core structure implications (*sadness*)
- fit of self and core role structure: dislodgement (*guilt*), good fit (*self-confidence*), or dislodgement of other's construing of self (*shame*)
- fit between own core structure and other's (*contempt* and *disgust*)
- recognition of construct system functionality: inadequate (*anxiety*), or adequate (*contentment*)
- sudden need to construe (*surprise*)
- behaviour associated with emotion: active elaboration of one's perceptual field (*aggressiveness*), or effort at validation without change (*hostility* and *anger*).

The definitions of the transitions are given in Table 5.1, together with the definition of *stress* given by Kelly (1991b/1955, p. 165) in addition to his discussion of the professional constructs relative to transitions.

5.4 Personal narratives: some illustrative plots

Even though every personal narrative differs from another, we maintain that it is possible and useful to construct some regularities in the guise of 'plots' which tend to be repeated with minor variations. This possibility arises from the partial sharing in the construction of experience (according to the commonality corollary), in turn deriving from the structure we have in common by belonging to the same species and culture. Different cultures give shape to narrative organisations of experience resulting in different plots. It is indirectly testified by the clinical presentation of psychiatric disorders described by transcultural psychiatry.

The following do not aim at being accounts of personal narratives relative to specific 'disorders', as we see our construction of clients' personal narratives as similar in certain core aspects. They may appear plausible to other clinical psychologists and psychotherapists who, based on similar epistemological and theoretical assumptions, try to understand their clients' narratives.

It is important to specify that the following accounts represent the form the personal narratives assume in an advanced phase of the psychotherapy process, when the elaboration of the complaint (see section 6.6) and of the person (see section 6.7) has encouraged an increased level of cognitive awareness in the client. We cannot exclude that, during the course of such an elaborative process, the therapists' experience of narratives construed as

Table 5.1 Professional constructs relative to transitions according to Kelly (*) and McCoy

Change in core structures	
Awareness of imminent comprehensive change in one's core structures	Threat*
Awareness of imminent incidental change in one's core structures	Fear*
Awareness of potential threat	Stress*
Change in non-core structures	
Awareness of imminent comprehensive change in non-core structures	Bewilderment
Awareness of imminent incidental change in non-core structures	Doubt
Validation of core structures	
Awareness of validation of one's core structure	Love
Awareness of validation of a portion of one's core structure	Happiness
Validation of non-core structure	
Awareness of validation of a non-core structure	Satisfaction
Awareness of validation of a small portion of some non-core structure	Complacency
Invalidation of core structure implications	
Awareness of the invalidation of implications of a portion or all of the core structure	Sadness
Fit of self and core role structure	
Awareness of the goodness of fit of the self in one's core role structure	Self-confidence
Awareness of dislodgement of the self from one's core role structure	Guilt*
Awareness of dislodgement of the self from another's construing of your role	Shame
Fit between own core structure and other's	
Awareness that the core role of another is comprehensively different from one's own and/or does not meet the norms of social expectation	Contempt (or disgust)
Recognition of construct system functionality	
Awareness that the events with which one is confronted lie outside the range of convenience of the construct system	Anxiety*
Awareness that the events with which one is confronted lie within the range of convenience of the construct system	Contentment
Sudden awareness of a need to construe events	Startle (or surprise)
Behaviour associated with emotion	
Active elaboration of one's perceptual field	Aggressiveness*
Continued effort to extort validational evidence in favour of a type of social prediction which has already been recognised as a failure	Hostility*
Awareness of invalidation of constructs leading to hostility	Anger

similar, encourages a co-construction that would therefore assume the value of a self-fulfilling prophecy. Moreover, the narrative of a single person may assume different versions depending on the context (as implied by the fragmentation corollary). Regarding this, Mair (1988, p. 127) suggests a distinction between a 'master-story' and its different 'subplots'.

5.4.1 Developmental paths of dependency

We regard personal narratives as the development of possible paths deriving from the person's construction of early relational experiences. In our opinion, it is such experiences, figured as initial conditions liable to a variety of subsequent variations, which channelise the person's develop-ment. That is why we shall refer to our hypothesis of 'personal paths of dependency' (Chiari *et al.*, 1994), as mentioned in section 3.7.1.

Briefly, children are likely to follow three main *developmental paths of dependency*, each of them traced by the main transition they experience within the early dependency relationship with their parents. Parenthetically, dependency paths are reminiscent of other two tripartite classifications: that of Ainsworth *et al.* (1978) of secure, ambivalent and avoidant patterns of infant–mother attachment, and that of Watzlawick, Beavin, and Jackson (1967) of confirmation, rejection and disconfirmation, seen as communica-tion response modes that summarise forms of relational feedback.

Aggressiveness (see section 5.3.5) can be seen as the transition more favourable to the development of a greater dispersion of dependency and of the greater, related emergence of role constructs. Defined as the active elaboration of the perceptual field the child's aggressiveness encourages social experimentations, giving a structure to the areas of anxiety relative to the social world, and contributing to a progressive differentiation and an increasing hierarchical integration of the system. A precondition for this process is that the children do not perceive the relationship with their parents as threatening. On the contrary, parents' relationship with their child is supposed to be characterised by *acceptance*, that is, by their readi-ness to understand and to take into account (not necessarily to approve) the child's experiences. As stated in the sociality corollary, 'to the extent that one person construes the construction processes of another, he may play a role in a social process involving the other person' (Kelly, 1991a/1955, p. 66). By extensively construing their child's construction processes, and relating with them on the basis of such an understanding, parents in turn offer their child the possibility of construing a variety of regularities as to their own processes, thus encouraging the elaboration of role constructs. This comprehensive role relation to the parents makes the child feel the relationship with them is highly enough structured and unlikely to fall apart. We refer to this developmental path as a *dependency path traced by aggressiveness*.

On the contrary, interpersonal conditions unfavourable to the process of dispersion of dependency limit the personal investment in role relations. One of them is characterised by the transition of threat (see section 5.3.1), the other by the transition of guilt (see section 5.3.4).

The children's dispersion of their dependencies on a number of people can be strongly limited by the particular interaction with their mother or caregiver. This interaction ultimately implies a restriction of the children's spontaneous activities that otherwise would be likely to result in a dispersion of their dependency. The restriction is usually obtained by the mother through her withdrawal from the relationship with the child, and the consequent threat relative to the loss of the dependency relation with her. Later, as the children will, more and more frequently, come into contact with people outside the family the relationship with them will be likely to involve threat, that is, the anticipation of the loss of the relationship with the mother on which they still locate most of their dependencies. Given the limitation to social experimentations, the social reality constructed by the children (and later on by the adults) is likely to remain simple and concrete, based prevailingly on dependency constructs. Thus, people are categorised as familiar people, upon which they can rely or as strangers, who are construed as figures rather than people, and viewed as unwilling and vaguely hostile. Each separation, manifested or anticipated, from the people on whom they depend can easily jeopardise their maintenance processes, and will therefore be avoided whenever possible. We refer to this early developmental path as *dependency path traced by threat*.

A different obstacle to the process of dispersion of dependency is represented by the invalidations the children's experience in their attempts to construe a role in the relationship with their mother. That is, a recurrent transition of guilt in the children characterises this kind of relationship, often triggered by a hostile mother. In turn, the mother's hostility is supposed to derive from two possible experiences. She strives to see her child as the child she strongly desires, e.g. a doll. The child behaves differently, and she, instead of revising her construction, looks for appeasement – being critical and disregarding whenever the child does not fit her construction. Kelly's description of 'loving' hostility (1991a/1955, p. 376) fits well with the preceding discussion. In other cases, the mother's hostility is relative to more comprehensive and core constructions. At a low level of cognitive awareness she has already experienced the failure of her experiments undertaken with respect to people. She faces guilt, that is, the loss of her core role. Hostility is a protection against guilt. She must do all she can to extort validational evidence in favour of the adequacy of her role. She must prove that she is right and the others are wrong. As a consequence, she cannot approve of her child: there is always something wrong in the child's behaviour. In both cases, the children experience difficulties in understanding their mother, in perceiving regularities in her behaviour relative to their own processes. The children try to understand the mother's demands and behave accordingly, but their anticipations keep being invalidated. We refer to this type of developmental path as *dependency path traced by guilt*.

The paths of ontogenic development traced by the prevailing transitions experienced by the child in early dependency relationships are likely to become increasingly divergent from each other in time, particularly during the pre-adolescent and adolescent period of the organisation of self. The dependency paths traced by threat and guilt, implying a lower dispersion of dependency and a lesser emergence of role constructs, are more likely to result in personal disorders in the adult. They are not 'pathological' paths in themselves, their problematic nature stems from the person's difficulty to conserve an adaptation when some kind of change is required.

The following are tentative, concise accounts of personal narratives as could be told by psychotherapy clients. The initial bifurcation into narratives referable to early relational experiences of threat and guilt is supposed to be followed by a series of successive branches, in relation to the structural changes 'chosen' by the child in order to conserve adaptation and identity. Of these branches we shall try to give a sketch, emphasising the progressive character of their development as opposed to the categorical classification of diseases of the DSM-IV-TR (American Psychiatric Association, 2000).

5.4.2 Narratives referable to early relational experiences of threat

The avoidance of separation from the figures the child relies upon, and the threat experienced following a separation or the anticipation of it, is best represented by the separation anxiety disorder. As adults such people are likely to develop one of the permutations of panic disorder and agoraphobia described by the DSM-IV.

From a personal construct perspective, the panic/agoraphobia complex may be construed by making reference to a dimension of undispersed dependency. However, the clients' personal narratives in the first phase of the psychotherapy process appear to disregard the experience of threat relative to events of separation or loss, instead being centred on the difficulty in giving a meaning to their experience. This finding, which traditional clinical psychology can describe in terms of low level of awareness and difficulty in discriminating different emotions, appears to us as the consequence of the child's limitation of social experimentations. The person's construction of self and others is not based on the construction of interpersonal processes channelised by role constructs, but prevailingly on dependency constructs. When confronted with a separation or a loss the adult experiences a sudden change in his or her core constructs (with consequent alterations of maintenance processes), which can be hardly construed in relation to personal elements. The mysteriousness and unpredictability of such a change only allows a construction of the experience implying the anticipation of, for example, 'losing control', 'having a heart attack' and 'becoming mad'.

Prior to the first 'panic attack' the person had shown signs of threat when unable to avoid situations vaguely construed as a limitation on the freedom of movement (crowded spaces, elevators, flying, etc.). Professionally, such a threat has to do with the difficulty (at a low level of cognitive awareness) in quickly reaching 'safe' places, meant as familiar places, or figures upon which the person depends. This same interpretation is applicable to the threat experienced when in 'open spaces', specifically by being equidistant from the ends of large spaces (squares, bridges, galleries). After the first experience, the person tries to limit the unpredictable occurrence of further 'attacks', by operating a constriction, ranging from staying at home to going out only if accompanied by 'trusted' people (i.e., those on whom he or she depends). The dramatic change following the first experience of threat is usually accompanied by a 'contrast reconstruction' in the person's construction of self, from a self-confident, independent and adventuresome person to an insecure, dependent and fearful one. Such a change is construed as deriving from some kind of disease.

A variety of personal narratives deriving from early relational experiences of threat derives from the child's choice of conserving an adaptation by means of the impermeability of the constructs superordinate to self. It is particularly the case for people diagnosed with obsessive-compulsive disorder and obsessive-compulsive personality disorder. Our personal experience, as well as some experimental studies (e.g., Clark & Bolton, 1985), seem to suggest that these people perceive, since their childhood, a high level of expectancies and demands by their parents. The high risk of not fully satisfying such expectancies – and the ensuing threat to the conservation of the relation with their parents – results in the distinctive feature of the obsessional client, whose superordinate structure, according to Kelly (1991a/1955, p. 62), 'is characteristically impermeable; he needs a separate pigeonhole for each new experience and he calculates his anticipations of events with minute pseudo-mathematical schemes'. Once their monolithic, highly tight organisation disintegrates it appears to become fragmented (Makhlouf-Norris et al., 1970), accounting for the observation that the people with obsessional behaviour construct subsystems concerning the self and their obsessional concerns which represent an island of structure amidst the vagueness and confusion of a system with a generally loose organisation (Fransella, 1974).

Impermeability, making a change in a person's construction system more difficult as predicted by the modulation corollary, justifies many of the characteristics of the obsessive-compulsive personality disorder such as the preoccupation with details and order, perfectionism, being overconscientious

and scrupulous, rigidity and stubbornness. Tight construing and impermeability have also been related to the dissociation implicit in both post-
traumatic stress disorder and dissociative identity disorder, based on the
proposal that 'the trauma produces isolated construct classes which cannot
be related by associative or transitive propositions to the rest of the
conceptual structure' (Cromwell *et al.*, 1996, p. 180).

5.4.3 Narratives referable to early relational experiences of guilt

In our experience, narratives referable to the construction of early relational
experiences of invalidation are particularly frequent in psychotherapy
clients. They usually rotate around personal dimensions of 'unlovability',
'personal inadequacy', 'worthlessness' and 'unworthiness'. While diction-
aries may define the above terms in rather distinct ways, their meaning is
often vague and confused in people who make them the core and the
principal subject of their narratives due to the fact that they are prevailingly
non-verbal construct dimensions that acquire a label and a clearer meaning
in the negotiation that occurs during the psychotherapeutic conversation.

When in a relationship with a mother or caregiver, who repeatedly
invalidates the children's tentative constructions of her, they can make the
elaborative choice to loosen their constructions so as to limit the possibility
of further invalidations.

An extreme example of this is represented by Bannister's (1960) serial
invalidation hypothesis on the genesis of schizophrenic thought disorder.
According to the hypothesis, subjected to experimental tests (Bannister,
1963, 1965; Bannister & Salmon, 1966), the bizarre thoughts characteristic
of the disorder derive from the progressive loosening of the construction of
others following repeated experiences of invalidation.

Several authors, supporting an interpersonal model of schizophrenia,
have observed the presence of contradictory, disqualifying or incoherent
communication between the future schizophrenic children and their
parents. Bateson *et al.* (1956) first introduced the concept of 'double
bind'; Laing and Esterson (1964) speak of the disintegrating effects of
'mystification' and Lidz (1964) of 'inculcation of confused and distorted
meanings'. These communications, in terms of personal construct theory,
are likely to be experienced as invalidations hindering the construction of
role relationships. Bannister's hypothesis, in line with a constructivist
assumption, emphasises the adaptive function of the loosening process
more than the interpersonal model, not to mention the cognitive models
and approaches to the therapy of schizophrenia which use the concepts of
erroneous controlling assumptions (Jacobs, 1980) and dysfunctional
schemes (Perris, 1990) according to a rationalistic perspective. The constructivist understanding of the schizophrenic process does not, in fact,

start off from the assumption that people affected by schizophrenic thought disorder have a sort of deficit due to dysfunctional cognitions or that they become incoherent due to incoherent information, but from the assumption that the person attempts to maintain a social adaptation by adopting different possible strategies consisting in particular structural changes. What allows the conservation of some understanding in the people labelled as schizophrenics from a psychiatric viewpoint is just the loosening of the construction of others.

Although not telling the stories that thought disordered schizophrenics tell and the stories they live by according to Mair (1989b, p. 6), Bannister tells 'stories of schizophrenic thought disorder as reflecting *ways of life*, manner of living'. Remaining in the area of schizophrenia and other psychotic disorders, as described by the DSM-IV, a reverse operation was made by Jacobs (1980) in terms of a cognitive approach applied within the psychoanalytic theory. Describing the self-narratives of patients with delusional beliefs, Jacobs observed that they rotate around a dimension of 'unlovability': 'I am worth nothing', 'I cannot be loved, therefore any attempt to relate to people is senseless', 'I must be careful because the others want to hurt me', 'If I stay on my own I may not get hurt'. From a personal construct interpretation of the preceding narratives, one can interpret them as narrative organisations of experiences implying a transition of threat of guilt, that is, the anticipation of a possible loss of core role. In addition to loosening, the person tries to face the threat of further invalidations by means of constriction, hence, by avoiding any relationship with others. Variants of the above narratives, referable to early relational experiences of invalidation, can be found, according to the DSM-IV, in clients affected by paranoid, schizoid, schizotypal and borderline personality disorders.

Sometimes, the child's anticipation of further invalidations – and the consequent threat to the dependency relationship – can see the predominance of constriction, consisting particularly in the exclusion from the child's perceptual field of all the aspects of self not meeting the mother's demands, in the attempt at satisfying them. In such a case the child – later on the adult – is likely to experience a divided self. Winnicott (1960) and Laing (1960) expounded – from a psychoanalytic and, respectively, phenomenological approach – a similar process. In a personal construct understanding it consists of a distinction between a 'façade self', a mask, by which the person constantly strives to anticipate the demands of others in order to maintain the relationship and an appearance of role, and a 'true self', in turn construed loosely as wrong, unlovable, inadequate and at the same time as special, unique, particularly lovable or admirable. In both cases, the possible revelation of the 'true self' implies a threat of guilt. Some people (psychiatrically diagnosed as avoidant-personality disordered patients) constrict their world and limit their activities so as to minimise the risk of being discovered as inadequate; central to their narratives is the 'fear of judgement'. Others (diagnosed as social phobics) make the choice of exposing themselves to threatening situations in the hope of conserving the role of brilliant and talented people, telling themselves the 'fear of being discovered as a bluff'.

A special case of constriction implying the emergence of a divided self can be seen in eating disorders, particularly anorexia nervosa. The child's relationship with her mother does not encourage social aggressiveness, since the mother 'prescribes' behaviours and feelings. The child's processes are progressively channelised by what the mother expects from her rather than by anticipations deriving from more comprehensive personal experiences. However, the very same attempts at understanding the mother's expectancies are frequently invalidated, since some are very clear (e.g., being obedient or a diligent student), others are vague and incoherent. Thus, in the child's narrative, a distinction between an 'intellectual self' (brilliant, bright) and an 'affective self' (unlovable, inadequate, maybe wrong) slowly emerges. The core construction of self as unlovable implies the anticipation of the impossibility of deep relationships with others. The role relationships can be played in terms of being helpful, if not essential (role of care, nurturance), or of being appraised, if not prestigious (role of competent). If threatened, the recourse to hostility is frequent. On the other hand, personal needs and desires cannot be taken into consideration. They must be excluded as much as possible by the perceptual field (constriction) or at least by the relational field, being incompatible with the conservation of the relationship. For the same reason, it is not possible for the person to rely upon other people or ask for help; all dependencies are located on the self. The alternative of being altruistic is that of being selfish, and therefore unacceptable to others.

The discrepancy between the core, usually non-verbal construction of self as unlovable, and the constricted role played in the relationships with other people, encourages the emergence of a distinction between a 'true self' and a 'façade self'. The 'real self' is overprotected in order to avoid further validations of the dimension of unlovability, but, at the same time, it often expresses its looseness through a sense of incomprehension ('if only one could see me for the person I really am. . .'). Fantasies of redemption are also frequent ('the ugly duckling' transforming in a swan, the 'prince charming' coming to take her away), as alternative constructions which could magically solve the sense of isolation, allowing a full expression of self.

A core theme of such a narrative concerns expectancies. The person conserves adaptation and identity by attempting to meet the other's demands. If the compliant role is invalidated ('you are not right anyway'), there can be a contrast reconstruction, that is, an opposing behaviour, and the onset of the eating disorder. The latter can be regarded as the only activity in which the person conserves a sense of personal agency, together with the sense of being somehow effective in the relationship with other people, particularly the mother.

Chapter 6

An ontological venture: the psychotherapy process

6.1 Being, becoming, and not-becoming in a hermeneutic constructivist framework: an overall view

A radically constructivist approach to the psychological study of the person begins from a simple assumption: it is not possible to observe the world from a privileged place. In other words, *we do not have the possibility of knowing the world abstracting from our structure.*

It may seem an easily shareable, if not trivial assumption. Husserl (1976/1936) observes that the evidence revealing the correlation between the world and the subjective ways of perceiving it, has never given rise to philosophical amazement, and did not ever become the subject of a particular scientificity, since everybody became trapped in the obviousness of the realisation that all things have a different aspect for different people. This sense of obviousness derives from a particular interpretation of the preceding statement, consistent with a deep-rooted realistic view of knowledge which one can reformulate by asserting that our structure *allows* us to know the world. Had we been without the sensory apparatus we have, and especially the cognitive capacities allowed by our brain, our knowledge of the world would be no *better* (closer to reality) than that of other less evolved living systems.

The 'constructivist' meaning of this statement is a different interpretation in that the type of correlation introduced by Husserl (and by constructivism) does not imply a generic relation between subject and world (obviously accepted by any philosophical theory of knowledge), but a relation which is intentional (see section 2.3.2). The implication is by no means obvious, since it becomes apparent that the foundation of knowledge does not lie 'in one pole or the other of the *correlation*, but in the correlation itself' (Armezzani *et al.*, 2003, p. 18, our translation, italics in the original). In other words, our knowledge of the world is *dependent on* our structure; is *related to* how we are made. If the world appears to us as it does, it is because of our structure. Our knowledge, therefore, is not one of a world external to us, but the result of our relation with the environment.

It tells us what we have become, rather than informing us on the invariant structures of a reality that seems to surround us. As Maturana affirms:

> we find ourselves as human beings here and now in the praxis of living, in the happening of being human, in language languaging, in an *a priori* experiential situation in which everything, that is, everything that happens, is and happens in us as part of our praxis of living.
>
> (1987, p. 326)

Every explanation of the praxis in which we live (experience) is given at a later time. It does not substitute or constitute it: the explanations take place operationally in a meta-domain in respect to what they intend to explain.

In the preceding chapters we have already thoroughly analysed the characteristics of the constructivist paradigm, pointing out its different expressions in the fields of philosophy, biology, cybernetics and psychology. In this chapter we intend to outline a reference frame which allows us to introduce the implications such a paradigm has for psychotherapy.

Relinquishing the idea that it is possible to observe the world *objectively*, without falling into the opposite alternative, that all knowledge is *subjectively* construed, is, according to us, the challenge (and the main difficulty) of constructivism, particularly hermeneutic constructivism (section 2.6). It is a challenge that can only be confronted by overcoming the conceptual categories that Western culture, prevalently oriented in a rationalistic way, makes easily available.

First, one must go beyond the idea that the subject and object of knowledge represent the terms, singularly meant, of a relation: that is, that there is an *interaction* between the person and the environment. Only if we attempt to conceive the relation between the person and the social environment – and, generally speaking, between a living system and the environment – in terms of a relation of *complementarity* (Chiari & Nuzzo, 2006), the implications that derive would lead to a radical rereading of the most fundamental aspects of the whole psychotherapeutic process.

As long as an adaptation, a structural coupling between the living system and the environment, is maintained the system preserves its autopoietic organisation undergoing structural changes that constitute its ontogenetic development.

Through successive, recursive structural changes in a living system provided with a complex nervous system, as is the human species (itself the outcome of a long phylogenetic path), language emerges, and, with it, the possibility to operate distinctions (see section 3.2). Such distinctions specify a world of 'objects', a reality, that is the counterpart of the system's constraints and possibilities, and that allow for further developments in terms of planning or anticipations (see section 3.4). The person also becomes part of such a reality following still another order of recursion that enables the system to acquire self-consciousness through a distinction of self as an entity (endowed with its own organisation) different from other person-entities (see section 3.6). Personal knowledge consists of the ways people organise their own experience. Such organisation of personal experience has to be distinguished from the subjective character of experience supposed to occur at many levels of animal life (see e.g. Nagel, 1981/1974). It consists in the construction of experience which becomes possible only when a living system can distinguish itself as an observer, and represents the way in which the autopoietic organisation realises itself in a linguistic, social domain.

If the conservation of organisation and adaptation has been a 'relational' matter since the cellular phase of ontogenesis, it becomes, from this moment on, a 'social' matter. Given their structural intersection (see section 3.2), adaptation in fact becomes dependent not only on the conservation of the living organisation (the autopoietic organisation), but also on the conservation of the organisation of self within a network of social relations.

Personal change is seen as the expression of the continuous structural changes the system encounters in its dialectical relation with the environment (see section 3.3). Being organisationally closed, the system necessarily subordinates any change ('becoming') to the conservation of its identity ('being').

Such structural changes can be usefully described in terms of the professional constructs relative to the structure of a personal construct system (section 5.1), with the assumption that any structural change represents the attempt at conserving the organisation of self and adaptation.

Some structural changes, however, can be experienced by the person as implying the disintegration of organisation and adaptation. To them, we propose to apply the professional constructs relative to transitions (section 5.3): the person is aware of the possibility to lose the organisation of self, and ceases to change.

It is the very suspension of movement in the person's relation with the social environment ('not-becoming') that, in a constructivist perspective, is seen as a disorder (see following section 6.2), as a halt in experiencing; and it is the possibility for the person to resume experiencing that represents the main object of psychotherapy. 'To define psychotherapy as a form of treatment – something that one person does to another – is misleading. Psychotherapy takes place when one person makes constructive use of another who has offered himself for that purpose' (Kelly, 1980/1967, p. 21). Psychotherapy is 'a form of experience' which 'follows an exploratory course, with many reappraisals based on the outcomes of yesterday's commitments' (ibid., p. 22). Its long-range objective:

> is not to conform to oneself, whole or fragment; or to society, lay or ordained; or to nature, whatever the latest version of that happens to

be. This objective is for man continually to determine for himself what is worth the price he is going to end up paying for one thing or another anyway, to keep moving toward what he is not – surmounting obstacles as best he can – and to keep on doing both as long as he has anything to invest. To render and to utilize technical aid in this ontological venture is the special transaction we call "psychotherapy".

(Ibid., p. 20)

This ontological venture sees the client and the therapist engaged in a joint enterprise, aimed at transforming the disordered area into an area of experience.

6.2 Disorder and diagnosis revisited

The view of psychotherapy as a reconstructive process is implied by the metatheoretical assumption of personal construct theory, that is, constructive alternativism (see section 1.1). In terms of the analogy of the person as a scientist people have their own views (elaborate theories) of the world, and these allow them to have their own expectations (to formulate hypotheses) about what will happen in given situations. It is on this basis that people act and at the same time, through their behaviour, put their hypotheses to test (make experiments), and revise their constructions (that is, modify their theories) in the light of the outcomes.

This continuous cycle of experience (see section 3.5) implies a particular understanding of what other perspectives regard as psychopathology. While in rationalistic perspectives a disorder is viewed as an entity which affects the person, in personal construct psychology it is seen as 'any personal construction which is used repeatedly in spite of consistent invalidation' (Kelly, 1991b/1955, p. 193, italics in the original). Simply speaking, disordered people use constructions that are no longer able to give a proper meaning to their experience, but nonetheless, they keep using them due to lack of viable alternatives. The conservation of the person's adaptation through recursive changes is jeopardised: the processes become repetitive (Chiari & Nuzzo, 2004).

A clinically relevant personal disorder consists of a cessation of movement in a core structure within the person's construction system: the person-as-scientist is no longer able to revise their most basic constructions, notwithstanding the negative outcomes of their experiments. Of particular importance is the failure of experiments in the social domain, given its close relation with the people's construction of core role, that is, their self-identity and the organisation of self. The client has difficulty in conserving a role in relation to other people. They experience a loss of social adaptation, or they anticipate such a loss. In our opinion, the understanding of the client's disorder is likely to be inadequate as long as the therapist is unable to trace back the client's complaint to a difficulty in maintaining a social adaptation. Briefly stated, 'any personal problem is a problem in the social domain' (Chiari & Nuzzo, 2004, p. 61).

The personal constructivist view of diagnosis is also informed by the assumption of constructive alternativism. The constructivist psychotherapist chooses to conceptualise the clinical diagnosis as the planning stage for the client's reconstruction. This is why Kelly uses the term 'transitive diagnosis'.

> The term suggests that we are concerned with transitions in the client's life, that we are looking for bridges between the client's present and his future. Moreover, we expect to take an active part in helping the client select or build the bridges to be used and in helping him cross them safely. The client does not ordinarily sit cooped up in a nosological pigeonhole; he proceeds along his way. If the psychologist expects to help him he must get up off his chair and start moving along with him.
>
> (1991b/1955, pp. 153–54)

The professional or diagnostic constructs introduced in the preceding chapter do not merely refer to the ways in which the therapist can distinguish the client from other people, but also to the most important ways in which the client can change. 'The diagnostic dimensions are avenues of movement as seen by the therapist, just as the client's personal constructs are potential avenues of movements as seen by the client' (ibid., p. 154). Accordingly, 'in diagnosis [. . .] we should indicate what we think will happen, how it can be made to happen, and when to check up and see if it has happened or not. Transitive diagnosis is a matter of a clinician's "sticking his neck out"' (ibid., p. 191).

Differently from the kind of diagnosis typical of psychiatry, as well as of other psychological approaches based on pre-emptive nosological categories, transitive diagnosis is founded on a dimensional system of structural and transitional processes. In illustrating some representative types of psychological disorders in terms of such set of axes, Kelly distinguishes between the 'disorders of construction' and 'disorders of transition', according to the diagnostic dimensions principally involved. The former include disorders involving dilation, tightening and loosening of constructs, core constructs and pre-emption. The latter include disorders involving aggression, hostility, anxiety, constriction, guilt, undispersed dependency, 'psychosomatic' symptoms, organic deficit, control and impulsivity. Moreover, Kelly briefly argues that some disorders arise out of content, that is, of the intrinsic meaning of personal constructs, rather than the general form they have assumed. We have already suggested (see section 6.1) a conception of personal disorders which can allow to give up the above differentiation, offering a more comprehensive and psychodynamic view of the processes involved.

This said, the healing process consists of the constructive elaboration by the clients of that structure of their construction system 'which appears to fail to accomplish its purpose' (Kelly, 1991b/1955, p. 195). The task of the therapist is to encourage such elaboration, joining the client in the role of a co-experimenter.

6.2.1 Notes on the indication for psychotherapy

Both experienced and inexperienced psychotherapists, of any theoretical orientation, sometimes feel inadequate to accomplish their task. We think that sometimes the problem originates from an inadequate assessment of the indications for psychotherapy.

According to the more traditional psychotherapies, the matter can be divided into three points:

1　if the client's complaint can be considered to have psychotherapeutic pertinence
2　if the specific psychotherapy for which the therapist is trained is indicated for the disorder presented by the client
3　if the particular psychotherapist, given his or her experience and personal characteristics, is capable of effectively meeting the client's request.

From the viewpoint of constructivist psychotherapy, the first two points are ascribable to a single question: does the client show a disorder, according to the definition described in the preceding section (see section 6.2)?

In fact, the indications for constructivist psychotherapy are not limited to particular categorical diagnoses, to particular age groups (children, adolescents, adults, elderly) or to particular settings (individual, couple, family, or group). The object of individual constructivist psychotherapy is the reactivation of movement in a person's construction of experience, and the disorder consists in the repetitive use of certain personal constructions (in particular relative to the core role), alternative constructions not being viable. Settings, other than the individual one, require a specific reformulation of the disorder. In constructivist couple therapy the disorder concerns the unmodifiability of a relationship, following a change in one or both of its members, resulting from a lack of alternative ways to construe one another. In the case of constructivist family therapy the disorder may be conceptualised in terms of the preservation of a family organisation constituted by the specific members and their relations, involving resistance to changing explanations and stories. Constructivist approaches to group therapy, in contrast to the preceding ones, do not have as object the group as a system, but the individual components of the group which, in a microsocial situation led by the therapists have the chance to elaborate their role constructions and to carry out controlled social experimentations.

Independently of the type of complaint and setting, the constructivist psychotherapist should assess the presence of a disorder in order to recognise the indication for psychotherapy. In negative cases, it would be advisable (for both client and therapist) to suggest a support therapist, a counsellor, a family mediator or even a social worker. At times, it may be more appropriate to advise the client to seek legal or medical help.

In regard to this last possibility, it is worth clarifying the following. Traditionally, the problem envisaged by the psychotherapist is whether certain symptoms derive from an organic disease (consequently of medical pertinence), or a mental disorder (therefore of psychiatric or psychological pertinence). Is the delusion shown by the client an expression of a mental disorder, or the result of a cerebral or metabolic condition? Is the tremor a manifestation of anxiety, or of a neurological pathology? Usually, when a client turns to a psychotherapist for help he or she has already undergone medical examinations that have excluded the organic nature of the symptoms. But the conclusion of the physician that the client shows a psychological disorder often is a diagnosis by exclusion: if there are no medical explanations for the client's complaint, then it must be a psychological problem. The constructivist psychotherapists should not be satisfied with such a conclusion. They should not take charge of the client's problem only because it is 'non-medical', therefore a 'psychological' disorder. The psychotherapists, as the physicians, should also wonder if they can account for the client's symptoms in terms of their system of reference and their expertise. Moreover, the constructivist psychotherapist (for sure, the personal construct therapist), unlike therapists of other approaches and the medical doctors, does not assume the existence of bodily and mental disorders or medical and psychological diseases. Bodily/mental and medical/psychological are constructs applicable to processes which have no intrinsic properties before being distinguished in this or that manner. Rather, the question the constructivist psychotherapists should pose themselves is, 'in the light of a psychological construction of the client's complaint, can I hope to help the client better than a medical doctor or a psychiatrist, who works in the light of a medical or psychiatric construction of the "same" problem?' We have put in quotations 'same' because it may be considered so only in the light of a naïve (non-professional) construction. Actually, in terms of a psychiatric construction, a delusion may be seen as an erroneous perception to which the person adheres inflexibly, whereas in constructivist terms it can be viewed as a legitimate personal construction, not shared by other people, and yet having an adaptive function.

6.3 The client–therapist conversation

Different schools conceive the relationship between therapist and client in different ways. Beyond such differences, however, a great many of the psychotherapeutic perspectives agree that the relationship that develops between the therapist and client is fundamental for the success of treatment. This is particularly the case for the perspectives which acknowledge the role of interpersonal processes in the development of personality and the genesis of disorders. Of course, how to define a 'successful' psychotherapeutic relationship, how exactly it influences process and outcome, what are its various components and which are most important for the healing process are all questions whose answers depend on the specific conceptions about the nature of interpersonal processes and of personal disorders.

The importance of the psychotherapeutic relationship clearly emerges from a view of the person as a socially embedded network of processes, and from the ensuing consideration that the process of socialisation involves the development of different social selves, or a 'community of selves' (Mair, 1977).

Such a view – held, in particular, by the social constructionist movement (Gergen, 1985) and by the therapeutic approaches which make reference to it (McNamee & Gergen, 1992) – is coherent with Kelly's theory, not only in the sense that other people are important for the testing of one's construing system and its resulting development, but also in the understanding of self as a social construction (see also section 3.7).

In a paper presented in 1965 at a symposium on *Cognitive and analytic conceptions of the therapeutic relationship*, Kelly (1969/1965) chose to differentiate the personal construct theory's view on the subject by resorting to the different ways devised to understand the relationship between the person and the environment. In elaborating the differences, Kelly referred to his understanding of the cognitive and psychoanalytic perspectives of that time. Hence, the cognitive perspective is equated to a stimulus–organism–response psychology; the psychoanalytic is anchored to Freud's drive theory, both of them far from conceiving the therapist's task in terms of the development of a role relationship with the client. The subsequent developments of both psychoanalytic and cognitive psy-chotherapies towards increasing attention to the interpersonal processes involved in the genesis of personal disorders, as well as in the psycho-therapeutic process, resulted in a progressive convergence between the two perspectives, and between both of them and personal construct psycho-therapy. The differences are still important, but the spreading of object relations theories in psychoanalysis (see e.g. Bacal & Newman, 1990), and the elaboration of interpersonal-developmental approaches within the cognitive perspective (see e.g. Safran & Segal, 1990) encourage the opening of a domain of conversation that personal construct psychotherapists can at last begin to join, thus putting an end to their long-established isolation.

The acknowledgement of the importance of early relational experiences (see section 3.7.1), the role given to the collaborative alliance between client and therapist and the attention to transference and countertransference dynamics are the principal indications of such a convergence.

6.3.1 The alliance between client and psychotherapist: psychoanalytic, cognitive-relational and personal construct perspectives

Kelly described the therapist–client relationship by making use of several analogies (Chiari & Nuzzo, 2005).

Basically, the relationship can be described as similar to that between a therapist-as-supervisor and a research student. The research supervisors must subsume crucial aspects of the students' research interest if they want to help them design the optimal methodology with which to answer their questions. Their talent lies in the methodology of how to ask a good experimental question. The students' level of expertness lies in their specialist knowledge of the subject. The clients' subject is themselves, but they are no longer in a position to learn from their experimentation. The therapist's task is to help the clients to formulate the questions they need to ask themselves, in order to put back in motion their incomplete cycle of experimentation. This illustrates why this model of the psychotherapeutic relationship is one of active co-experimentation.

The dyad client–therapist is described as a team: 'The team of client and therapist can go about their task in a variety of ways' (Kelly, 1969b/1958, p. 231). More figuratively, 'the client and his therapist embark together as shipmates on the very same adventure' (ibid., p. 235). The psychotherapeutic process is described as an undertaking in which:

> the fortunate client has a partner, the psychotherapist. But the psychotherapist does not know the final answer either – so they face the problem together. Under the circumstances there is nothing for them to do except for both to inquire and both to risk occasional mistakes. So that it can be a genuinely cooperative effort, each must try to understand what the other is proposing and each must do what he can to help the other understand what he himself is ready to try next. They formulate their hypotheses jointly. They even experiment jointly and upon each other. Together they take stock of outcomes and revise their common hunches. Neither is the boss, nor are they merely well-bred

neighbors who keep their distance from unpleasant affairs. It is, as far as they are able to make it so, a partnership.

(Ibid., p. 229)

The personal construct psychotherapist dismisses the role of expert, that characterises so many helping professions, to join the client in the exploration of a personal world of meanings, a journey where they walk forward not following a particular, already beaten path, but 'laying down a path in walking' (Varela, 1987).

The preceding descriptions of the psychotherapeutic relationship appear to have much in common with the contemporary psychoanalytic concept of 'therapeutic alliance' (Zetzel, 1956). The term refers to a relationship between analyst and patient which provides an atmosphere of basic acceptance, understanding and safety. Zetzel, in her seminal paper, had in mind the early mother–infant object relationship. She emphasised that the development of the therapeutic alliance is a mutual and reciprocal process, not only requiring that the patient identifies with the analyst, but also that the analyst be able to identify with the patient.

Actually, Kelly's early consideration is that the whole therapeutic process is subordinate to the task of 'teaching the client how to be a "patient"' by giving specific instructions since the task involves 'much more than the recitation of a formal charge [insomuch that] it may take months to teach the client how he should respond to the therapeutic situation in order to get the most out of it' (1991b/1955, p. 62). Kelly's consideration suggests a similarity to another concept of the orthodox psychoanalytic tradition, that is, the 'working alliance' (Greenson, 1965). This refers to the more circumscribed and rational phenomenon in which the patient comes to identify with the work-ego of the analyst, gradually becoming an analytic collaborator – being the 'work-ego' defined as 'the temporarily built-up person who [functions] under the circumstances and for the period of his work' (Fliess, 1942, p. 225). The working alliance has been regarded as sequential to, and made possible by, the therapeutic alliance (Rather, 2001).

Cognitive therapists also require from the client an active and conscious collaboration to the therapeutic task, more similar to the working than to the therapeutic alliance. This collaboration – described in terms of 'collaborative empiricism' by Beck *et al.* (1979) – is viewed as crucial for the success of the therapeutic process. However, in line with the rationalistic assumption of cognitive therapy, collaborative empiricism is seen as the process by which the therapist and patient, working together, frame the patient's cognitive distortions as hypotheses to be tested and then examined logically, so as to arrive at new conclusions as a consequence of confronting and incorporating new evidence.

The concepts of therapeutic alliance and working alliance are supposed to occupy an intermediate ground in which elements of transference and non-transference (that is, relative to a 'real' relationship) co-mingle (Greenson, 1978/1971).

6.3.2 Transference and countertransference

The acknowledgement of the role of interpersonal processes in the personal construction of self and in the genesis of personal disorders implies a different way of considering the relationship between client and therapist: as an experience having a central role in the therapeutic process, rather than as the means for the application of therapeutic techniques. 'Psychotherapy may be defined as the attempt to change pathological ways of organizing experience through the use of an interpersonal relationship' (Leitner, 1985, pp. 94–95), that is, the psychotherapeutic relationship is not a means to the end of a change, but the social medium in which a personal change can happen. It follows therefore, that there are no particular personal problems that can be dealt with any better than others by working on the relationship with the client. Every personal disorder can be understood as a personal difficulty in relating with other people and can therefore be dealt with in the ambit of the client–therapist relationship.

The way personal construct psychotherapy deals with the therapeutic aspect of the therapist–client relationship is so similar to the psychoanalytic one that Kelly (1991b/1955, pp. 75–90) chose to make use of the terms transference and countertransference.

Kelly underlines that the notion of transferring is an essential feature of the psychology of personal constructs, since 'a person, in staking a prediction on the future, must lift a construct from his repertory and use it to determine the nature of his bet'. In a similar way, a client confronted with the therapist 'lifts a construct from his repertory and goggles at the therapist through it' (ibid., p. 75). The therapist's understanding of the way the client construes them – referred to as 'construction of transference' – allows them to extricate themselves from those constructions which are not useful to the client, and to assume an orthogonal position (see following section 6.3.3).

According to personal construct theory, transference can be based upon the client's role constructs or dependency constructs.

In the former case, the constructs tend to be used in a constellatory manner, partly due to the therapist's lack of self-disclosure. Once the therapists are seen, for example, as 'father figures', they are cast into a stereotype which can be hard for the client to modify, to the detriment of the experimental potential of the psychotherapeutic relationship. On the other hand, 'if the psychotherapist conducts himself in such a manner as to become an intimately known person and a sharply delineated personality for the client, he is handicapped in his reconstructive role' (Kelly, 1991b/1955, p. 45).

Should the therapists be construed by means of the client's dependency constructs, they will be expected to respond as if the client's life depended upon them. The client is likely to bring forward an increasing series of demands, whose refusal can jeopardise the relationship. Sometimes a 'transference of dependency' can be inadvertently encouraged by the therapist. For example, 'if the therapist takes the stand that "he is the doctor", that "he knows what is best for the client", he leaves himself wide open for being construed as an authoritarian father' (ibid., p. 80).

Even though an interim dependency transference can serve a useful purpose when used as a starting point for the working out of alternatives, this cannot be the case when the therapists also look at the client through their dependency constructs. Such a 'counter-dependency transference' is more likely to occur when the therapists are not well trained, and therefore not experienced in the practice of subsuming their understanding of the clients under an adequate repertoire of professional constructs.

Even though some psychotherapeutic approaches maintain that the emotions of the therapist arising from a personal involvement in the relationship with the client can play a therapeutic role (e.g. Safran & Greenberg, 1991), we are more inclined to consider countertransference (counter-dependency transference in particular) as an indication of the therapist's failure to maintain a professional role. This of course can happen, but the therapist should strive to avoid it, and not consent to it thereby adopting it in a therapeutic way. As long as the therapists succeed in subsuming their understanding of the client under a set of permeable professional constructs the person of the therapist is not involved in the relationship with the client, and the therapists experience neither emotions nor feelings. When they fail, the relationship comes to be structured by the complementary roles played by the two participants, based upon their personal construction of each other. Of course, when aware of a countertransference the therapist can try to recover a professional role by asking for supervision.

An elaboration of the notion of transference unique to personal construct psychotherapy consists in the distinction between primary and secondary transference. By 'primary transference' – or 'whole figure transference' (Kelly, 1969/1965, p. 223) – Kelly refers to the client's pre-emptive construction of the therapist. When this is the case, 'the therapist becomes "typed" in his part. No longer can he cast himself in a variety of supporting roles' (1991b/1955, p. 83). As a consequence, therapeutic movement may take place within the therapy room, but no new approaches are tried outside. Probably, the therapist has contributed to the structuration of this kind of transference by disclosing him or herself to the client thus allowing to be construed as 'the only one that. . .' for example, 'the only one man who can understand and accept me'. On the contrary, in the case of a 'secondary transference' – or 'propositional construct transference' (1969/1965, p. 223) – the client applies to the therapist a sequence of constructs from former experiences, and the latter can encourage the development of a versatile capacity for role relationships with different kinds of people.

Once again, the recent developments of some cognitive approaches appear to share the view that the client's relationship with the therapist can encourage the change of central beliefs about the self in interaction with others. Moreover, they attach to the emotions of the therapist the value of important sources of information as to the patient's way of relating with others. The differences among the psychoanalytic, cognitive and personal constructivist perspectives lie at a metatheoretical level, and imply specific theories about personal and interpersonal processes, change and disorder.

Broadly speaking, the psychoanalytic perspective is aimed at encouraging a change in intrapsychic or relational conflicts by means of their *interpretation* whenever they are expressed in the psychotherapeutic relationship through transference. Interpretation, in turn, is aimed at increasing the clients' understanding of themselves and their symptoms, thus allowing a greater mastery of their relational problems (Luborsky, 1984).

The cognitive-relational perspectives direct their efforts towards the *correction* of maladaptive interpersonal schemata and the recovery of a sense of integration of experience, mainly by means of the 'good quality' of the relationship between client and therapist, and the consequent development of metacognitive abilities (Liotti, 1999). This view reminds us of the psychoanalytic notion of 'corrective emotional experience', aimed at encouraging the client toward 're-experiencing the old unsettled conflict, but with a new ending' (Alexander & French, 1946, p. 338).

Finally, the personal construct perspective is aimed at the reactivation of an elaborative movement through the *reconstruction* of the client's experience. The purpose of personal construct psychotherapy, to use Kelly's expression, 'is not to produce a state of mind but to produce a mobility of mind that will permit one to pursue a course through the future' (1991b/1955, p. 65). It is not a question of increasing the clients' awareness of the interpersonal pattern they use, in order to prevent it from being repeatedly used. In fact, according to the choice corollary, the client will keep using the usual pattern in absence of a viable, at least equally meaningful alternative. Neither it is a question of letting the client experience a fixed, 'positive' type of relationship, as if it were the only worthy alternative. Rather, it is a question of helping the clients in inventing and elaborating some viable, alternative ways of relating within the experimental field of the psychotherapeutic relationship, so as to give new meaning to their social world and to their role in it. It is in this very sense that the relationship between client and therapist can be regarded as a reconstructive relationship.

6.3.3 Orthogonal relationships

As implied by the choice corollary, the clients seek to structure the relationship with the therapist by resorting to the dimensions they are used to applying when in relation with other people (Chiari & Nuzzo, 2005). The notion of transference described previously arises from the observation of such tendencies. Whether the clients succeed in this endeavour or not, also depends on the therapists who could or could not lend themselves to be construed in the way expected by the clients. If the former is the case, a personal change is not encouraged since the clients can keep playing the very same role compatible with their disorder. Sometimes inexperienced therapists, eager to establish a good rapport with their clients, encourage such a therapeutically ineffective relationship.

Instead, the therapists' ability consists of understanding the clients' tried role constructions in order to extricate themselves from them and present themselves to their clients so as to encourage the pursuit of new ways of relating. In this way, 'through the construal of the therapist, the patient has an opportunity for in vivo experimentation with alternative ways of construing other people in her life' (Soldz, 1993, p. 191).

With regard to this, the therapist's construction of transference is a prior requisite. In line with the view that an interpersonal relation cannot be reduced to what takes place independently within each of its members (Chiari & Nuzzo, 2006), the constructivist psychotherapists are aware that the clients' processes are dependent on the relationship with them: they assume a reflexive attitude, and regard themselves as an integrating and fundamental part of the relationship (Chiari & Nuzzo, 2005). Both the client and therapist bring their own structures into the psychotherapeutic relationship, and the realities co-constructed within it bear the stamp of those structures. Incidentally, a similar understanding of the shared responsibility in the shaping of the psychotherapeutic relationship is one of the principles of I. Hoffman's (1998) dialectical-constructivist view of the psychoanalytic process (see section 2.7.1).

A careful and continuous consideration of the relation with the client as one of complementarity, allows the therapist to assume an orthogonal position. By 'orthogonal position' we mean the therapists' way of proposing themselves so that the client cannot adequately construe them under either poles of the constructs usually applied to other people: the client is requested to recur to other constructs, whose axes of reference are perpendicular to the first ones (Chiari & Nuzzo, 1996a, 2005). An orthogonal position is likely to encourage a psychotherapeutic relationship being made which is based on role constructs other than those related to the disorder.

The notion of orthogonal position can be elaborated by referring to Maturana's (1988) treatment of change in human social systems. Given our existence as participants in networks of conversations, a personal change can take place through the encounter with other human beings in a conversation which is not confirmatory of the social systems we usually belong to, and which can trigger changes in our 'bodyhoods'. Efran has interpreted Maturana's point by using the label 'orthogonal interaction' (Efran *et al.*,

1990, pp. 144–146), coming to regard it as 'the key to therapeutic change' (Efran & Clarfield, 1992, p. 214).

On the basis of such understanding, the constructivist psychotherapist can hope to encourage a relationship which allows the client to elaborate new construct dimensions, while maintaining an optimal therapeutic distance (Leitner, 1985). The attainment of an optimal distance concerns the whole relationship, not only one of its members. Within a psychotherapeutic relationship characterised by such a distance, the client's core role constructs are not directly involved in the relation with the therapist, and therefore, are more likely to be explored and worked out.

To this regard the personal construct psychotherapist can draw from a repertoire of techniques, most of which fit into the conversational flow between client and therapist. The question as to whether psychotherapeutic change derives from the client–therapist relationship, or from the utilisation of specific techniques, becomes meaningless in the light of the understanding that the efficacy of all techniques originates in the context of the psychotherapeutic relationship, while contributing to its shaping through their contribution to the therapeutic conversation. To repeat, this is that the psychotherapeutic relationship can be considered not as a container *in which* a conversation is brought forth, but as a process that takes shape *through* the conversation between the therapist and the client.

6.4 Techniques as conversational acts

Most of the techniques of personal construct psychotherapy can be considered as conversational techniques. They are, actually, contributions to the conversation that the therapist anticipates could encourage a certain process in the client's construction of experience. That is why we prefer to consider them 'conversational acts', rather than techniques. The distinction of different conversational acts derives from the segmentation of the conversational flow on the basis of the anticipation of the particular process the client's system will undergo following the perturbation they are likely to represent.

Such conversational acts do not differ significantly from the traditional interview techniques used in clinical psychology. The difference arises from the particular theory of personal change at the origin of the constructivist theory of knowledge. The latter views the change (more peripheral or more nuclear) as an expression of the continuous movement of the person in relation with the environment (especially the social one), subordinate to the conservation of organisation and adaptation (see section 3.3). Given this conceptualisation, the clinical interview cannot be seen as an instrument used to assess the clients, to 'picture' them, leaving them unchanged. The questions asked by the interviewer can make the client's construction in relation to the question under consideration more precise (tight) or vague (loose), more open to a re-consideration (permeable) or more immodifiable (impermeable), more similar to an hypothesis (propositional) or to a definitive truth (pre-emptive); they can make the client's view of the world broader (dilated) or narrower (constricted); and, almost inevitably, they increase the level of cognitive awareness. All this happens on the grounds of an 'emotional flow' (transitions) which can make the clients feel, from time to time, confused by what is said by the interviewer (anxiety), faced with a possible, important change of their view of the world (threat), confronted with a different view of themselves (guilt), aimed at searching new answers (aggressiveness) or, on the contrary, to defend with obstinacy their point of view (hostility). Following the clinical interview, the client leaves somewhat different to how she or he was beforehand. In fact, it is this very same movement that the therapists strategically attempt to encourage in the therapeutic conversation with the clients, guided by choosing step by step the conversational acts by their understanding of the clients subsumed by their professional construction of them.

At the beginning of the psychotherapy process, the object of the conversation is usually the client's narrative regarding the complaint. Progressively, the conversation glides into the client's self-narrative. This process offers the client the possibility to place the complaint in relation to his or her construction of experience, and successively to the construction of core role. Such a progressive understanding is aimed at encouraging the construction of alternative ways of relating to others, as well as their subsequent experimentation.

In order to have the possibility of a therapeutically effective conversation, it is crucial that the therapist creates initially the conditions likely to encourage the client's willingness to engage in it.

6.5 Setting the stage for a therapeutic conversation

The therapeutic conversation takes place in the therapy room. To encourage the conversation and the structuring of a psychotherapeutically effective relationship, the room should be free of non-essential gadgets, objects revealing or suggesting the private life or the interests of the therapist and disturbing noises. The therapist should be able to adjust the lighting at will. The therapist and the client should be seated on comfortable chairs, preferably at an angle of 90 degrees to each other. This permits the client either to face or to turn away from the therapist. The telephone should be silenced and the door kept closed. If the therapist decides to audio record the conversation, a digital recorder seems to us the best choice: it is not cumbersome, the sound quality is high and it is easy to transfer and store the recording onto a PC or CD. If the therapist intends to record the session this should be communicated to the client without undue emphasis, for example by saying, 'If you do not particularly mind, I would prefer to record the conversation, so as to limit taking notes and give full attention to what you will tell me'. Switching on the recorder may be accompanied by an invitation to begin talking, such as, 'Please, do tell me'.

Two sets of conversational acts can be usefully selected from the first phase of the psychotherapy process: reassurance, and support. Kelly (1991b/1955, pp. 65–74) names them *palliative techniques*, since he considers their function temporary and limited. On the contrary, we regard them as particularly precious in setting the stage for the therapeutic conversation, as well as for overcoming difficult moments throughout the psychotherapy process. Both of them are based on the acceptance of the client by the therapist which provides a background for their discriminating use.

6.5.1 Reassurance: 'Your story is meaningful to me'

Reassurance is defined as 'a simplified superordinate construction placed upon the clinical situation. It is communicated to the client so that his behaviour and ideas will temporarily appear to him to be consistent, acceptable, and organized' (ibid., p. 65). Essentially, they consist of the formulation of a summarising statement, likely to temporarily stabilise the client's construction system when it appears badly shaken. Usually the suggested construction does not coincide with the therapist's subsuming construction of the client's viewpoint, since it could appear meaningless to the client in the initial phase of the psychotherapy. 'What the therapist uses as reassurance is the proverbial string and baling wire. It keeps things together until a more substantial structure can be built' (ibid., p. 66). Of course, if the aim is to allow the clients to keep their personal constructs intact and operative, the superimposed construction should not question either the clients or their constructs. Many common-sense ways of reassuring people are not at all reassuring. It is not reassuring to say to a worried person, 'Don't worry!', or 'There is no reason to be worried'; it is reassuring, instead, to say, 'I can understand your worry' (implicitly, 'as far as I know you'). Kelly's example is particularly illustrative: 'if the client is suddenly and disruptively disillusioned regarding his parents, the therapist is scarcely reassuring when he murmurs, "Well, your parents are probably human just like other people". He is more reassuring if he says, "Well, you have known your parents for a good many years. Let's not suddenly decide that everything you have believed about them is completely wrong"' (ibid., p. 66).

There are various ways, consistent with the preceding general definition, for providing reassurance. One of the most effective consists of the *prediction of outcomes*, for example, the prediction about how the client will feel between the present session and the next. ('Considering the issues we dealt with today, I would not be surprised if in the next days you felt a bit upset. We can expect it.') In a similar way, the *postdiction of outcomes* ('I wonder if in the last days you felt more confused than usual. Am I right?') is likely to produce a somewhat reassuring effect, as well as the *acceptance of all new and anxiety-laden material offered by the client as if it were not wholly unexpected.* The *use of value labels* (such as 'That is good' or 'You were quite right') should be employed sparingly, since they are likely to make the client feel more trapped than the preceding conversational acts.

It is clear that in all the previous instances the therapist appears to have an overall frame of reference within which to embrace the client's construction system, thus suggesting that it maintains some measure of consistency, acceptability and organisation. The client will feel able to go on without their whole world falling apart. For this same reason, reassurance risks confirming those constructs which represent the basis of the client's difficulties. Furthermore, too much reassurance tends to encourage a primary transference (see section 6.3.2). Reassurance should be therefore used carefully, to set the stage for a therapeutic conversation aimed at achieving long-range goals.

6.5.2 Support: 'I am interested in knowing your story'

The hazards in the use of reassurance are a bit less risky in the case of *support*, defined as 'a broad response pattern on the part of the therapist which permits the client to experiment widely and *successfully*' (ibid., p. 71, italics in the original). In this case, the therapist's validation of the client's attempts to participate in the psychotherapeutic relationship follows their experimentations. For example, the therapist, 'instead of saying "You are absolutely right" (*reassurance*), may respond by saying, "I think I am beginning to understand what you mean"' (ibid., p. 71). Support suggests that the client's attempts at communication are getting positive results, with 'a minimum of implication that the client's way of looking at things is the only way of looking at things or that the therapist agrees with the client' (ibid., p. 71).

Again, the therapist can support the client in various ways: by keeping the appointments promptly; by recalling clinical material at appropriate times; by demonstrating correct construing of events within the client's own construction system; by making immediate adjustments to changes in the client's construction system without emphasising possible inconsistencies; by helping the client to verbalise new constructs, or already available superordinate constructs; by being compliant with the client's wishes, or providing services for the client (being aware of what this can imply for the psychotherapeutic relationship).

As in the case of reassurance, support should be measured and used as a preliminary basis for helping the clients revise their narratives.

6.6 Conversing on the client's narrative about the complaint

The first session is of the utmost importance, as the therapist's main object is to evaluate the presence of indications for psychotherapy and, if so, set the grounds for the continuation of the psychotherapy process. Such an assessment does not require the administration of psychological tests. It can be done adequately through a conversation about the client's narrative.

6.6.1 Uncontrolled elaboration: 'You are the storyteller'

The client usually presents a complaint. During the first session, the therapists should *allow the client to present the problem spontaneously*, limiting as much as possible their own interventions. By doing this, the therapists can avoid allowing themselves to be construed as 'expert'. The client's pre-construction of the relation with the psychotherapist is often similar to that with the doctor. That is, the client usually expects to be questioned, and therefore waits for the therapist to begin asking questions. If the therapist falls into the temptation of taking charge of leading the interview (see section 6.10), it is likely that the relation will go on this way, without ever assuming the form of a conversation. The therapist's ability mainly consists of accompanying the clients in their own personal elaboration. It is important to remember that the therapist's task is not that of coming to know things about the client, but that of encouraging a change in the client's organisation of experience through the construction of alternatives.

For this reason, we prefer to simply signal to the client that he or she can start talking about their request for an appointment. A starting sentence such as, 'Do tell me, what is your problem?' implies the therapist's assumption that the client believes themselves to have, or is willing to recognise to have, a problem, but this is not always the case. A nod, at the most accompanied by 'Tell me', is very often enough to communicate to the client that he or she may start saying what he or she likes, and lay the foundation for a relationship that shall progressively be built in terms of a collaboration (see section 6.3.1).

The tacit rules that shall guide the relationship are negotiated from the very first interactions and tend to remain, in order not to be sanctioned by the dissolution of the relation itself (Jackson, 1965). Especially at the beginning of the psychotherapy process, therefore, the therapist will give ample space to the client's 'uncontrolled elaboration' of the complaint (Kelly, 1991b/1955, pp. 279–282). There are two reasons for this choice. The first, is to show the clients the therapist's interest in knowing what they retain important to communicate. Actually, the therapist's understanding of the client's narrative about the complaint is the basis for further understanding and, at the same time, for a professional construction of the disorder. The second reason directly concerns the understanding of what the client expects from psychotherapy and the psychotherapist. In Kelly's words, 'What elements does the client collect as being amenable to psychotherapy? What elements does he mention in such a manner as to indicate that he specifically excludes them from "treatment"?' (ibid., p. 9.)

For example, if the client says that his problem consists in the fact that his wife pays no attention to him and this infuriates him, he is implicitly asking for help to 'make my wife understand she should listen to me'. In this case, the therapist is seen as a person who can intervene in the client's relationship with other members of the family, in the hope of explaining how they should behave.

The therapists risk losing their clients if they do not pay proper attention to their clients' expectancies from psychotherapy as they are likely to answer their questions in a way that, from the clients' point of view, is not pertinent. On the contrary, if the therapists understand the request implicit in the client's complaint, they can offer the client a therapeutically adequate reformulation likely to be accepted. Only a few people asking for psychotherapeutic help have adequate expectancies about what it can provide, and the therapist should not elude the gap, or disregard it.

During this first phase, the therapists will limit themselves to encouraging the client's spontaneous narration by showing attention and non-verbal signs of comprehension. The interventions will be aimed at a diversion from the course of the client's narrative, only when the therapist anticipates that the client might go towards untimely processes, such as the elaboration of the loss of role, or the further loosening of already loose constructions. The therapist shall also control the elaboration when the client's spontaneous narration will have stopped, or would have become repetitive (see following).

About Kelly's distinction between 'uncontrolled' and 'controlled elaboration', a personal specification appears useful to us. The term 'controlled' brings to mind the power to influence or direct people's behaviour; a view that contrasts both with the assumption of the person as an autonomous system, and the role of the therapist as traced by constructivist psychotherapy. We think that the uncontrolled/controlled distinction should be used to point out the lesser or greater participation of the therapist in the development of the client's narrative, and that 'controlled elaboration' should have the meaning of 'strategically oriented'.

Throughout the psychotherapy process (and particularly during the first session), the constructivist psychotherapist should try *to understand the client's point of view*. This attempt requires the therapists should:

- avoid interpretations, both in the sense of giving the client explanations, and of giving themselves interpretations deriving from their own way of constructing reality; in other words, the therapists should hold an attitude of 'not-knowing' (Anderson & Goolishian, 1992), and avoid giving a personal meaning to the client's statements

• attribute their perception of a lack of meaning or of contradictions to their insufficient understanding, before attributing it to the client's meaninglessness or incoherency; maybe the client's contradiction depends on their understanding

• 'put out' or 'put aside' any personal and/or moral judgement: to judge is not part of the professional role of a constructivist psychotherapist; whether the therapists indulges in a personal rather than professional construction of the client, could signal a difficulty requiring supervision

• ask themselves the question, 'from which assumption does the client derive the statement that. . .?': the answer can facilitate the individuation of superordinate constructs, thus encouraging their understanding of the client and furthermore, to give back to the client such an understanding will be particularly important in the following phases of the psychotherapy process

• test their understanding, by re-formulating what is expressed by the client and looking for a sharing of meanings ('Let us see if I have really understood what you mean'), or by trying to anticipate covertly the course of the client's uncontrolled elaboration.

6.6.2 Controlled elaboration: 'Tell me more'

The therapist should start intervening in the conversation (that is, controlling the elaboration of the complaint) only when the client's uncontrolled elaboration stops or becomes repetitive.

To this end, Kelly (1991b/1955, p. 282) suggests *seven basic questions*. Starting with the question 'Upon what problems do you wish help?', they are designed to get the client to place the problems on a time line ('When were these problems first noticed?', 'Under what conditions did these problems first appear?'), and to see them as fluid and transient, and therefore likely to change in response to treatment ('What corrective measures have been attempted?'), the passing of time ('What changes have come with treatment or the passing of time?') and varying conditions ('Under what conditions are the problems most noticeable?', 'Under what conditions are the problems least noticeable?').

Furthermore, the therapists can strategically steer the client's elaboration in a variety of ways.

They can ask for *the client's interpretation of causes* ('And you, what do you think? Why this happens to you? How can you explain it?'). This conversational act risks encouraging the client's rationalisation of his or her behaviour, but it may also lead to an understanding of the client's personal construction of life, and may represent an expression of the therapist's interest.

The therapist can cast the complaint into a social framework; by asking the clients if they consider their problem strange, if they know other people having or having had a similar problem and in this case how they think these people solved it. This kind of enquiry can also give indications of a possible guilt, that is, of social alienation ('I am the only one who has ever had such a problem').

They can confront the clients with complaints not yet mentioned; that is, setting them down in the midst of a situation which is not of their own choosing. This conversational act may serve, according to Kelly (1991b/1955, pp. 285–286), at least three useful purposes: *to clarify the diagnostic picture*, allowing to know how the clients are likely to deal with issues not yet mentioned; *to clarify the therapeutic relationship*, by providing a broader base for it through the inclusion in the conversation of problems that the clients hoped not having to discuss; *to produce transition*, adding new problem areas after the clients' elaboration of one or two areas only.

The therapist can resort to *reflection procedures*. The reflection may be relative to 'feelings' (in the style of Rogers), to 'key' or 'used terms' (in the manner of Deutsch, 1949), or elaboration can be encouraged simply by picking up and reflecting the terminal phrase of the client's last sentence. A case of reflection requiring considerable skills by the therapist is *thematic reflection*, used 'to develop chains into narratives and narratives into thema'. In a way similar to the interpretation of Thematic Apperception Test (Murray, 1938) protocols, 'if the narrative involves a plot or theme which can be abstracted from it and [. . .] recognized as similar to that abstracted from other contents, the therapist may set about to make a thematic analysis of the client's production' (Kelly, 1991b/1955, p. 288). Reflecting selected elements from the client's production back to the client, the therapist anticipates the possibility that the client will delineate a theme, as in the following example. 'You have told me about the relationship with your first partner. Now you are talking about your disappointment with your job. What follows?. . . Can you tell me just why it follows?' The final form of reflection is *review reflection*, consisting in reflecting a review of the material produced in past sessions. The procedure shows the client that the therapist has been listening attentively, and sets the stage for elaborations to be attempted in the remainder of the session, usually at a higher level of superordination (abstraction).

6.6.3 The contract: 'We can go on conversing'

As previously discussed in connection with acceptance (see section 4.2), the constructivist psychotherapists can adequately play their role to the extent that they are able to subsume their construction of the client as a person within a professional construction. One of the most common mistakes made by trainees consists of giving a professional construction of the clients, not adequately based on an understanding of them. In other words, in order to strategically steer the therapeutic conversation it is extremely important to apply diagnostic constructs to specifiable personal elements.

At the end of the first session, an experienced therapist can already be able to decide if there are indications for psychotherapy (see also section 6.10). The answer is not to be taken for granted since, of course, it is not enough that the client asks for it. Only the therapist has the adequate competence to decide; and it is the therapist, having come to the resolution that there is the indication for psychotherapy, to decide if he or she is disposed to personally take charge of it.

The decision may be determined by the therapist's availability of time, but not only that. It can also depend on the therapist's self-knowledge, which should allow foreseeing whether he or she will be able to maintain a professional role with that particular client, without undesiderable countertransferential interferences. If the therapist thinks, for example, that the potential client could try structuring a dependency relationship, and this eventuality is experienced as threatening since the therapist anticipates that he or she could meet such a request, it may be appropriate, for the benefit of both, to invite the client to begin the psychotherapy with a colleague the therapist knows to be immune from such a 'flaw'.

In both the previous cases, and in case the therapist decides to personally take charge of the client, the client will be generically informed of the nature of the psychotherapy process. In our opinion (though aware of the different views of many therapists), the so-called 'therapeutic contract' should not be precise in the specification of the goal to be achieved. To indicate the removal of the complaint as the objective of the therapy would be obvious, and sometimes ambitious. Furthermore, the objective identified as such in the first phase of the psychotherapy process, could reveal itself secondary following further elaboration. Finally, the view of the psycho-therapy process as a path to trace step by step would be compromised since its onset. It will be enough to indicate to the client the usefulness of understanding psychologically the nature of the complaint and, based on that, the likelihood of finding a solution. Talking about elaboration, reconstruction or search for alternatives would be meaningless to most clients.

Instead, it is important to precisely and clearly define frequency and duration of sessions (usually, once a week, for 45–50 minutes) and the fee, clarifying the amount, as well as the procedure in case the session is cancelled by the client.

Constructivist psychotherapy, as we conceive and practice it, lasts for a minimum of one year to a maximum of three to four years, exceptionally more, at which time Kelly suggests rapidly arriving at the conclusion; after one or two bi-weekly sessions. The choice made by some therapists (and often welcomed by clients) of making the sessions less frequent (bi-weekly or monthly) without a definite term, aimed at 'monitoring' the outcome, is likely to conceal separation difficulties. It is, however, important not to present the completion of psychotherapy as an end, but instead as an interruption. It is expedient that the clients know that whenever they should ask for it, they can rely on the therapist's help.

6.7 Conversing on the client's self-narrative

The elaboration of the client's self-narrative will progressively replace the uncontrolled or controlled elaboration of the complaint. Technically, the gradual transition from the elaboration of the *problem* the client is facing, to the elaboration of the *person* presenting the problem, can be defined as 'dilation' (see section 5.1.2).

Encouraging dilation is not to be confused with 'confrontation' (see section 6.6.2). Once the elaboration of the complaint consisting, for example, in problems in relationship with the partner, is finished, if the therapist were then to say, 'Now tell me, how is your working life?' would imply a sudden shift of the conversational theme from the complaint to areas the client has not mentioned. On the contrary, dilating means introducing into the conversation other elements, supposedly related with the present ones, such as, 'Did you ever have similar problems with past partners, or in the relationship with your parents?' The new elements can lead the client to consider the present relational problem as the instance of a more comprehensive one, maybe as a personal way of relating with significant people.

Of course, such a dilation can be threatening, and the therapist should encourage it based on the anticipation of what the client will be confronted with. On the other hand, a dilation offers greater possibilities of elaboration and reconstruction. It is important that the therapists carry on such a process by maintaining a collaborative alliance, and utilising a professional construction to find the right timing for such a therapeutic choice.

6.7.1 Elaborating the client's self-narrative: 'Tell me the story of the storyteller'

To understand and encourage the elaboration of the client's construction system, Kelly takes also into consideration the *use of psychological tests*, particularly those suitable for the production of narratives (discussed in section 4.4), aware of the possible threat to the psychotherapeutic relationship. The Thematic Apperception Test can help in discovering the underlying themes in the stories told by the client. The repertory grids (see section 4.4.1) and other forms of grids (see sections 4.4.2–4.4.4), in addition to allow remarks about the outcome which are likely have therapeutic repercussions, require a concept-formation task and encourage an increase in the level of cognitive awareness during their administration.

Undoubtedly, self-characterisation (see section 4.4.8) is the most suitable means by which to encourage the *elaboration* of the self-narrative *through self-description*. The request to write a sketch can be given soon after the elaboration of the narrative about the complaint, and its analysis may serve as a starting point for further elaboration of the person. But also, the request for verbal self-narratives have their usefulness (such as, 'What kind of child were you? or 'What kind of person do you expect to become?'), as well as the request of an *autobiography*, to be read by the therapist as a historian rather than as a chronicler. 'As a historian he can lift the vibrant themes out of the tumult of context' instead of falling 'into step the fateful tread of seasonal events'. The autobiography should be seen as 'a present structure which is, in part, documented by selected memories of the past, and is, in part, a viewing screen upon which the events of the past seem to have form and consequences' (Kelly, 1991b/1955, p. 301).

A more specific *elaboration of life-role structure* is preferable when clients present problems which might be attributed to a lack of overall purpose and outlook in their life, and the therapist strives to encourage the elaboration of 'those constructs having to do with the development of the client's personality over the changing years, his construction of himself in terms of his life cycle [. . .], and his view of himself as a gradually aging person' (ibid., p. 302). In this case, earlier versions of the life role (such as, 'What were some of your plans for the future when you were a child?') or projective elaboration of it, can throw light upon the client's life-role structure.

To encourage the elaboration of alternatives, the therapist can repeatedly recur to the C-P-C cycle (see section 1.1.6) and ask the client to pursue a *progressive confrontation with alternatives*. 'The therapist keeps asking such questions as, "What does one *do* about such things?", "What could you have done?", "What else could you have done?", [. . .] "Having done that, what comes next?"' (ibid., p. 304), and so on. As a result of this type of elaboration, the clients may decide to act upon some of the alternatives chosen, and therefore the therapist should be aware of the principal consequences of the projected actions.

If the above conversational acts within the therapy room can help the clients to put ideas into action, *controlled elaboration* may be produced *by means of prescribed activities*. Whether occupational, recreational or social activities they are aimed at encouraging the elaboration of the clients' core roles. To minimise the risk of catastrophic repercussions, the social experimentations should be preceded by verbal elaboration of the situations the clients are likely to face, a careful choice of the activity programme and the subsequent discussion of their outcome. Similar functions, and similar precautions, are relevant to *elaboration through play and creative production*, particularly effective in cases of prevailing features of hostility, impulsivity, and preverbality in the client's construction system.

6.7.2 From structuration to construction: 'This yes, that no'

One of the constructivist psychotherapist's greatest concerns regards the choice of material to be elaborated during the conversation with the client. Initially, the therapists make a classification or *structuration* of what they observe, putting aside for possible further elaboration much of the material arising during the session. As psychotherapy progresses and the therapists acquire a better understanding of the client, they are more and more able to substitute *construction* for structuration. Furthermore, the therapists' understanding of the client will help them to decide if the client is ready to discuss the topics they regard as significant. 'What the therapist chooses for further elaboration is partly determined by its suspected significance and partly by the client's readiness to deal with the kind of material the cue seems to represent' (Kelly, 1991b/1955 p. 312). The following are the *criteria for selection of material to be elaborated* as suggested by Kelly: *strange or unexpected material*, a sign that the therapist has to revise the construction of the client; *material which is possibly indicative of an expected therapeutic movement or revision of the construct system*, in order to facilitate the new development; *material possibly relating to an area of the construct system which is under intensive study*; *context material to be utilised in psychotherapeutic experimentation*, which can be used as safe ground on which to erect a new structure; *validation material*, that is, material referring to past experience, which can be used to test the validity of new constructs; *documentary material*, a kind of validational material, clearly illustrative of some construct the therapist wants the client to 'nail down'; *material representing an extended range of convenience for constructs already in use*.

The therapist may choose to elaborate the preceding material by means of several conversational acts.

After recapitulating what has been discussed in past sessions, the therapist may ask the client to check it. In addition to allowing the therapist to show acceptance, the *recapitulation procedure* requires the client to consider, in an organised manner, what they have been saying, thus testing its internal consistency.

Probing consists in controlling the clients' participation in the conversation, by either pushing them into dealing with matters that they might not otherwise mention or by keeping them from talking about matters that, according to the therapist, they (the therapist) are not willing to discuss at the moment.

The *detection of impending changes*, usually revealed by new experimentations before they are verbally announced, will allow the therapist to validate them in the relationship with the client.

Elaboration of self-narratives can also be encouraged during the client's description of incidents or experiences. The therapist may ask the client to describe the incident in greater detail (*elaboration by citing detail*), aimed at discovering cues the client can link with repetitive themes which begin to manifest themselves in the psychotherapy process, or at surrounding the implied construct with enough content to make it more easily recalled in a later session. The therapist may ask the client to describe the events leading to the incident and those following it or appearing to be affected by it (*elaboration of antecedents and consequents*), revealing the client's view of cause–effect relationships. The therapist may ask the client to think of some other experiences which aroused the same feeling (*citation of material which is construed to be similar*), so as to explore experiences without a precise verbal definition. Similarly, the therapist may call the client's attention to two or three experiences described, asking to construe them (*elaboration by construing a series of experiences*), for example saying, 'As you see it, how do all of these experiences seem to be alike?' (ibid., p. 323).

Usually, the changes which are taking place are not verbally expressed by the client. If the therapists choose to encourage a construction of these changes at a higher level of cognitive awareness, they can ask the client to construe three experiences: one occurring before therapy, one early during the therapy, and one recently (*elaboration of therapeutic movement*).

As an alternative to the above conversational acts, the therapist may decide to enact the part of one of the protagonists of the event, by saying, for example, 'Let's see if we can get a clearer picture of how this happened. Suppose I am. . .' (ibid., p. 325), and immediately playing the character (*elaboration through enactment*). The client's possible resistance, once overcome, to play the part, brief enactments, reciprocal suggestions and exchange of parts represent a powerful tool for the client's elaboration and the therapist's understanding of the client.

6.8 Encouraging new narratives

6.8.1 The golden rule of change: 'Create a new story before leaving the old'

The conversational acts previously described, aimed at elaborating the client's narratives about the complaint and the self, are part of a strategy directed at encouraging the construction of alternative narratives which can allow the client to resume construing and re-construing experience. However, following the choice corollary, such alternatives should also allow the client to give meaning to his or her experience, at least as much as the old narrative. This is also the case when the new narrative can appear decidedly desirable if human nature is conceived in hedonistic terms, that is, in terms of calculations of pleasures and pains, rewards and punishments.

The following extract describes the effect of the disintegration of the client's organisation of self, not adequately preceded by the construction of an alternative organisation.

> The response of an anxious client who has been prematurely thrust into meaningful experimental situations may be very puzzling to the therapist. Why does the client go to pieces when seemingly the experiment was so successful and the client reaped such 'rewards'? The answer often lies in the extent of the implications, not in their 'rewarding' features. For example, a student who has long considered himself to be dull, and who is anxious, may be encouraged by his counsellor to use a certain new approach in his studies. This is by way of an experiment. The student, seeking any kind of new structure that will serve him, agrees to cooperate. The experiment turns out 'successfully', or so the counsellor thinks! The student gets a mark of 'A' in his course. But then the student begins to show great anxiety and confusion. The counsellor, still believing that human nature is governed by rewards and punishments, is at as loss to explain the student's reaction.
>
> What has happened is that the student begins to see the far-reaching implications of his experiment. For a long time he has conceptualized himself as a stupid person and has organized a great deal of his life around that conceptualization. The organization has been disintegrating lately, and he has been faced with larger and larger areas of chaos in his construct system. In the midst of this teetering structure he finds that one of the major beams, his construction of himself as being a dull student, is faulty. Perhaps he never 'liked' the idea of being stupid but nevertheless a great deal of reliance had been based on that postulate. Worry, worry, what is he to do now that he is 'bright'?
>
> (Kelly, 1991b/1955, p. 404)

The common-sense approach to personal change, as well as many psychotherapeutic approaches, shares the view that what is more desirable for a person is also preferable. The fundamental postulate of personal construct theory goes against such understanding of human nature. To the extent that 'a person's processes are psychologically channelised by the ways in which he anticipates events', and 'a person anticipates events by construing their replications' (construction corollary), only a different construction of events, an alternative, can give way to a personal change. In addition, it has to be an alternative 'through which he anticipates the greater possibility for extension and definition of his system' (choice corollary), that is, more meaningful than other 'viable paths'.

Examples of the non sustainability of the desirable preferable equation are obvious to all. Consider the case of the obese person who succeeded in losing weight after a strict diet, or following a surgery. She or he is happy to have gained a silhouette she or he had probably never had, wear fashionable clothes and feel admired at last. But she or he also feels uneasy with her or his new appearance, maybe she or he has difficulty in relating with others in his or her new role. How could it be otherwise? Ever since being an overweight child, he or she has been relating to others as a fat person. Being obese has become a core aspect of his or her role. He or she knows the meaning of being obese very well (even though unhappily), whereas to be slim confronts him or her with too many obscurities, anxiety and guilt. In a few months he or she will regain his or her weight, sad but confident of anticipating again his or her social life.

This 'way of life' theory has been suggested by Fransella for application to people with long-standing behavioural complaints (ticqueurs, smokers, people with obsessions, obese people), and its efficacy has been proven for people who stutter (Fransella, 1972). But the preceding are instances of the same general rule followed by constructivist psychotherapists (and applicable both to 'normal' and 'disordered' people): *no personal change will be achieved until the meaning of being for some core aspect a different person is at least as meaningful as being the usual person.*

The same rule, implied by the fundamental postulate, can explain the phenomenon of 'resistance'. Indeed, people resist, but not to treatment: they resist changing, independently of their suffering or not. They strive to maintain a narrative of their relation with the world, which they try to make as meaningful as they can and they are the stories they tell (see section 5.4). Their narratives also tell of their 'resistance' to change.

The therapeutic object of encouraging the creation of new narratives calls the creativity cycle into play (see section 1.3).

Sometimes, the clients' superordinate constructs are so impermeable and pre-emptive (for example in people psychiatrically diagnosed as obsessive), that their narratives cannot accept variations. Actually, it could be better to say that the superordinate constructs are impermeable *so as* not to accept variations, given that – according to the choice corollary – their impermeability has to be seen as the result of an elaborative choice: a variation could jeopardise the integrity of the system. Under such conditions, experiences either have to be accommodated within tightly structured organisations, or put aside (through constriction). The clients are easily faced with threat or guilt, anticipating devastating repercussions when they are unable to keep using their narrative. In the framework of the theory of autopoiesis, environmental perturbations are likely to imply the disintegration of organisation.

Sometimes, the superordinate constructs are so permeable and propositional (for example in people psychiatrically diagnosed as schizophrenic), that their narratives are suitable for whichever experience, at the cost of a dreamlike construction of reality, of a difficulty in making decisions (due to a halt of the C-P-C cycle at the phase of circumspection), and of the impossibility of undergoing variations due to the impossibility of verifing the validity of such vague anticipations. In the framework of the theory of autopoiesis, the structure of the unity specifies a domain of 'sparse' possible perturbations.

However, it is extremely important not to forget that the preceding conditions have to be viewed as the result of structural changes aimed at conserving adaptation and organisation. Consequently, the constructivist psychotherapist should not try to encourage a change of the actual condition without an understanding of its adaptive function and anticipating what will ensue from it. On the other hand, this is why the conversational acts aimed at producing loosening or tightening encounter difficulties and could imply hazards if the therapist is not careful in setting the stage for providing the client with other ways of maintaining adaptation.

6.8.2 Loosening: 'Can you wander around your story?'

Kelly has observed how psychoanalytic theory utilises loose hypotheses, and psychoanalytic techniques are likely to encourage loosening (see section 5.1.1) in the client's construct system. In fact, the conversational acts described by personal construct psychotherapy and aimed at encouraging loosening, are reminiscent of the psychoanalytic armamentarium.

Chain association consists in telling the clients to express whatever comes to their mind, sometimes beginning *from an initial point* suggested by the therapist. In this case, the initial take-off point can be a tightly construed experience which the client could associate with experiences loosely construed as similar. In order to explore the clients' preverbal constructs, the therapist can give them an initial point and then suggest associating *away from* it. If the therapist cautions the clients *not to try to say anything 'important'*, they can reveal the contrast poles of underlying loose preverbal constructs.

Assuming that 'dreams represent about the most loosened construction that one can put into words' (Kelly, 1991b/1955, p. 334), *reporting dreams* can also encourage loosening. The constructivist psychotherapist is not interested in the interpretation of dreams (even though the clients' interpretation may provide interesting preverbal material), as in the process of reporting them. Therefore, a discussion about 'the dream that the client cannot remember' can also achieve the purpose.

Producing loosening by relaxation (think of the psychoanalytic couch) can require the use of systematic relaxation techniques. We prefer not to break the conversational flow, and encourage relaxation – and the ensuing, looser material produced by the client when relaxed – by means of the relaxed manner of the therapist (including speaking slowly, in a low voice, and with a regular rhythm), and the dimming of the light in the room.

Another conversational act suitable for encouraging loosening consists in *uncritical acceptance*. The clients' point of view is passively accepted by the therapist, who avoids questioning them as to what they mean, thus offering no ground for validation or invalidation.

6.8.3 Tightening: 'Can you detail your story?'

Kelly (1991b/1955, pp. 355–361) describes a variety of techniques to produce tightening (see section 5.1.1). Their function is essentially that of facilitating experimentation by making the client's anticipations more easily subjected to verification. All of them can be regarded as conversational acts aimed at making the client's system more organised and stable.

The therapist can ask the clients to put a superordinate construction upon a group of constructs which they have been expressing unsystematically ('Now just what have you been saying today that you have not told me before?', 'You have told me about a lot of incidents and feelings but it is not clear to me how you see these matters as fitting together. Are they simply illustrations of something?', and so on).

The therapist can ask the clients to summarise what they have been saying, or to give an historical explanation ('When did you first start having these thoughts?', 'Have you ever felt like this before?'), or to relate their thinking to that of others ('Do you know of anyone else who may feel this way?', 'Can you remember hearing anyone else express these kinds of thoughts?', and so on).

Furthermore, the therapist can use a direct approach, consisting of asking the clients to be more explicit; to explain what they mean ('I don't understand; could you make it clearer to me just what you mean?', 'Could you explain just how it is to feel this way? What happens inside of you?', and so on).

In some cases, the therapist can decide to challenge the clients' constructions, at any one of several levels depending on how much threat they are able to manage. The questions can go from 'I don't want to misunderstand you, so could you go back over what you were just saying?', to 'I find this a little confusing; first you said. . . and now you say. . . Can you help me understand?', to 'Can you reconcile what you are saying now with. . . ?' Sometimes the therapist can deliberately misinterpret what the clients have said: 'If I understand you correctly, this is what you really mean. . . You say it's not?. . . Then just what do you mean?'

If the therapist chooses to use the technique of *enactment*, the clients can be asked to portray the part of another person, or to explain the therapist who enacts the part how it should be played. In both cases, the clients have to become more explicit in their construction of that person.

To encourage tightening the therapists can resort to the basic formula of concept formation, how are two of these alike yet different from the third?:

'You have mentioned this, this, and this. Let's see if we can understand these three things better. Think about them. Are two of them alike in some way that seems to set them off from the third?', and so on; or they can ask for validating evidence ('How do you know that?', 'What kind of evidence would it take to convince you that you were mistaken?', and so on).

Finally, *binding*; a conversational act that goes further than mere tightening, tending also to encourage impermeability. For example, in *word binding* the clients are asked to name each of their constructs, and when talking about these constructs the therapist is careful to use the given label; once a word is accepted as a tight symbol, the constructs become more 'rigid'. The therapist can also encourage *time binding*, asking the clients to date their constructs, so that they are urged to think, for example, 'This is a view which was applicable to what I experienced when I was in high school but it is no longer applicable'. *Other forms of symbol binding* (place binding, person binding, situation binding, and so on) can reduce the constructs to impermeability, thus contributing to a narrowing of their ranges of convenience and opening the way to alternative constructions.

In the course of a psychotherapy process, the constructivist psychotherapist is likely to encourage a series of adjustments by means of repeated processes of loosening and tightening. 'After a form of adjustment has been worked out at the tightened level for a time, the therapist may open up the construction again, perhaps dealing with the same contextual elements, perhaps in a new area'. This can lead the clients to reconsider their last 'insights', looking for new kinds of insights. 'After a period of loosened construing, the therapist may move in the direction of tightening again and seek to establish a mode of adjustment at a new level'. In this circularity, 'the welcome "insights" emerging from the present cycle may become the irritating "resistances" of the next' (Kelly, 1991b/1955, p. 367).

We see in this weaving back and forth between tightening and loosening in the search of new narratives, so central to Kelly's view of the psychotherapy process, something similar to Derrida's (1976/1967) deconstructive strategy, or to the movement of interpretation described as 'hermeneutic circle' (Schleiermacher, 1998/1828), both leading to a successive and progressive shifting of meaning. There is no end to this endeavour, no 'final truth' to achieve. There is instead the emergence of 'further meanings' (Gadamer, 1960) both in the therapist and the client; meanings that were not there before the process of interpretation (Chiari & Nuzzo, 2000). Such new meanings can allow the clients to invent and adopt new narratives about themselves and their worlds.

6.9 Reactivating movement

Kelly deals with the importance of the client's experimentation by recurring again to the metaphor of the person as a scientist. Once the implications of the theoretical systems (through elaboration) necessary before designing a meaningful experiment are explored and once a creative but testable hypothesis is formulated (through loosening and tightening), the person-as-scientist is ready to experiment. Sometimes, the client begins spontaneously to do so reporting the outcome to the therapist. At times, the client objects to the idea of experimenting, somehow fearful of the outcome.

We could also adopt the metaphor of the person as storyteller, in which case, we could say that the clients have begun to tell themselves new stories, but are reluctant to live them. They keep living according to the old narratives; though ready to play new roles. The constructivist psychotherapist now has the task of encouraging experimentation; of helping the client to come on stage. This is necessary to check the applicability of the narrative, to open new vistas of experience, to put him or her in touch with other people and seeing, within the framework of the new narrative, how they tell their worlds so as to adjust his or her role to a more effective relationship to others.

The psychotherapeutic relationship is likely to be the first social environment in which the clients dare to live the new stories they tell. The conversation with the therapist has encouraged their creation, and the very same relationship should encourage their experimentation, due to the therapist's attitude of permissiveness and responsiveness. Furthermore, the therapist can set the stage posing a series of 'what would happen if. . .', as well as helping the client to detail the characters of the play (and indirectly the client's role) by discussing the points of view of others, how these view themselves and how a certain other person views the client. But the new story has to be acted also outside the favourable conditions of the therapy room.

This is one of the most critical moments of the psychotherapy process, since the appropriateness of the social milieu can have a crucial importance in the success or failure of the experimentation. The client and the therapist can both rely on luck and it could be given a boost. The clients can be encouraged to experiment with novel social situations, to associate with new people and to attend groups which have interests in which they might be expected to become involved. All the above, and much more, can be helpful, and left to the inventiveness of both client and therapist.

6.10 Concluding remarks: the difficulty of being a constructivist psychotherapist

In the preceding chapters we outlined a possible therapeutic praxis based on a constructivist assumption. We tried to illustrate this assumption by dedicating several pages, first to those developments of philosophical thought of which contemporary psychological constructivism can be considered a derivation, second to constructivist epistemology in its various forms, and third to the contributions of psychology, as well as cybernetics and biology, in the formalisation of psychotherapeutic approaches definable, broadly speaking, as constructivist. We then chose to dwell on the psychotherapy deriving from Kelly's personal construct theory which we view as the forerunner of such approaches. At the same time, once reinterpreted in the light of the most recent developments, Kelly's theory put into practice constructivist epistemology in the most revolutionary, original, integrated and rigorous way. We gave a sketch of our elaboration of such an outlook which sees the psychotherapist aimed at penetrating the clients' lived worlds to explore them, in a joint journey, through the telling of their narratives, questing not only for the paths of knowledge already beaten by them – which led them to a dead-end street – but also for the opening, along the way, of new paths, allowing them to resume the interrupted walk. It is this very intent and the way in which it is pursued, that leads us to connote our particular approach as narrative and hermeneutic.

The use we have just made of the metaphor of exploration does not meet poetical purposes; instead, it meets the difficulty in expounding with greater clarity ideas and concepts which appear unfamiliar and strange to our culture and also are hard to articulate, so much so that some authors felt the necessity to coin new words. German phenomenology is full of new (often difficult to translate) words: *dasein* (being-there/here), *mitwelt* (with-world), *mitdasein* (being-in-themselves within-the-world). The theory of autopoiesis is rich with expressly coined words and expressions, and personal construct theory is abundant with new terms or words whose meanings differ from the usual one. Thus, one is confronted with the necessity of choosing – or wavering – between a precise, rigorous and technical exposition resulting in a difficult reading (like great part of Maturana's writings, or the Kelly of *The psychology of personal constructs*), and a metaphorical, evocative narration, which turns out to be vague, and hardly acceptable for most of the scientific community (like Maturana when speaking about love, or like Kelly's latest writings). The preceding has significant consequences also in relation to the formation and the practice of constructivist psychotherapists.

The profession of a psychotherapist is a difficult one, requiring prolonged training and personal inclination. Studies show that the latter can be traced back to personal experiences of psychological distress in themselves and in their families of origin (Murphy & Halgin, 1995), sometimes in the form of childhood trauma and emotional deprivation (Fussell & Bonney, 1990; Nikcevic et al., 2007), resulting in an early occupation of caring roles within the family (DiCaccavo, 2002). Consequently, the psychotherapist has been described as a 'wounded healer' (Sussman, 2007). If these early childhood experiences can explain the choice of psychotherapy as a career, they can, at the same time, go well together with underlying motives and aims, such as the wish to be needed, or to enjoy the prospect of receiving aid and comfort. Consequently, therapists run the risk of exploiting clients for their own needs. Moreover, one should add the difficulty of learning (as well as teaching) psychotherapy, particularly those approaches which emphasise the greater importance of the interpersonal relationship as a vehicle for therapeutic change, compared to the mere administration of techniques.

Efran, Lukens and Lukens (1990) show intellectual honesty by saying what is not usually said in the world of psychotherapy; by telling their experience as students that we believe can be extended to most students in psychotherapy. Trainees are inclined to feel confused about their role of therapist and wait 'to be admitted to that inner circle where the secrets of the profession would be laid bare' (p. 2), feeling 'as if there is a conspiracy of silence about the fundamental underpinnings of psychotherapeutic practice' (p. 4). When they begin to see clients, they use a number of ploys to cover their lack of confidence in their role: they lapse into nondirective 'reflective' mode even though not being Rogerian, assume a posture of psychoanalytic silence even though having no affinity with analytic tenets, indulge in information-gathering in order to postpone 'that awful moment of truth when *actual treatment* would need to begin' (p. 3, italics in the original). When the clients appear to demand more concrete help, they 'launch into "lecturettes" on the principles of good living', or offer titbits of practical advice 'usually invented on the spot, derived loosely from a combination of common sense and personal experience', being 'plagued by the nagging concern that "real therapists" don't do this' (p. 3). 'In later years', the authors add, 'we discovered to our surprise that students were not the only ones experiencing distress about playing the role of therapist. Even seasoned therapists report finding themselves in an agonizingly ambiguous role, feeling somehow obliged to offer solutions they do not think they possess' (p. 4). The picture is made even more deceptive by the observation that 'the unending supply of smoothly run cases with simple diagnoses and happy outcomes that is apparently available to writers and workshop presenters seems to be denied to most of the rest of us' (p. 15).

The preceding thoughts apply presumably to psychotherapists of any theoretical orientation. We are tempted to go even further, on the basis of some evidence that the very same choice of a specific theoretical orientation is likely to be linked with personality and epistemological values and beliefs (Arthur, 2001; Vasco & Dryden, 1997). Therefore, the aim of these concluding remarks is to increase the level of awareness of constructivist psychotherapists on what could be defined as 'temptations', deriving from the very epistemological assumptions of psychological constructivism.

All constructivist psychotherapists share the fundamental importance of accepting the client by adopting what Kelly names a 'credulous approach' (see section 4.1). Acceptance is the necessary prior condition for playing a therapeutic role within a constructivist perspective. Not all, however, have come to embody such understanding. Usually the 'signs' of such a failure show up in an advanced phase of the psychotherapy process. At the beginning, the therapists may have been successful in understanding the clients by accepting them as they know they should. Yet, the therapist's acceptance of the client can also be viewed as an elaborative choice (see section 1.1.8). That is, one is accepting, and remains so, to the extent that this choice allows the anticipation of events better than alternative choices. If, in the continuation of a therapy, the therapist encounters difficulties in encouraging a therapeutic movement, he or she may slide into the most usual alternative to acceptance, that is, judgement, based on what we could call a 'normative approach', at times accompanied by the therapist's hostility. The therapists begin to replace the professional construction of the clients based on their understanding of them, with a pre-emptive construction founded on criteria of normality. The client's problem is thus interpreted in terms of defect or excess with respect to cognitive (if not common-sense) dimensions which have little or nothing to do with the client's own construction of experience: the client is 'little assertive', 'too insecure', has a 'low tolerance to frustration', is 'too demanding', 'too sensitive to criticisms', and so on. Sometimes, this pre-emptive and normative construction may concern the diagnostic constructs, giving the therapists the illusion of keeping a professional construction: the clients are 'too loose' in their construction of themselves, 'too rigid' (better still, 'too impermeable') or show 'little aggressiveness'. These 'diagnoses' may result in the therapist giving advice in an attempt to increase what is lacking in the clients or to reduce what exceeds, into the overt expression of judgements, or sometimes into an open contestation of the clients and their choices.

When the therapists succumb to the temptation of judgement, having experienced the inefficiency of therapeutic acts initially coherent with an adequate transitive diagnosis, problems may arise from a pre-emptive use of such a diagnosis. Also, a formally proper diagnostic construction may be used in a pre-emptive way: the client's disorder is 'nothing but. . .'. Keeping the diagnosis as propositional as possible would allow the therapist the search for alternatives, still remaining acceptant of the client.

The temptation of judgement is not to be mistaken for the temptation of truth. Whereas the former derives from a loss of acceptance, the latter retains it, but the therapist falls into a paradox: that of sustaining that the diagnostic conclusion he or she reached, based on the professional construction of an understanding of the client, is the only true conclusion. In such cases, it is the philosophical assumption of constructivist psychotherapy, that is, constructive alternativism that is given up. It is a deceitful temptation which can affect, even more than the inexperienced, the more experienced psychotherapists. Certain of their diagnosis, the therapists discourage the clients' attempts at exploring alternative constructions, insisting they accept their diagnostic conclusion and face the 'evidence'. What is it due to, and how can we prevent the temptation of truth?

The therapists probably neglected carrying out the therapeutic process in collaboration with the client, and directed the conversation towards those aspects of the client's construction of experience which, according to their experience, would have quickly and easily lead to a clarification of the diagnostic picture. They selected, among the client's suggestions, only those they saw as congruent to the impression they had already formed, showing the client the non-plausibility (!) of those aspects that would have led to different directions. They assumed a 'conclusive' attitude rather than an 'invitational' one (McWilliams, 1996), by the abundant use of the verb 'to be' and assertions of truth. Obedience to the therapist's knowledge is requested of the clients as a prerequisite to the solution of their problems.

Maybe the temptation of truth represents a natural development of the temptation of authority. By putting aside the necessity of constructing a therapeutic alliance and of bringing forward the therapeutic process in collaboration with the client, the therapist copes with his or her anxiety by taking charge and leading the conversation, rapidly and inadvertently assuming the role of expert.

It is from the very early phases of the psychotherapeutic relationship that the constructivist therapist should avoid this temptation, because it is at the very first interactions with the client that the outcome of the game is decided. Should the client initially have difficulty in the spontaneous elaboration of the complaint, and the therapist feels he or she should help out and start asking questions, from that moment the rules have been set (and they will be very difficult to change). The client will gladly answer the therapist, and then await the ensuing questions. This is, on the other hand, what the client usually expects, founded on a pre-construction of psycho-therapeutic relationship similar to that between a patient and the doctor. Soon (at times during the very first session) the therapist begins to wonder, 'And now, what shall I ask?', 'How shall I go on?' In turn, the client does not feel involved in the therapeutic process, and waits for the solution to his or her problem, according to the replies given to the therapist's questions. The sessions will rapidly become a burden for the therapist, who is likely to tell him or herself, 'I have to prepare the session', bearing all alone the choice of the subjects to deal with, maybe searching for a hint in notes from previous sessions.

About notes: usually the inexperienced psychotherapists try during the session to put down whatever they can, maybe regretting not having done a course in stenography. They may also record the session and then listen to it before the following one. Our advice is to limit notes as much as possible. We consider it useful to write the names of people who populate the social world close to the clients, because it can allow the therapists to accede more rapidly in their world and to jot down a few phrases or expressions the clients uses which we see as particularly significant, because they could represent coordinates which may help us to put together our construction of the clients. At the end of the session, we usually write a memo (a phrase, or just a word), to facilitate the continuity with the following session. As to the rest, we confide to memory! What we forget, evidently we consider of little importance (and anyway, if we do not fall into the temptation of authority, we can ask help from our client).

Pursuing a psychotherapy process without a strategy is giving way to the temptation of negligence, which may easily lead to endless psychotherapies. Therapeutically effective conversations ended a long time ago, but the relation continues on the basis of 'drawing-room' talk. The therapists usually play their role by asking at the beginning of the sessions, 'How are things?', 'How did this week go?', and so on. The 50 minute session turns out to be a report on the events of the week, maybe with some interventions of the therapists (in the guise of an emotional participation, a reflection on certain aspects of the client that surfaced in previous sessions, or a fragmentary elaboration of what was narrated without including it in a wider frame of reference). The sole aim is self-reassurance on the fact that they are correctly carrying out their task, supported by considerations such as, 'If he continues coming. . .'. But the reasons why the client still continues the therapy may differ from those pertinent with the role of a therapist (and it would be wise for the therapist to wonder about such reasons). In other words, the therapists may have lost, for some time, their professional role, and be seen by the clients as confidants, friends, people with whom to take it out on (maybe receiving appeasement for their hostility). In these cases, it would be decidedly appropriate for the therapists to ask for supervision or to end the therapy, thus recuperating their professional role.

If understanding the clients by putting themselves in their shoes is fundamental for a constructivist psychotherapist, the very same understanding can become a trap. For instance, when analysing the family relationships in which the client has grown up, he 'may begin to appear so utterly plausible that the clinician sees no problem to be solved, save that of "the society which made him this way" or of the "mother who projected her own neurosis upon him"' (Kelly, 1991b/1955, p. 167).

The temptation of justification is more likely to be attractive to therapists who start from realistic and deterministic assumptions. Constructivist psychotherapists should be exempt from it, constructive alternativism being the starting point in their formation and practice. Moving from a constructivist assumption, in fact:

what the clinician must plan to correct is not the behaviour which is implausible or irrational, but the behaviour which he has come to see as plausible and wholly rational. There are many clinicians who cannot do this. They think that what is plausible and rational is therefore 'true' or 'realistic'. They see no alternatives to what is 'true' or 'realistic'. Not fully realizing that there are such things as alternative truths and alternative realities they are unprepared to help their clients find psychological solutions for personal problems.

(Kelly, 1991b/1955, p. 167)

The philosophical assumption of constructive alternativism has to be applied circularly to itself, to avoid falling into self-contradiction. Even though, at the beginning of this book, we stated that personal construct theory is the avant-garde of psychological constructivism, especially in its application to psychotherapy, we should not forget that:

a theory is a construction, an invention, and not a discovery. Constructively speaking a theory, as long as we accept its assumptive structure, can be applied in its original form, elaborated or even revised in its subordinate implications; otherwise, it can be rejected in favour of an alternative theory if we choose to move from different assumptions.

(Chiari & Nuzzo, 1996, p. 27)

Kelly is particularly clear about this requisite of a theory: 'our theory is frankly designed to contribute effectively to its own eventual overthrow and displacement' (Kelly, 1969a/1958, p. 66).

When introducing his theory during a conference in Moscow, Kelly invited the attendants to join him aboard his 'theoretical vessel and set out on a voyage of discovery [. . .] to observe the islands we pass' (Kelly, 1969/1961, p. 95). The metaphor can also be applied to the psychotherapeutic venture, where the clients have a companion, the therapist. Later, the clients can cross other vessels, and exchange impressions with their crews. As a result, they can decide to change their course, and see with their own eyes what others have told them, turning others' experience into their own, and 'press the voyage further'.

Glossary

Key:
PCT = Personal construct theory
PGE = Piaget's genetic epistemology
ToA = Theory of autopoiesis
Sources: Bannister and Fransella, 1986; English and English, 1958; Scheer and Walker, 2003; Whitaker, 1998.

Accommodation [PGE]:   the modification of an organised structure as a consequence of a process of *assimilation*.

Adaptation [ToA]:   the relation of dynamic structural correspondence with the *medium* in which a *unity* conserves its class identity (*organisation* in the case of a *composite unity*, and operation of its properties in the case of a *simple unity*).

Aggressiveness [PCT]:   the active elaboration of one's *perceptual field*.

Anticipation [PCT]:   it is implied by any personal *construct*, given that this is an abstraction of something that repeats itself, of a regularity.

Anxiety [PCT]:   the awareness that the events with which one is confronted lie mostly outside the *range of convenience* of one's *construct* system.

Assimilation [PGE]:   integration into previous structures, which may remain unaffected or else be modified (*accommodation*) to a greater or lesser degree by this very integration, but without any break of continuity with the former state. (See also *recursion*.)

Autonomy [ToA]:   autonomous systems are systems defined as *unities* by their *organisation*. The *autopoietic organisation* that characterises living systems is the basis of their autonomy.

Autopoiesis [ToA]:   a term coined by Maturana, which connotes the *organisation* of living systems. An autopoietic system is a *composite unity* whose organisation can be described as a closed network of productions of components that, through their interactions, constitute the network of productions that produce them, and specify its extension by constituting its boundaries in their domain of existence.

Autopoietic organisation [ToA]:   see *autopoiesis*.

C-P-C cycle [PCT]:   a sequence of construction involving, in succession, circumspection, pre-emption and control, and leading to a choice precipitating the person into a particular situation.

Composite unity [ToA]:   a *unity* distinguished as a *simple unity* that through further operations of distinction is decomposed by the *observer* into components that through their composition would constitute the original simple unity in the domain in which it is distinguished.

Comprehensive construct [PCT]:   a *construct* which subsumes a wide variety of events. (See also *incidental construct*.)

Constellatory construct [PCT]:   a *construct* which fixes the other realm membership of its *elements*. This is stereotyped or typological thinking. (See also *pre-emptive construct*, *propositional construct*.)

Constriction [PCT]:   constriction occurs when a person narrows their *perceptual field* in order to minimise apparent incompatibilities. (See also *dilation*.)

Constructivism: an epistemology, a metatheory, a theory of knowledge, the generic definitions of which is centred on the active participation of the subject in construing reality, rather than on reflecting or representing it. (See also *radical constructivism*, *trivial constructivism*, *epistemological constructivism*, *hermeneutic constructivism*.)

Context [PCT]:   comprises those *elements* among which the user ordinarily discriminates by means of the *construct*. It is somewhat more restricted than the *range of convenience*, since it refers to the circumstances in which the construct emerges for practical use and not necessarily to all the circumstances in which a person might eventually use the construct. It is somewhat more extensive than the *focus of convenience*, since the construct may often appear in circumstances where its application is not optimal.

Contrast [PCT]:   the relationship between the two *poles* of a *construct* is one of contrast.

Contrast end [PCT]:   when referring specifically to *elements* at one *pole* of a *construct*, one may use the term 'contrast end' to designate the opposite pole.

Core construct [PCT]:   a *construct* which governs a person's *maintenance processes*. (See also *peripheral construct*.)

Creativity cycle [PCT]:   one which starts with loosened construction and terminates with tightened and validated construction. (See also *loose construct*, *tight construct*.)

Dilation [PCT]:   dilation occurs when a person broadens their *perceptual field* in order to reorganise it on a more comprehensive level. It does not, in itself, include the comprehensive reconstruction of those *elements*. (See also *constriction*.)

Distinction [ToA]:   in the operation of distinction an *observer* brings forth a *unity* (an entity, a whole) as well as the *medium* in which it is distinguished.

Elements [PCT]: the things or events which are abstracted by a person's use of a *construct*.

Emergent [PCT]: the emergent *pole* of a *construct* is that one which embraces most of the immediately perceived *context*. (See also *submergence*.)

Epistemological constructivism: epistemological constructivism, according to Chiari and Nuzzo, espouses ontological realism in that it acknowledges a real world. Yet, from an epistemological viewpoint, it asserts that it is not possible to know reality except through personal constructions. (See also *constructivism, radical constructivism, trivial constructivism, hermeneutic constructivism*.)

Equilibration [PGE]: the process that, by coordinating the regulatory activities of a living system with external *perturbations*, allows it to conserve its equilibrium.

Experience cycle [PCT]: on the basis of any construction, the persons anticipate some event, invest themselves in this *anticipation*, actively encounter the event, verify whether anticipation has been validated or invalidated, and revise their construction accordingly. The fulfillment of the whole process is followed by a new anticipation giving rise to a subsequent experiential cycle.

Fear [PCT]: the awareness of an imminent incidental change in one's core structures. (See also *core construct*.)

Focus of convenience [PCT]: a *construct*'s focus of convenience comprises those particular things to which the user would find its application maximally useful. (See also *range of convenience*.)

Guilt [PCT]: the awareness of dislodgement of the self from one's core role structure. (See also *core construct*.)

Hermeneutic constructivism: hermeneutic constructivism, according to Chiari and Nuzzo, views knowledge and truth as an interpretation historically founded rather than timeless, contextually verifiable rather than universally valid, and linguistically generated and socially negotiated rather than cognitively and individually produced. It is contrasted with epistemological constructivism. (See also *constructivism, radical constructivism, trivial constructivism, epistemological constructivism*.)

Hostility [PCT]: the continued effort to extort validational evidence in favour of a type of social prediction which has already been recognised as a failure.

Implicit [PCT]: the implicit *pole* of a *construct* is that one which embraces contrasting *context*. It contrasts with the *emergent* pole. Frequently the person has no available *symbol* or name for it; it is symbolised only implicitly by the emergent term.

Incidental construct [PCT]: a *construct* which subsumes a narrow variety of events. (See also *comprehensive construct*.)

Level of cognitive awareness [PCT]: the level of cognitive awareness ranges from high to low. A high-level *construct* is one which is readily expressed in socially effective *symbols*; whose alternatives are both readily accessible; which falls well within the *range of convenience* of the client's major construction; and which is not suspended by its superordinating constructs. (See also *preverbal construct, submergence, suspension*.)

Likeness end [PCT]: when referring specifically to *elements* at one *pole* of a *construct*, one may use the term 'likeness end' to designate that pole.

Loose construct [PCT]: a *construct* which leads to varying predictions but which retains its identity. (See also *tight construct*.)

Maintenance processes [PCT]: those processes by which a person maintains his or her identity and existence.

Medium [ToA]: the medium of a *unity* is the containing background of *distinctions* with respect to which an *observer* distinguishes it in his or her praxis of living, and in which it realises its domain of existence.

Objectivity in parenthesis [ToA]: putting objectivity in parenthesis implies that reality is a domain specified by the operations of the *observer*, according to a constitutive rather than transcendental ontology.

Observer [ToA]: a human being, a person, a living system who can make *distinctions* and specify that which he or she distinguishes as a *unity*, as an entity different from himself or herself that can be used for manipulations or descriptions in interactions with other observers.

Ontogenic structural drift [ToA]: the ontogeny of a living system as its history of structural changes with conservation of class identity (*organisation*) and *adaptation* (structural coupling).

Organisation [ToA]: it is constituted by the relations between components in a *composite unity* that make it a composite unity of a particular kind, specifying its class identity as a *simple unity* in a meta-domain with respect to its components.

Organisational closure [ToA]: organisational closure can be attributed to any discriminable *unity* defined as a configuration of processes such that: (1) the relationships among these processes comprise a network; (2) the processes are mutually interdependent for their own generation and realisation; and (3) the set of processes constitute the system as a unity recognisable in the space (domain) in which the processes exist.

Perceptual field [PCT]: all those aspects of the world to which at a given time an animal makes a discriminating response. It consists of what the animal perceives, not what is there.

Peripheral construct [PCT]: a *construct* which can be altered without serious modification of the core structure. (See also *core construct*.)

Permeability [PCT]: a *construct* is permeable if it admits newly perceived *elements* to its *context*. It is impermeable if it rejects elements on the basis of their newness.

Personal construct [PCT]: a way of seeing two or more things or persons as similar, and at the same time different from the third; an abstraction whereby people make discriminations among the events that they encounter in their daily lives.

Perturbation [ToA]: the effect of an agent which affects an organisationally closed system, triggering in it structural changes.

Pole [PCT]: each *construct* discriminates between two poles, one at each end of its dichotomy. The *elements* abstracted are like each other at each pole with respect to the construct and are unlike the elements at the other pole.

Pre-emptive construct [PCT]: a *construct* which pre-empts its *elements* for membership in its own realm exclusively. This is the 'nothing but' type of construction—'if this is a ball it is nothing but a ball'. (See also *constellatory construct, propositional construct.*)

Preverbal construct [PCT]: one which continues to be used, even though it has no consistent word *symbol*. It may or may not have been devised before the client had command of speech symbolism.

Propositional construct [PCT]: a *construct* which carries no implications regarding the other realm membership of its *elements*. This is uncontaminated construction. (See also *constellatory construct, pre-emptive construct.*)

Radical constructivism: radical constructivism, according to von Glasersfeld, breaks with convention and develops a theory of knowledge in which knowledge does not reflect an 'objective' ontological reality, but exclusively an ordering and organisation of a world constituted by our experience. Radical constructivism is contrasted with trivial constructivism. (See also *constructivism, trivial constructivism, epistemological constructivism, hermeneutic constructivism.*)

Range of convenience [PCT]: a *construct*'s range of convenience comprises all those things to which the user would find its application useful. (See also *focus of convenience.*)

Recursion [ToA]: there is a recursion whenever the *observer* can claim that the application of an operation occurs on the consequences of its previous application. Maturana contrasts it with *repetition*.

Regnant construct [PCT]: a kind of *superordinate construct* which assigns each of its *elements* to a category on an all-or-none basis, as in classical logic. It tends to be non-abstractive.

Repetition [ToA]: there is a repetition whenever an observer can claim that a given operation is realised again with independency of the consequences of its previous realisation. Maturana contrasts it with *recursion*.

Simple unity [ToA]: a *unity* brought forth in an operation of *distinction* that constitutes it as a whole by specifying its properties as a collection of dimensions of interactions in the *medium* in which it is distinguished.

Structural coupling [ToA]:   see *adaptation.*

Structural determinism [ToA]:   since the *structure* of a *composite unity* consists in its components and their relations, any change in a composite unity consists in a structural change, and arises in it at every instant necessarily determined by its structure at that instant through the operation of the properties of its components.

Structural intersection [ToA]:   in the structural realisation of a *composite unity,* its components may participate in the realisation of the *organisation* of many other composite unities, which thus intersect structurally with it.

Structure [ToA]:   in a *composite unity,* be this static or dynamic, the actual components plus the actual relations that take place between them while realising it as a particular composite unity characterised by a particular *organisation,* constitute its structure.

Submergence [PCT]:   the submerged *pole* of a *construct* is the one which is less available for application to events. (See also *emergence.*)

Subordinate construct [PCT]:   a *construct* which is included as an *element* in the *context* of another. (See also *superordinate construct.*)

Superordinate construct [PCT]:   a *construct* which includes another as one of the *elements* in its *context.* (See also *subordinate construct.*)

Suspension [PCT]:   a suspended *element* is one which is omitted from the *context* of a *construct* as a result of revision of the client's construct system.

Symbol [PCT]:   an *element* in the *context* of a *construct* which represents not only itself but also the construct by which it is abstracted by the user is called the construct's symbol.

Threat [PCT]:   the awareness of an imminent comprehensive change in one's core structures. (See also *core construct.*)

Tight construct [PCT]:   a *construct* which leads to unvarying predictions. (See also *loose construct.*)

Trivial constructivism: while recognising the agency of the learner in forming knowledge, still postulates an external reality knowable by all individuals in the same way. Von Glasersfeld contrasts it with radical constructivism. (See also *constructivism, radical constructivism, epistemological constructivism, hermeneutic constructivism.*)

Unity [ToA]:   an entity, a whole, brought forth by an *observer* through an operation of *distinction* together with the *medium* in which it is distinguished.

Validation [PCT]:   represents the compatibility (subjectively construed) between one's *anticipation* and the outcome one observes. *Invalidation* represents incompatibility (subjectively construed) between one's anticipation and the outcome one observes.

References

Adams-Webber, J. R. (1979) *Personal construct theory: Concepts and applications*, New York: Wiley.

Adams-Webber, J. R. (1990) 'Personal construct theory and cognitive science', *International Journal of Personal Construct Psychology*, 3: 415–421.

Adams-Webber, J. R. and Mancuso, J. C. (Eds) (1983) *Applications of personal construct theory*, Toronto: Academic Press.

Ainsworth, M. D. S., Blehar, M. C., Waters, E. and Wall, S. (1978) *Patterns of attachment: A psychological study of the Strange Situation*, Hillsdale, NJ: Lawrence Erlbaum Assocaites, Inc.

Alexander, F. and French, T. M. (1946) *Psychoanalytic therapy: Principles and application*, New York: Ronald Press.

American Psychiatric Association (2000) *Diagnostic and statistical manual IV (text revision)*, Washington, DC: APA.

Amundson, J. K. (2001) 'Why narrative therapy need not fear science and "other" things', *Journal of Family Therapy*, 23: 175–188.

Anderson, H. and Goolishian, H. (1992) 'The client is the expert: A not-knowing approach to therapy', in S. McNamee and K. J. Gergen (Eds), *Therapy as social construction* (pp. 25–39), London: Sage.

Angus, L. E. and McLeod, J. (Eds) (2004), *The handbook of narrative and psychotherapy: Practice, theory, & research*, Thousand Oaks, CA: Sage.

Armezzani, M. (2002) *Esperienza e significato nelle scienze psicologiche [Experience and meaning in psychological sciences]*, Roma, Italy: Laterza.

Armezzani, A., Grimaldi, F. and Pezzullo, L. (2003) *Tecniche costruttiviste per la diagnosi psicologica [Constructivist techniques for the psychological diagnosis]*, Milano: McGraw-Hill.

Armon-Jones, C. (1986) 'The thesis of constructionism', in R. Harré (Ed.), *The social construction of emotions* (pp. 32–56), Oxford: Basil Blackwell.

Aron, L. (1993) 'Working toward operational thought: Piagetian theory and psychoanalysis', *Contemporary Psychoanalysis*, 29: 289–313.

Arthur, A. R. (2001) 'Personality, epistemology and psychotherapists' choice of theoretical model: a review and analysis', *European Journal of Psychotherapy, Counselling and Health*, 4: 45–64.

Atwood, G. E. and Stolorow, R. D. (1984) *Structures of subjectivity*, Hillsdale, NJ: Analytic Press.

Bacal, H. A. and Newman, K. M. (1990) *Theories of object relations: Bridges to self psychology*, New York: Columbia University Press.

Bannister, D. (1960) 'Conceptual structure in thought-disordered schizophrenics', *Journal of Mental Science*, 106: 1230–1249.

Bannister, D. (1963) 'The genesis of schizophrenic thought disorder: A serial invalidation hypothesis', *British Journal of Psychiatry*, 109: 680–686.

Bannister, D. (1965) 'The genesis of schizophrenic thought disorder: Re-test of the serial invalidation hypothesis', *British Journal of Psychiatry*, 111: 377–382.

Bannister, D. (1968) 'The myth of physiological psychology', *Bulletin of the British Psychological Society*, 21: 229–231.

Bannister, D. (1983) 'Self in personal construct theory', in J. R. Adams-Webber and J. C. Mancuso (Eds), *Applications of personal construct theory* (pp. 379–386), Toronto: Academic Press.

Bannister, D. (Ed.) (1985) *Issues and approaches in personal construct theory*, London: Academic Press.

Bannister, D. and Fransella, F. (1965) 'A repertory grid test of schizophrenic thought disorder', *British Journal of Social and Clinical Psychology*, 2: 95–102.

Bannister, D. and Fransella, F. (1966) *Grid Test of Thought Disorder*, Barnstaple, UK: Psychological Test Publications.

Bannister, D. and Fransella, F. (1986) *Inquiring man: The psychology of personal constructs* (3rd edn), London: Routledge.

Bannister, D. and Salmon, P. (1966) 'Schizophrenic thought disorder: specific or diffuse?', *British Journal of Medical Psychology*, 39: 215–219.

Bateson, G. (1976) 'Foreword: A formal approach to explicit, implicit and embodied ideas and to their forms of interaction', in C. E. Sluzki and D. C. Ransom (Eds), *Double bind: The foundation of the communicational approach to the family* (pp. xi–xvi), New York: Grune & Stratton.

Bateson, G. (1979) *Mind and nature: A necessary unity*, Cresskill, NJ: Hampton Press.

Bateson, G., Jackson, D. D., Haley, J. and Weakland, J. H. (1956) 'Toward a theory of schizophrenia', *Behavioral Science*, 1: 251–264.

Beail, N. (Ed.) (1985) *Repertory grid technique and personal constructs: Applications in clinical & educational settings*, London: Croom Helm.

Beck, A. T. (1976) *Cognitive therapy and the emotional disorders*, New York: International Universities Press.

Beck, A. T., Rush, A. J., Shaw, B. F. and Emery, G. (1979) *Cognitive therapy of depression*, New York: Guilford Press.

Bentham, J., and Ogden, C. K. (1932) *Bentham's theory of fictions*, London: K. Paul, Trench, Trubner & Co.

Berger, P. L. and Luckmann, T. (1966) *The social construction of reality: A treatise in the sociology of knowledge*, Garden City, NY: Doubleday.

Berkeley, G. (1710) *A treatise concerning the principles of human knowledge*, Dublin: Aaron Rhames.

Bieri, J., Atkins, A. L., Briar, S., Leaman, R. L., Miller, H. and Tripodi, T. (1966) *Clinical and social judgment: The discrimination of behavioural information*, New York: Wiley.

Binswanger, L. (1963) *Being-in-the world: Selected papers of Ludwig Binswanger*, New York: Basic Books.

Bloom, D., Spagnuolo Lobb, M. and Staemmler, F. M. (2007) 'Editorial', *Studies in Gestalt Therapy: Dialogical Bridges*, 1: 5–9.

Bocchi, G. and Ceruti, M. (1981) *Disordine e costruzione. Un'interpretazione epistemologica dell'opera di Jean Piaget* [*Disorder and construction: An epistemological interpretation of the work of Jean Piaget*], Milano: Feltrinelli.

Bodner, G. M., Klobuchar, M. and Geelan, D. R. (2001) 'The many forms of constructivism', *Journal of Chemical Education*, 78: 1107.

Bonarius, H., Holland, R. and Rosenberg, S. (Eds) (1981) *Personal construct psychology: Recent advances in theory and practice*, New York: St. Martin's Press.

Boscolo, L., Cecchin, G. F., Hoffman, L. and Papp, P. (1987) *Milan systemic family therapy*, New York: Basic Books.

Botella, L., Herrero, O., Pacheco, M. and Corbella, S. (2004). 'Working with narrative in psychotherapy: A relational constructivist approach', in L. E. Angus and J. McLeod (Eds), *The handbook of narrative and psychotherapy: Practice, theory, and research* (pp. 119–136), Thousand Oaks, CA: Sage.

Botella, L., Corbella, S., Gómez, T., Herrero, O. and Pacheco, M. (2005) 'A personal construct approach to narrative and post-modern therapies', in D. A. Winter and L. L. Viney (Eds), *Personal construct psychotherapy: Advances in theory, practice and research* (pp. 69–80), London: Whurr.

Bowlby, J. (1958) 'The nature of the child's tie to his mother', *International Journal of Psycho-Analysis*, 39: 350–373.

Bowlby, J. (1969) *Attachment, Vol. 1 of Attachment and loss*, New York: Basic Books.

Bowlby, J. (1973) *Separation: Anxiety, and anger, Vol. 2 of attachment and loss*, New York: Basic Books.

Bowlby, J. (1979) *The making and breaking of affectional bonds*, London: Tavistock.

Bowlby, J. (1980) *Loss: Sadness and depression, Vol. 3 of Attachment and loss*, New York: Basic Books.

Bowlby, J. (1988) *A secure base: Clinical applications of attachment theory*, London: Routledge.

Brentano, F. (1995) *Psychology from an empirical standpoint* (Trans. L. L. McAlister), London: Routledge. (Original work published 1874.)

Bridgman, P. W. (1936) *The nature of physical theory*, Princeton: Princeton University Press.

Bruner, J. S. (1956) 'A cognitive theory of personality: You are your constructs', *Contemporary Psychology*, 1: 355–357.

Bruner, J. S. (1986) *Actual minds, possible worlds*, Cambridge, MA: Harvard University Press.

Bruner, J. S. (1990) *Acts of meaning*, Cambridge, MA: Harvard University Press.

Buber, M. (1937) *I and thou* (Trans. R. G. Smith), Edinburgh: T. & T. Clark. (Original work published 1923.)

Bunge, M. (1999) *The philosophy–sociology connection*, New Brunswick, NJ: Transaction Publishers.

Burkitt, I. (1996) 'Social and personal constructs: A division left unresolved', *Theory & Psychology*, 6: 71–77.

Burr, V. and Butt, T. (1992) *Invitation to personal construct psychology*, London: Whurr.

Butler, R. J. and Green, D. (2007) *The child within: Taking the young person's perspective by applying personal construct psychology* (2nd edn), London: Wiley.

Butt, T. (1998a) 'Sociality, role, and embodiment', *Journal of Constructivist Psychology*, 11: 105–116.

Butt, T. (1998b) 'Sedimentation and elaborative choice', *Journal of Constructivist Psychology*, 11: 265–281.

Butt, T. (2000) 'Pragmatism, constructivism, and ethics', *Journal of Constructivist Psychology*, 13: 85–101.

Butt, T. (2001) 'Social action and personal constructs', *Theory & Psychology*, 11(1): 75–95.

Butt, T. (2004) 'Understanding, explanation, and personal constructs', *Personal Construct Theory & Practice*, 1: 21–27. Retrieved from http://www.pcpnet.org/journal/pctp04/butt04.pdf

Butt, T. (2006) 'Personal construct therapy and its history in pragmatism', in P. Caputi, H. Foster and L. L. Viney (Eds), *Personal construct psychology: New ideas* (pp. 20–34), London: Wiley.

Butt, T. (2008) *George Kelly and the psychology of personal constructs*, Basingstoke: Palgrave.

Button, E. J. (Ed.) (1985) *Personal construct theory & mental health: Theory, research and practice*, London: Croom Helm.

Carlson, J. and Sperry, L. (1998) 'Adlerian psychotherapy as a constructivist psychology', in M. F. Hoyt (Ed.), *The handbook of constructive therapies: Innovative approaches from leading practitioners* (pp. 68–82), San Francisco, CA: Jossey-Bass.

Ceccato, S. (1964–66) *Un tecnico fra i filosofi* [*A technician among philosophers*], Padova: Marsilio.

Chiari, G. (2000) 'Personal construct theory and the constructivist family: A friendship to cultivate, a marriage not to celebrate', in J. W. Scheer (Ed.), *The person in society: Challenges to a constructivist theory* (pp. 66–78), Gießen: Psychosozial Verlag.

Chiari, G. and Nuzzo, M. L. (1983) 'Conoscenza e metaconoscenza individuale. Il problema dell'"Inconscio" in psicoterapia cognitiva' [Individual knowledge and meta-knowledge: The issue of "unconscious" in cognitive psychotherapy], in A. Balestrieri and C. L. Cazzullo (Eds), *L'inconscio e le scienze* [*Unconscious and the sciences*] (pp. 127–134), Roma: Il Pensiero Scientifico.

Chiari, G. and Nuzzo, M. L. (1985) 'La ragione dell'emozione. La conoscenza individuale in una concezione costruttivista monista' [The reason of emotion: Individual knowledge in a monist constructivist view], in F. Mancini and A. Semerari (Eds), *La psicologia dei costrutti personali. Saggi sulla teoria di G. A. Kelly* [*The psychology of personal constructs: Essays on the theory of G. A. Kelly*] (pp. 175–194), Milano: Angeli.

Chiari, G. and Nuzzo, M. L. (1987, August 4–9) *Constructs and trinities: Kelly and Varela on complementarity and knowledge.* Paper presented at the 7th International Congress on Personal Construct Psychology, Memphis, TN. (Available from http://www.aippc.it/articles/aippc1.pdf)

Chiari, G. and Nuzzo, M. L. (1988) 'Embodied minds over interacting bodies: A constructivist perspective on the mind–body problem', *Irish Journal of*

Psychology, 9: 91–100. (A special issue edited by V. Kenny on *Radical constructivism, autopoiesis and psychotherapy*.)

Chiari, G. and Nuzzo, M. L. (Eds) (1992) *La ricerca psicologica sul cancro. Teorie psicobiologiche, psicogenetiche e psicosociali [The psychological research on cancer: Psychobiological, psychogenetic, and psychosocial theories]*, Milano: Angeli.

Chiari, G. and Nuzzo, M. L. (1993) *Personal construct theory within psychological constructivism: Precursor or avant-garde*? Paper presented at the Xth International Congress of Personal Construct Psychology, Townsville, Australia.

Chiari, G. and Nuzzo, M. L. (1996a) 'Personal construct theory within psychological constructivism: Precursor or avant-garde?', in B. M. Walker, J. Costigan, L. L. Viney and B. Warren (Eds), *Personal construct theory: A psychology for the future* (pp. 25–54), Sydney: The Australian Psychological Society.

Chiari, G. and Nuzzo, M. L. (1996b) 'Psychological constructivisms: A meta-theoretical differentiation', *Journal of Constructivist Psychology*, 9: 163–184.

Chiari, G. and Nuzzo, M. L. (1998) 'Lo scienziato e il narratore: sugli approcci paradigmatici e narrativi in psicoterapia' [The scientist and the storyteller: About paradigmatic and narrative approaches in psychotherapy], in G. Chiari and M. L. Nuzzo (Eds), *Con gli occhi dell'altro. Il ruolo della comprensione empatica in psicologia e in psicoterapia costruttivista [Through the eyes of the other: The role of empathic understanding in constructivist psychology and psychotherapy]*, Padova: Unipress.

Chiari, G. and Nuzzo, M. L. (2000) 'Hermeneutics and constructivist psychotherapy: The psychotherapeutic process in a hermeneutic constructivist framework', in J. W. Scheer (Ed.), *The person in society: Challenges to a constructivist theory* (pp. 90–99), Gießen: Psychosozial Verlag.

Chiari, G. and Nuzzo, M. L. (2003a) 'Kelly's philosophy of constructive alternativism', in F. Fransella (Ed.), *International handbook of personal construct psychology* (pp. 41–49), Chichester: Wiley.

Chiari, G., and Nuzzo, M. L. (Eds) (2003b) *Psychological constructivism and the social world*, Milano, Italy: Angeli.

Chiari, G. and Nuzzo, M. L. (2004) 'Steering personal construct theory toward hermeneutic constructivism', in S. K. Bridges and J. D. Raskin (Eds), *Studies in meaning 2: Bridging the personal and social in constructivist psychology* (pp. 51–65), New York: Pace University Press.

Chiari, G. and Nuzzo, M. L. (2005) 'The psychotherapeutic relationship from a personal construct perspective', in D. A. Winter and L. L. Viney (Eds), *Personal construct psychotherapy: Advances in theory, practice and research* (pp. 43–53), London: Whurr.

Chiari, G. and Nuzzo, M. L. (2006) 'Exploring the sphere of between: The adoption of a framework of complementarity and its implications for a constructivist psychotherapy', *Theory & Psychology*, 16: 257–275.

Chiari, G., Nuzzo, M. L., Alfano, V., Brogna, P., D'Andrea, T., Di Battista, G., Plata, P. and Stiffan, E. (1994) 'Personal paths of dependency', *Journal of Constructivist Psychology*, 7: 17–34.

Chiari, G., Kalekin-Fishman, D. and Nuzzo, M. L. (2001, July 15–21) *Discourses about time: From phenomenological and hermeneutic perspectives to constructivist understandings*. Paper presented at the 14th International Congress on Personal Construct Psychology, Wollongong, NSW, Australia.

Cionini, L. (1999) 'La psicoterapia cognitivo-costruttivista' [Cognitive-constructivist psychotherapy], in O. Codispoti and C. Clementel (Eds), *Psicologia clinica. Modelli, metodi, trattamenti* [*Clinical psychology: Models, methods, treatments*] (pp. 387–399), Roma: Carocci.

Clark, D. A. and Bolton, D. (1985) 'Obsessive-compulsive adolescents and their parents: A psychometric study', *Journal of Child Psychology and Psychiatry*, 26: 267–276.

Clifford, J. and Marcus, G. E. (Eds) (1986) *Writing culture: The poetics and politics of ethnography*, Berkeley, CA: University of California Press.

Cooley, C. H. (1912) *Human nature and the social order*, New York: Scribner's.

Cornelius, N. (Ed.) (2002) *Building workplace equality: Ethics, diversity and inclusion*, London: Thomson.

Cromwell, R. L., Sewell, K. W. and Langelle, C. (1996) 'The personal construction of traumatic stress', in B. M. Walker, J. Costigan, L. L. Viney and B. Warren (Eds), *Personal construct theory: A psychology for the future* (pp. 173–197), Sydney: The Australian Psychological Society.

Dauenhauer, B. (2005) 'Paul Ricoeur', in E. N. Zalta (Ed.), *The Stanford encyclopedia of philosophy* (*winter 2005 edition*). (Available from http://plato.stanford.edu/archives/win2005/entries/Ricoeur)

Denicolo, P. and Pope, M. L. (2001) *Transformative professional practice: Personal construct approaches to education and research*, London: Whurr.

Derrida, J. (1976) *Of grammatology* (Trans. G. C. Spivak), Baltimore, MD: Johns Hopkins University Press. (Original work published 1967.)

Deutsch, F. (1949) *Applied psychoanalysis: Selected objectives of psychotherapy*, New York: Grune and Stratton.

Dewey, J. (1993) 'Philosophies of freedom', in D. Morris and I. Shapiro (Eds), *John Dewey: The political writings* (pp. 133–141), Indianapolis, IN: Hackett. (Original work published 1928.)

DiCaccavo, A. (2002) 'Investigating individuals' motivations to become counselling psychologists: The influence of early caretaking roles within the family', *Psychology and Psychotherapy: Theory, Research and Practice*, 75: 463–472.

Dilthey, W. (1924) *Gesammelte Schriften* (Vol. V: Die geistige Welt. Einleitung in die Philosophie des Lebens. 1: Abhandlungen zur Grundlegung der Geisteswissenschaften). Leipzig: Verlag Von B. G. Teubner.

Domenici, D. J. (2004, June 17–20) *Perspective and possibility: Exploring and expanding hermeneutic constructivism.* Paper presented at the Constructivism 3-D: Diversity, development and dialogue. The 11th Biennial Conference of the North American Personal Construct Network Memphis, TN.

Dooley, J. (1993) 'Piaget, self-organizing knowledge, and critical systems practice'. *Systemic Practice and Action Research*, 6: 359–381.

Downing, J. N. (2000) *Between conviction and uncertainty: Philosophical guidelines for the practicing psychotherapist*, Albany, NY: State University of New York Press.

Dubois, D. M. (2000) 'Review of incursive, hyperincursive and anticipatory systems: Foundation of anticipation in electromagnetism', in D. M. Dubois (Ed.), *Third International Conference on Computing Anticipatory Systems: CASYS'99* (pp. 3–30), The American Institute of Physics, AIP Conference Proceedings 517.

Dunnett, G. (Ed.) (1988) *Working with people: Clinical uses of personal construct psychology*, London and New York: Routledge.

du Preez, P. (1980) *Social psychology of politics*, Oxford: Basil Blackwell.

Dymond, R. F. (1950) 'Personality and empathy', *Journal of Consulting Psychology*, 14: 343–350.

Edwards, D. and Potter, J. (1992) *Discursive psychology*, London: Sage.

Efran, J. S., Lukens, M. D. and Lukens, R. J. (1990) *Language, structure, and change: Frameworks of meaning in psychotherapy*, New York: Norton.

Efran, J. S. and Clarfield, L. E. (1992) 'Constructionist therapy: Sense and nonsense', in S. McNamee and K. J. Gergen (Eds), *Therapy as social construction* (pp. 200–217), London: Sage.

Ekman, P., Friesen, W. V. and Ellsworth, P. (1972) *Emotion in the human face*, New York: Pergamon Press.

Ellenberger, H. F. (1970) *The discovery of the unconscious: The history and evolution of dynamic psychiatry*, New York: Basic Books.

Ellis, A. (1962) *Reason and emotion in psychotherapy*, New York: Lyle Stuart.

Ellis, A. (1998) 'How rational emotive behavior therapy belongs in the constructivist camp', in M. F. Hoyt (Ed.), *The handbook of constructive therapies: Innovative approaches from leading practitioners* (pp. 83–99), San Francisco: Jossey-Bass.

English, H. B. and English, A. C. (1958) *A comprehensive dictionary of psychological and psychoanalytical terms: A guide to usage*, New York: Longmans, Green and Co.

Epting, F. R. (1984) *Personal construct counseling and psychotherapy*, New York: Wiley.

Epting, F. R. (1988) 'Journeying into the personal constructs of children', *International Journal of Personal Construct Psychology*, 1: 53–61.

Epting, F. R. and Amerikaner, M. (1980) 'Optimal functioning: A personal construct approach', in A. W. Landfield and L. M. Leitner (Eds), *Personal construct psychology: Psychotherapy and personality* (pp. 55–73), New York: Wiley.

Epting, F. R. and Landfield, A. W. (Eds) (1985) *Anticipating personal construct psychology*, Lincoln, NE: University of Nebraska Press.

Epting, F. R. and Leitner, L. M. (1992) 'Humanistic psychology and personal construct theory', *The Humanistic Psychologist*, 20: 243–259.

Epting, F. R. and Paris, M. E. (2006) 'A constructive understanding of the person: George Kelly and humanistic psychology', *The Humanistic Psychologist*, 34: 21–37.

Faidley, A. J. and Leitner, L. M. (1993) *Assessing experience in psychotherapy: Personal construct alternatives*, Westport, CN and London: Praeger.

Feixas, G. (1995) 'Personal constructs in systemic practice', in R. A. Neimeyer and M. J. Mahoney (Eds), *Constructivism in psychotherapy* (pp. 305–337), Washington, DC: American Psychological Association.

Feldman, C. F. (1994) 'Genres as mental models', in M. Ammaniti and D. N. Stern (Eds), *Psychoanalysis and development: Representations and narratives* (pp. 111–121), New York: New York University Press.

Ferrari, M., Pinard, A. and Runions, K. (2001) 'Piaget's framework for a scientific study of consciousness', *Human Development*, 44: 193–211.

Feyerabend, P. K. (1976) *Against method*, New York: Humanities Press.

Flavell, J. H. (1963) *The developmental psychology of Jean Piaget*, Princeton: Van Nostrand.

Fliess, R. (1942) 'The metapsychology of the analyst', *The Psychoanalytic Quarterly*, 11: 211–227.

Foucault, M. (1965) *Madness and civilization: A history of insanity in the age of reason* (Trans. R. Howard), London: Tavistock. (Original work published 1961.)

Foucault, M. (1977) *Discipline and punish: The birth of the prison*, New York: Pantheon Books. (Original work published 1975.)

Frankl, V. E. (1962) *Basic concepts of logotherapy*, Greenville, Delaware: Psychosynthesis Research Foundation.

Fransella, F. (1972) *Personal change and reconstruction: Research on a treatment of stuttering*, London: Academic Press.

Fransella, F. (1974) 'Thinking in the obsessional', in H. R. Beech (Ed.), *Obsessional states* (pp. 175–196), London: Methuen.

Fransella, F. (1983) 'What sort of scientist is the person-as-scientist?', in J. R. Adams-Webber and J. C. Mancuso (Eds), *Applications of personal construct theory* (pp. 127–135), Toronto: Academic Press.

Fransella, F. (1995) *George Kelly*, London: Sage.

Fransella, F. (2000) 'George Kelly and mathematics', in J. W. Scheer (Ed.), *The person in society: Challenges to a constructivist theory* (pp. 114–121), Giessen, Germany: Psychosozial Verlag.

Fransella, F. (Ed.) (2003a) *International handbook of personal construct psychology*, Chichester, UK: Wiley.

Fransella, F. (2003b) 'Some skills and tools for personal construct practitioners', in *International handbook of personal construct psychology* (pp. 105–121), Chichester, UK: Wiley.

Fransella, F. (Ed.) (2005) *The essential practitioner's handbook of personal construct psychology*, Chichester, UK: Wiley.

Fransella, F. and Dalton, P. (1990) *Personal construct counseling in action*, Thousand Oaks, CA: Sage.

Fransella, F., Bell, R. C. and Bannister, D. (2003) *A manual for repertory grid technique* (2nd revised edn), Chichester, UK: Wiley.

Freud, S. (1899) 'Screen memories', in J. Strachey (Ed. and Trans.), *Standard edition of the complete psychological works of Sigmund Freud* (Vol. 3, pp. 301–322), London: Hogarth Press.

Freedman, J. and Combs, G. (1996) *Narrative therapy: The social construction of preferred realities*, New York: Norton.

Friedman, T. L. (1978) 'Piaget and psychotherapy', *Journal of American Academy of Psychoanalysis*, 6: 175–192.

Frijda, N. H. (1986) *The emotions*, Cambridge, MA: Maison des Sciences de l'Homme and Cambridge University Press.

Fromm, M. (2004) *Introduction to the repertory grid interview*, Münster: Waxmann.

Fussell, F. W. and Bonney, W. C. (1990) 'A comparative study of childhood experiences of psychotherapists and physicists: Implications for clinical practice', *Psychotherapy: Theory, Research, Practice, Training*, 27: 505–512.

Gadamer, H. G. (1960) *Truth and method*, New York: Thomas Crowell.

Gadamer, H. G. (1976) *Philosophical hermeneutics* (Trans. D. E. Linge), Berkeley: University of California Press.

Gadamer, H. G. (1989) *Truth and method* (Trans. J. Weinsheimer and D. G. Marshall) (2nd edn.), New York: Seabury Press.

Garrison, J. (1995) 'Deweyan pragmatism and the epistemology of contemporary social constructivism', *American Educational Research Journal*, 32: 716–740.

Gash, H. (1983) 'Vico's theory of knowledge and some problems in genetic epistemology', *Human Development*, 26: 1–10.

Gash, H. and von Glasersfeld, E. (1978) 'Vico (1668–1744): An early anticipator of radical constructivism', *Irish Journal of Psychology*, 4: 22–32.

Geelan, D. R. (1997) 'Epistemological anarchy and the many forms of constructivism', *Science & Education*, 6: 15–28.

Gergen, K. J. (1973) 'Social psychology and history', *Journal of Personality and Social Psychology*, 26: 309–320.

Gergen, K. J. (1982) *Toward transformation in social knowledge*, New York: Springer.

Gergen, K. J. (1985) 'The social constructionist movement in modern psychology', *American Psychologist*, 40: 266–275.

Gergen, K. J. and Davis, K. (Eds) (1985) *The social construction of the person*, New York: Springer.

Gergen, K. J. and Gergen, M. M. (1991) 'Toward reflexive methodologies', in F. Steier (Ed.), *Research and reflexivity* (pp. 76–95), London: Sage.

Gibson, J. J. (1979) *The ecological approach to visual perception*, Boston: Houghton Mifflin.

Good, R. (1993) 'The many forms of constructivism, Editorial', *Journal of Research in Science Teaching*, 30: 1015.

Goodman, N. (1976) *Languages of art: An approach to a theory of symbols*, Indianapolis and Cambridge: Hackett.

Goodman, N. (1978) *Ways of worldmaking*, Hassocks, Sussex, UK: Harvester Press.

Goodman, N. (1984) *Of mind and other matters*, Cambridge, MA: Harvard University Press.

Goolishian, H. and Anderson, H. (1981) 'Including non-blood related persons in treatment: Who is the family to be treated?', in A. Gurman (Ed.), *Questions and answers in family therapy*, New York: Bruner/Mazel.

Green, D. (2005) 'Personal construct theory and paediatric health care', *Clinical Child Psychology and Psychiatry*, 10: 33–41.

Greenberg, J. R. and Mitchell, S. A. (1983) *Object relations in psychoanalytic theory*, Cambridge, MA: Harvard University Press.

Greenberg, L. S. and Safran, J. D. (1987) *Emotion in psychotherapy: Affect, cognition, and the process of change*, New York: Guilford.

Greenberg, L. and Pascual-Leone, J. (1995) 'A dialectical constructivist approach to experiential change', in R. A. Neimeyer and M. J. Mahoney (Eds), *Constructivism in psychotherapy* (pp. 169–191), Washington, DC: American Psychological Association.

Greenson, R. R. (1965) 'The working alliance and the transference neurosis', *Psychoanalytic Quarterly*, 34: 155–181.

Greenson, R. R. (1978) 'The "real" relationship between the patient and the psychoanalyst', in R. R. Greenson (Ed.), *Explorations in psychoanalysis* (pp. 425–440), New York: International Universities Press. (Original work published 1971.)

Greenwald, H. (1973) *Decision therapy*, New York: Wyden.

Guidano, V. F. (1987) *The complexity of Self: A developmental approach to psychopathology and therapy*, New York: Guilford.

Guidano, V. F. (1991) *The Self in process: Toward a post-rationalist cognitive therapy*, New York: Guilford.

Guidano, V. F. and Liotti, G. (1983) *Cognitive processes and emotional disorders: A structural approach to psychotherapy*, New York: Guilford.

Habermas, J. (1971) *Knowledge and human interests*, Boston: Beacon Press.

Harré, R. (1979) *Social being*, Oxford: Blackwell.

Harré, R. (1983) *Personal being*, Oxford: Blackwell.

Harré, R. (Ed.) (1986) *The social construction of emotions*, Oxford: Basil Blackwell.

Harré, R. and Gillett, G. R. (1994) *The discursive mind*, London: Sage.

Heidegger, M. (1962) *Being and time* (Trans. J. Macquarrie and E. Robinson), New York: Harper. (Original work published 1927.)

Heidegger, M. (1998) *Pathmarks*, Cambridge: Cambridge University Press. (Original work published 1976.)

Held, B. S. (1995) *Back to reality: A critique of postmodern theory in psychotherapy*, New York: Norton.

Hillman, J. (1983) *Healing fiction*, Barrytown, NY: Stanton Hill Press.

Hinkle, D. N. (1965) *The change of personal constructs from the viewpoint of a theory of construct implications*. Unpublished PhD dissertation, Ohio State University, Columbus.

Hoffman, I. Z. (1998) *Ritual and spontaneity in the psychoanalytic process: A dialectical-constructivist view*, Hillsdale, NJ: The Analytic Press.

Hoffman, L. (1993) *Exchanging voices: A collaborative approach to family therapy*, London: Karnac.

Horley, J. (Ed.) (2003) *Personal construct perspectives on forensic psychology*, Hove, UK, and New York: Brunner-Routledge.

Howard, G. S. (1990) 'Narrative psychotherapy', in J. K. Zeig and W. M. Munion (Eds), *What is psychotherapy?*, San Francisco: Jossey-Bass.

Husserl, E. (1900–1901) *Logische Untersuchungen* [*Logical investigations*], Halle a. d. S.: Max Niemeyer.

Husserl, E. (1931) *Ideas: General introduction to pure phenomenology* (Trans. W. R. Boyce Gibson), London: George Allen & Unwin. (Original work published 1913.)

Husserl, E. (1976) 'Die Krisis der europaeischen Wissenschaften und die Traszendentale Phenomenologie' [The crisis of European sciences and transcendental phenomenology], in W. Biemel (Ed.), *Husserliana* (Vol. VI), Den Haag: Martinus Nijhoff. (Original work published in 1936.)

Ihde, D. (1986) *Experimental phenomenology*, Albany: SUNY Press.

Iser, W. (1978) *The act of reading*, Baltimore: John Hopkins University Press.

Izard, C. E. (1971) *The face of emotion*, New York: Appleton-Century-Crofts.

Jackson, D. (1965) 'The study of the family', *Family Process*, 4: 1–20.

Jacobs, L. (1980) 'A cognitive approach to persistent delusions', *American Journal of Psychotherapy*, 34: 556–563.

James, W. (1890) *The principles of psychology*, New York: Holt.

James, W. (1978) *Pragmatism*, Cambridge, MA: Harvard University Press. (Original work published 1907.)

Jankowicz, A. D. (2003) *The easy guide to repertory grids*, Chichester, UK: Wiley.

Jaspers, K. (1968) 'The phenomenological approach in psychopathology', *British Journal of Psychiatry*, 114: 1313–1323. (Original work published 1912.)

Jaspers, K. (1997) *General psychopathology* (Trans. J. Hoenig and M. W. Hamilton),. Baltimore, MD: Johns Hopkins University Press. (Original work published 1913.)

Jones, J. V., Jr. (1995) 'Constructivism and individual psychology: Common ground for dialogue', *Individual Psychology: Journal of Adlerian Theory, Research and Practice*, 51: 231–243.

Jones, J. V., Jr. and Lyddon, W. J. (1997) 'Adlerian and constructivist psychotherapies: A constructivist perspective', *Journal of Cognitive Psychotherapy*, 11: 195–210.

Kalekin-Fishman, D. and Walker, B. M. (Eds) (1996) *The construction of group realities: Culture, society, and personal construct psychology*, Malabar, FL: Krieger.

Kant, I. (1929) *Critique of pure reason*, London: Macmillan. (Original work published 1781.)

Keeney, B. P. (1983) *Aesthetics of change*, New York: Guilford.

Kelly, G. A. (1966) *Experimental dependency*. Unpublished manuscript, Brandeis University.

Kelly, G. A. (1969a) 'Man's construction of his alternatives', in B. A. Maher (Ed.), *Clinical psychology and personality: The selected papers of George Kelly* (pp. 66–93), New York: Wiley. (Original work published 1958.)

Kelly, G. A. (1969b) 'Personal construct theory and the psychotherapeutic interview', in B. A. Maher (Ed.), *Clinical psychology and personality: The selected papers of George Kelly* (pp. 224–264), New York: Wiley. (Original work written 1958.)

Kelly, G. A. (1969) 'A mathematical approach to psychology', in B. Maher (Ed.), *Clinical psychology and personality: The selected papers of George Kelly* (pp. 94–113), New York: Wiley. (Original work written 1961.)

Kelly, G. A. (1969) 'In whom confide: On whom depend for what?', in B. A. Maher (Ed.), *Clinical psychology and personality: The selected papers of George Kelly* (pp. 189–206), New York: Wiley. (Original work written 1962.)

Kelly, G. A. (1969) 'The autobiography of a theory', in B. A. Maher (Ed.), *Clinical psychology and personality: The selected papers of George Kelly* (pp. 46–65), New York: Wiley. (Original work written 1963.)

Kelly, G. A. (1969) 'The language of hypothesis: Man's psychological instrument', in B. A. Maher (Ed.), *Clinical psychology and personality: The selected papers of George Kelly* (pp. 147–162), New York: Wiley. (Originally published in *Journal of Individual Psychology*, 20: 137–152, 1964.)

Kelly, G. A. (1969) 'The psychotherapeutic relationship', in B. A. Maher (Ed.), *Clinical psychology and personality: The selected papers of George Kelly* (pp. 216–223), New York: Wiley. (Original work written 1965.)

Kelly, G. A. (1969) 'Ontological acceleration', in B. A. Maher (Ed.), *Clinical psychology and personality: The selected papers of George Kelly* (pp. 7–45), New York: Wiley. (Original work written 1966.)

Kelly, G. A. (1970a) 'A brief introduction to personal construct theory', in D. Bannister (Ed.), *Perspectives in personal construct theory* (pp. 1–29), London: Academic Press. (Original work written 1966.)

Kelly, G. A. (1970b) 'Behaviour is an experiment', in D. Bannister (Ed.), *Perspectives in personal construct theory* (pp. 255–269), London: Academic Press. (Original work written 1966.)

Kelly, G. A. (1977) 'The psychology of the unknown', in D. Bannister (Ed.), *New perspectives in personal construct theory* (pp. 1–19), London: Academic Press. (Original work written 1963.)

Kelly, G. A. (1980) 'A psychology of the optimal man', in A. W. Landfield and L. M. Leitner (Eds), *Personal construct psychology: Psychotherapy and personality* (pp. 18–35), New York: Wiley. (Original work published 1967.)

Kelly, G. A. (1991a) *The psychology of personal constructs: Vol. 1. A theory of personality*, London: Routledge. (Original work published 1955.)

Kelly, G. A. (1991b) *The psychology of personal constructs: Vol. 2. Clinical diagnosis and psychotherapy*, London: Routledge. (Original work published 1955.)

Kenny, V. (1988) 'Autopoiesis and alternativism in psychotherapy: Fluctuations and reconstructions', in F. Fransella and L. F. Thomas (Eds), *Experimenting with personal construct psychology* (pp. 36–47), London: Routledge & Kegan Paul.

Kenny, V. and Gardner, G. (1988) 'Constructions of self-organising systems', *The Irish Journal of Psychology*, 9: 1–24. (A special issue on *Radical constructivism, autopoiesis and psychotherapy* edited by V. Kenny.)

Knorr-Cetina, K. D. (1981) *The manufacture of knowledge: An essay on the constructivist and contextual nature of science*, Oxford: Pergamon Press.

Kuhn, T. S. (1962) *The structure of scientific revolutions*, Chicago: Chicago University Press.

Kvale, S. (Ed.) (1992) *Psychology and postmodernism*, London: Sage.

Laing, R. D. (1960) *The divided self: A study of sanity and madness*, London: Tavistock.

Laing, R. D. and Esterson, A. (1964) *Sanity, madness and the family: Families of schizophrenics*, London: Tavistock Publications.

Landfield, A. W. (1951) *A study of threat within the psychology of personal constructs*. Unpublished doctoral dissertation, Ohio State University.

Landfield, A. W. (1971) *Personal construct systems in psychotherapy*, Chicago: Rand McNally.

Landfield, A. W. (1980) 'Personal construct psychotherapy: A personal construction', in A. W. Landfield and L. M. Leitner (Eds), *Personal construct psychology: Psychotherapy and personality* (pp. 122–139), New York: Wiley.

Landfield, A. W. and Epting, F. R. (1987) *Personal construct psychology: Clinical and personality assessment*, New York: Human Sciences Press.

Landfield, A. W. and Leitner, L. M. (Eds) (1980) *Personal construct psychology: Psychotherapy and personality*, New York: Wiley-Interscience.

Lazarus, R. (1991) *Emotion and adaptation*, New York: Oxford University Press.

Leitner, L. M. (1985) 'The terrors of cognition: On the experiential validity of personal construct theory', in D. Bannister (Ed.), *Issues and approaches in personal construct theory* (pp. 83–103), London: Academic Press.

Leitner, L. M. (1988) 'Terror, risk, and reverence: Experiential personal construct psychotherapy', *International Journal of Personal Construct Psychology*, 1: 251–261.

Leitner, L. M. and Dunnett, G. (Eds) (1993) *Critical issues in personal construct psychotherapy*, Malabar, FL: Krieger.

Leitner, L. M. Faidley, A. J., Dominici, D., Humphreys, C. L., Loeffler, V., Schlutsmeyer, M. and Thomas, J. (2005) 'Encountering an other: Experiential personal construct psychotherapy', in D. A. Winter and L. L. Viney (Eds), *Personal construct psychotherapy: Advances in theory, practice and research* (pp. 54–68), London: Whurr.

Lewis, M. and Brooks-Gunn, J. (1979) *Social cognition and the acquisition of self*, New York: Plenum Press.

Lidz, T. (1964) *The family and human adaptation*, London: Hogarth Press.

Liotti, G. (1999) 'Understanding the dissociative processes: The contribution of attachment theory', *Psychoanalytic Inquiry*, 19: 757–783.

Luborsky, L. (1984) *Principles of psychoanalytic psychotherapy*, New York: Basic Books.

Ludwig, S. (1998) 'Cybernetic signs of life: Pragmatism's cognitive lineage and the grounding of realism', in W. Fluck (Ed.), *Pragmatism and literary studies* (pp. 281–301), Tübingen, Germany: Gunter Narr Verlag.

Lyddon, W. J. (1995) 'Forms and facets of constructivist psychology', in R. A. Neimeyer and M. J. Mahoney (Eds), *Constructivism in psychotherapy* (pp. 69–92), Washington, DC: American Psychological Association.

Lyotard, J. F. (1979) *La condition postmoderne: Rapport sur le savoir [The postmodern condition: A report on knowledge]*, Paris: Les Éditions de Minuit.

McArthur, C. (1956) 'Review of *The psychology of personal constructs* by G. A. Kelly', *Journal of Counseling Psychology*, 3: 306–307.

McCoy, M. M. (1977) 'A reconstruction of emotion', in D. Bannister (Ed.), *New perspectives in personal construct theory* (pp. 93–124), London: Academic Press.

MacIntyre, A. (1981) *After virtue*, Notre Dame, IN: University of Notre Dame Press.

Mackay, D. (1975) *Clinical psychology: Theory and therapy*, London: Methuen.

Mackay, N. (2003) 'Psychotherapy and the idea of meaning', *Theory & Psychology*, 13(3): 359–386.

McNamee, S. and Gergen, K. J. (Eds) (1992) *Therapy as social construction*, London: Sage.

McWilliams, S. A. (1996) 'Accepting the invitational', in B. M. Walker, J. Costigan, L. L. Viney and W. G. Warren (Eds), *Personal construct theory: A psychology for the future* (pp. 57–78), Melbourne: Australian Psychological Society.

Maharg, P. (2000) 'Rogers, constructivism and jurisprudence: educational critique and the legal curriculum', *International Journal of the Legal Profession*, 7: 189–203.

Mahoney, M. J. (1988) 'Constructive metatheory: I. Basic features and historical foundations', *International Journal of Personal Construct Psychology*, 1: 1–35.

Mahoney, M. J. (1991) *Human change processes: The scientific foundations of psychotherapy*, New York: Basic Books.

Mahoney, M. J. and Lyddon, W. J. (1988) 'Recent developments in cognitive approaches to counseling and psychotherapy', *The Counseling Psychologist*, 16: 190–234.

Mair, J. M. M. (1977) 'The community of self', in D. Bannister (Ed.), *New perspectives in personal construct theory* (pp. 125–149), London: Academic Press.

Mair, J. M. M. (1985) 'The long quest to know', in F. R. Epting and A. W.

Landfield (Eds), *Anticipating personal construct theory* (pp. 3–14), Lincoln, NE: University of Nebraska Press.

Mair, J. M. M. (1988) 'Psychology as storytelling', *International Journal of Personal Construct Psychology*, 1: 125–137.

Mair, J. M. M. (1989a) *Between psychology and psychotherapy: A poetics of experience*, London and New York: Routledge.

Mair, J. M. M. (1989b) 'Kelly, Bannister, and a story-telling psychology', *International Journal of Personal Construct Psychology*, 2: 1–14.

Makhlouf-Norris, F., Jones, H. G. and Norris, H. (1970) 'Articulation of the conceptual structure in obsessional neurosis', *British Journal of Social and Clinical Psychology*, 9: 264–274.

Mancuso, J. C. (1986) 'The acquisition and use of narrative grammar structure', in T. R. Sarbin (Ed.), *Narrative psychology: The storied nature of human conduct* (pp. 91–110), New York: Praeger.

Mancuso, J. C. (1996a) 'Constructionism, personal construct psychology, and narrative psychology', *Theory & Psychology*, 6: 47–70.

Mancuso, J. C. (1996b) 'The socializing of personal constructions', *Theory & Psychology*, 6: 85–92.

Mancuso, J. C. and Hunter, K. V. (1985) 'Assunti costruttivisti nelle teorie di G. A. Kelly e J. Piaget' [Constructivist assumptions in the theories of G. A. Kelly and J. Piaget], in F. Mancini and A. Semerari (Eds), *La psicologia dei costrutti personali. Saggi sulla teoria di G. A. Kelly* [*The psychology of personal constructs: Essays on the theory of G. A. Kelly*] (pp. 73–103), Milano: Angeli.

Matthews, M. R. (1992) 'Old wine in new bottles: A problem with constructivist epistemology', in H. Alexander (Ed.), *Philosophy of Education 1992, Proceedings of the Forty-Eighth Annual Meeting of the Philosophy of Education Society* (pp. 303–311), Urbana, IL: Philosophy of Education Society.

Maturana, H. R. (1970) 'Neurophysiology of cognition', in P. L. Garvin (Ed.), *Cognition: A multiple view* (pp. 3–24), New York: Spartan.

Maturana, H. R. (1978) 'Biology of language: The epistemology of reality', in G. A. Miller and E. Lenneberg (Eds), *Psychology and biology of language and thought: Essays in honor of Eric Lenneberg* (pp. 27–63), New York: Academic Press.

Maturana, H. R. (1987) 'The biological foundations of self-consciousness and the physical domain of existence', in E. R. Caianiello (Ed.), *Physics of cognitive processes* (pp. 324–379), Singapore: World Scientific.

Maturana, H. R. (1988) 'Reality: The search for objectivity or the quest for a compelling argument', *Irish Journal of Psychology*, 9: 25–82.

Maturana, H. R. (1995a) 'Biology of self-consciousness', in G. Trautteur (Ed.), *Consciousness: Distinction and reflection* (pp. 145–175), Napoli: Bibliopolis.

Maturana H. (1995b) *The nature of time*, Santiago de Chile: Instituto de Terapia Cognitiva. (Available from http://www.inteco.cl/biology/nature.htm)

Maturana, H. R. (2001) *Emociones y lenguaje en educación y política* [*Emotions and language in education and politics*] (10th edn), Santiago de Chile: Dolmen.

Maturana, H. R. (2005) 'The origin and conservation of self-consciousness: Reflections on four questions by Heinz von Foerster', *Kybernetes*, 34: 54–88.

Maturana, H. R. and Varela, F. J. (1987) *The tree of knowledge: The biological roots of human understanding*, Boston and London: New Science Library. (Original work published 1984.)

Maturana, H. R. and Verden-Zöller, G. (1996) 'Biology of love', in G. Opp and F. Peterander (Eds), *Focus Heilpädagogik*, Munchen/Basel: Reinhardt Verlag.

Maturana, H. R., Mpodozis, J. and Letelier, J. C. (1995) 'Brain, language and the origin of human mental functions', *Biological Research*, 28: 15–26.

Mays, W. and Smith, L. (2001) 'Harré on Piaget's sociological studies', *New Ideas in Psychology*, 19: 221–235.

Mead, G. H. (1934) *Mind, self and society*, Chicago: University of Chicago Press.

Melnick, J. (1997) 'Welcome to *Gestalt Review*: An editorial', *Gestalt Review*, 1: 1–8.

Merleau-Ponty, M. (1962) *Phenomenology of perception*, London and New York: Routledge. (Original work published 1945.)

Merleau-Ponty, M. (1963) *The structure of behavior*, Boston: Beacon Press.

Metzger, W. (1941) *Psychologie: Die Entwicklung ihrer Grundannahmen seit der Einführung des Experiments* [*Psychology: The development of basic principles since the introduction of the experimental method*], Dresden, Germany: Steinkopff.

Minkowski, E. (1970) *Lived time: Phenomenological and psychopathological studies* (Trans. N. Metzel), Evanston: Northwestern University Press.

Moran, D. (1985) 'Nature, Man and God in the philosophy of John Scottus Eriugena', in R. Kearney (Ed.), *The Irish mind* (pp. 91–106; 324–332), Dublin and New Jersey: Wolfhound Press and Humanities Press.

Moshman, D. (1982) 'Exogenous, endogenous, and dialectical constructivism', *Developmental Review*, 2: 371–384.

Murphy, R. A. and Halgin, R. P. (1995) 'Influences on the career choice of psychotherapists', *Professional Psychology: Research and Practice*, 26: 422–426.

Murray, H. A. (1938) *Explorations in personality*, New York: Oxford University Press.

Nagel, T. (1981) 'What is it like to be a bat?', in D. R. Hofstadter and D. C. Dennett (Eds), *The mind's I: Fantasies and reflections on self & soul* (pp. 391–403), New York: Basic Books. (Original work published 1974.)

Natterson, J. M. and Friedman, R. J. (1995) *A primer of clinical intersubjectivity*, Northvale, NJ: Jason Aronson.

Neimeyer, R. A. (1985) *The development of personal construct psychology*, Lincoln, NE: University of Nebraska Press.

Neimeyer, R. A. (1987) 'An orientation to personal construct therapy', in R. A. Neimeyer and G. J. Neimeyer (Eds), *Personal construct therapy casebook* (pp. 3–19), New York: Springer.

Neimeyer, R. A. (1993a) 'An appraisal of constructivist psychotherapies', *Journal of Consulting and Clinical Psychology*, 61: 221–234.

Neimeyer, R. A. (1993b) 'Constructivism and the cognitive psychotherapies: Some conceptual and strategic contrasts', *Journal of Cognitive Psychotherapy*, 7: 159–171.

Neimeyer, R. A. (1994) 'The role of client-generated narratives in psychotherapy', *Journal of Constructivist Psychology*, 7: 229–242.

Neimeyer, R. A. (1995) 'Constructivist psychotherapies: Features, foundations, and future directions', in R. A. Neimeyer and M. J. Mahoney (Eds), *Constructivism in psychotherapy* (pp. 11–38), Washington, DC: American Psychological Association.

Neimeyer, R. A. (2000) 'Narrative disruptions in the construction of the self', in R. A. Neimeyer and J. D. Raskin (Eds), *Constructions of disorder: Meaning-making frameworks for psychotherapy* (pp. 207–242), Washington, DC: American Psychological Association.

Neimeyer, R. A. (2001) 'Reauthoring life narratives: Grief therapy as meaning reconstruction', *Israel Journal of Psychiatry and Related Sciences*, 38: 171–183.

Neimeyer, R. A. and Neimeyer, G. J. (Eds) (1987) *Personal construct therapy casebook*, New York: Springer.

Neimeyer, R. A. and Stewart, A. E. (2000) 'Constructivist and narrative psychotherapies', in C. R. Snyder and R. E. Ingram (Eds), *Handbook of psychological change: Psychotherapy processes & practices for the 21st century* (pp. 337–357), New York: Wiley.

Neisser, U. (1967) *Cognitive psychology*, Englewood Cliffs, NJ: Prentice-Hall.

Neisser, U. (1976) *Cognition and reality: Principles and implications of cognitive psychology*, San Francisco: Freeman.

Neubert, S. (2001) 'Pragmatism and constructivism in contemporary philosophical discourse'. Retrieved December 2, 2007, from wwwuni-koeln.de/ew-fak/paedagogik/dewe/texte/texte/pragmatism%20constructivism.pdf

Nikcevic, A. V., Kramolisova-Advani, J. and Spada, M. M. (2007) 'Early childhood experiences and current emotional distress: What do they tell us about aspiring psychologists?', *Journal of Psychology: Interdisciplinary and Applied*, 141: 25–34.

Nuzzo, M. L. and Chiari, G. (1987, August 4–9) *The personal construction of cancer: A constructivist framework for exploring malignancies*. Paper presented at the seventh International Congress on Personal Construct Psychology, Memphis, TN.

Nuzzo, M. L. and Chiari, G. (1992) 'Il cancro come costruzione personale' [Cancer as a personal construction], in G. Chiari and M. L. Nuzzo (Eds), *La ricerca psicologica sul cancro. Teorie psicobiologiche, psicogenetiche e psicosociali* [*The psychological research on cancer: Psychobiological, psychogenetic, and psychosocial theories*] (pp. 179–192), Milano: Angeli.

O'Hara, M. (1995) 'Carl Rogers: Scientist and mystic', *Journal of Humanistic Psychology*, 35: 40–53.

Payne, M. (2000) *Narrative therapy: An introduction for counselors*, London: Sage.

Peck, D. and Whitlow, D. D. (1975) *Approaches to personality theory*, London: Methuen.

Pepper, S. C. (1942) *World hypotheses: A study in evidence*, Berkeley and Los Angeles: University of California Press.

Perris, C. (1990) *Cognitive therapy with schizophrenic patients*, New York: Guilford Press.

Peterfreund, E. (1983) *The process of psychoanalytic therapy*, Hillsdale, NJ: Analytic Press.

Petitot, J., Varela, F. J., Pachoud, B. and Roy, J. M. (Eds) (1999) *Naturalizing phenomenology: Issues in contemporary phenomenology and cognitive science*, Stanford, CA: Stanford University Press.

Pfuetze, P. E. (1954) *The social self: A full-scale exposition, comparison, and criticism of the concept of the social self in the writings of George Herbert Mead and Martin Buber*, New York: Bookman Associates.

Phillips, D. C. (Ed.) (2000) *Constructivism in education: Opinions and second opinions on controversial issues*, Chicago, IL: National Society for the Study of Education Yearbooks.

Piaget, J. (1937) *La construction du réel chez l'enfant* [*The child's construction of reality*], Neuchâtel: Delachaux et Niestlé.

Piaget J. (1946) *Le développement de la notion de temps chez l'enfant* [*The development of the notion of time in the child*], Paris: Presses Universitaires de France.

Piaget, J. (1952) *The origins of intelligence in children*, New York: International Universities Press. (Original work published 1936.)

Piaget, J. (1954) 'The problem of consciousness in child psychology: Developmental changes in awareness', in H. Abramson (Ed.), *Problems of consciousness* (pp. 136–147), New York: Josiah Macy Foundation.

Piaget, J. (1962) 'The relation of affectivity to intelligence in the mental development of the child', *Bulletin of the Menninger clinic*, 26: 129–137.

Piaget, J. (1967) 'Les courants de l'épistémologie scientifique contemporaine', in J. Piaget (Ed.), *Logique et connaissance scientifique* (pp. 1225–1271), Paris: Gallimard.

Piaget, J. (1970a) 'Piaget's theory', in P. H. Mussen (Ed.), *Carmichael's manual of child psychology* (3rd edn, Vol. 1, pp. 703–732), New York: Wiley.

Piaget, J. (1970b) *Genetic epistemology* (Trans. E. Duckworth), New York: Norton.

Piaget, J. (1971) *Biology and knowledge: An essay on the relations between organic regulations and cognitive processes*, Edinburgh: Edinburgh University Press. (Original work published 1967.)

Piaget, J. (1974a) *La prise de conscience* [*The grasp of consciousness*], Paris: Presses Universitaires de France.

Piaget, J. (1974b) *Réussir et comprendre* [*To succeed and understand*], Paris: Presses Universitaires de France.

Piaget, J. (1981) *Intelligence and affectivity: Their relationship during child development*, Palo Alto, CA: Annual Reviews. (Original work published 1954.)

Piaget, J. (1995) *Sociological studies* (Ed. Leslie Smith), London: Routledge.

Piaget, J. and Garcia, R. (1983) *Psychogénèse et histoire des sciences*, Paris: Flammarion.

Plato (1921) *Theaetetus. Sophist* (Trans. H. N. Fowler), Cambridge, MA: Harvard University Press (Loeb Classical Library).

Polkinghorne, D. E. (1988) *Narrative knowing and the human sciences*, Albany, NY: State University of New York Press.

Polkinghorne, D. E. (1992) 'Postmodern epistemology of practice', in S. Kvale (Ed.), *Psychology and postmodernism* (pp. 146–165), Thousand Oaks, CA: Sage.

Polkinghorne, D. E. (1995) 'Piaget's and Derrida's contributions to a constructivist psychotherapy', *Journal of Constructivist Psychology*, 8: 269–282.

Pons, F. and Harris, P. (2001) 'Piaget's conception of the development of consciousness: An examination of two hypotheses', *Human Development*, 44: 220–227.

Pope, M. L. and Denicolo, P. (2001) *Transformative education: Personal construct approaches to practce and research*, London: Whurr.

Popper, K. R. (1959) *The logic of scientific discovery*, London: Hutchinson. (Original work published 1934.)

Popper, K. R. and Eccles, J. C. (1977) *The self and its brain: An argument for interactionism*, Berlin: Springer.

Purdy, D. E. (2000) 'The principles for financial reporting in the UK and personal construction', in J. M. Fisher and N. Cornelius (Eds), *Challenging the boundaries:*

PCP perspectives for the new millennium (pp. 140–155), Farnborough: EPCA Publications.

Putnam, H. (1981) *Reason, truth, and history*, Cambridge: Cambridge University Press.

Raskin, J. D. (2002) 'Constructivism in psychology: Personal construct psychology, radical constructivism, and social constructionism', in S. K. Bridges and J. D. Raskin (Eds), *Studies in meaning: Exploring constructivist psychology* (pp. 1–25), New York, NY: Pace University Press.

Raskin, J. D. and Neimeyer, R. A. (2003) 'Coherent constructivism: A response to Mackay', *Theory & Psychology*, 13(3): 397–409.

Rasmussen, J. (1998) 'Constructivism and phenomenology: What do they have in common, and how can they be told apart?', *Cybernetics and Systems*, 29: 553–576.

Rather, L. (2001) *The therapeutic and working alliances revisited*. Retrieved January 6, 2004, from www.fortda.org/spring_01/therapeutic.html

Ravenette, A. T. (1999) *Personal construct theory in educational psychology: A practitioner's view*, London: Whurr.

Ricoeur, P. (1984, 1985, 1988) *Time and narrative* (Trans. K. McLaughlin and D. Pellauer), Chicago and London: University of Chicago Press. (Original works published 1983, 1984, 1985.)

Ricoeur, P. (1992) *Oneself as another* (Trans. K. Blamey), Chicago and London: University of Chicago Press. (Original work published 1990.)

Riegler, A. (2001) 'The role of anticipation in cognition', in D. M. Dubois (Ed.), *Computing anticipatory systems* (pp. 534–541). Proceedings of the American Institute of Physics 573.

Rockmore, T. (2005) *On constructivist epistemology*, Lanham, MD: Rowman & Littlefield.

Rogers, C. R. (1951) *Client-centered therapy*, London: Constable.

Rogers, C. R. (1956) 'Intellectual psychotherapy', *Contemporary Psychology*, 1: 357–358.

Rogers, C. R. (1959) 'A theory of therapy, personality and interpersonal relationships, as developed in the client-centred framework', in S. Koch (Ed.), *Psychology: A study of science. Volume 3: Formulation of the person and the social context* (pp. 184–256), New York: McGraw-Hill.

Rogers, C. R. (1961) *On becoming a person: A therapist's view of psychotherapy*, London: Constable.

Rokeach, M. (1960) *The open and closed mind: Investigations into the nature of belief systems and personality systems*, New York: Basic Books.

Rorty, R. (1967) *The linguistic turn: Recent essays in philosophical method*, Chicago: University of Chicago Press.

Rorty, R. (1979) *Philosophy and the mirror of nature*, Princeton, NJ: Princeton University Press.

Rosen, H. (1985) *Piagetian dimensions of clinical relevance*, New York: Columbia University Press.

Rosen, H. (1996) 'Meaning-making narratives: Foundations for constructivist and social constructionist psychotherapies', in H. Rosen and K. T. Kuehlwein (Eds), *Constructing realities: Meaning-making perspectives for psychotherapists* (pp. 3–51), San Francisco, CA: Jossey-Bass.

Rychlak, J. F. (1981) *Introduction to personality and psychotherapy: A theory-construction approach* (2nd edn), Boston: Houghton Mifflin.

Rychlak, J. F. (1990) 'George Kelly and the concept of construction', *International Journal of Personal Construct Psychology*, 3: 7–19.

Ryle, A. (1975) *Frames and cages: The repertory grid approach to human understanding*, London: Sussex University Press.

Ryle, A. (1979) 'The focus in brief interpretive psychotherapy: Dilemmas, traps and snags as target problems', *British Journal of Psychiatry*, 134: 46–54.

Ryle, A. and Breen, D. (1972) 'A comparison of adjusted and maladjusted couples using the double dyad grid', *British Journal of Medical Psychology*, 45: 375–382.

Safran, J. D. and Segal, Z. V. (1990) *Interpersonal process in cognitive therap*, New York: Basic Books.

Safran, J. D. and Greenberg, L. (Eds) (1991) *Emotion, psychotherapy, and change*, New York: Guilford.

Salmon, P. (Ed.) (1980) *Coming to know*, London: Routledge & Kegan Paul.

Salmon, P. (1985) *Living in time: A new look at personal development*, London: Dent.

Sarbin, T. R. (Ed.) (1986a) *Narrative psychology: The storied nature of human conduct*, New York: Praeger.

Sarbin, T. R. (1986b) 'The narrative as a root metaphor for psychology', in T. R. Sarbin (Ed.), *Narrative psychology: The storied nature of human conduct* (pp. 3–21), New York: Praeger.

Schafer, R. (1976) *A new language for psychoanalysis*, New Haven, CT: Yale University Press.

Schafer, R. (1980) 'Narration in the psychoanalytic dialogue', *Critical Inquiry*, 7: 29–53.

Schafer, R. (1983) *The analytic attitude*, New York: Basic Books.

Schafer, R. (1992) *Retelling a life: Narration and dialogue in psychoanalysis*, New York: Basic Books.

Scheer, J. W. (1996) 'After the Wall: Construct systems in united Germany', in J. W. Scheer and A. Catina (Eds), *Empirical constructivism in Europe: The personal construct approach* (pp. 52–55), Giessen, Germany: Psychosozial Verlag.

Scheer, J. W. (2008) *Computer programmes for the analysis of Repertory Grids*. Retrieved May 26, 2008, from www.pcp-net.de/info/comp-prog.html

Scheer, J. W. and Walker, B. M. (Eds) (2003) *The internet encyclopaedia of personal construct psychology*. Retrieved December 7, 2008, from www.pcp-net.org/encyclopaedia/main.html

Schiller, F. C. S. (1907) *Studies in humanism*, London: Macmillan.

Schleiermacher, F. (Ed. A. Bowie) (1998) *Hermeneutics and criticism and other writings*, Cambridge, UK and New York: Cambridge University Press. (Original work published 1828.)

Segal, L. (1986) *The dream of reality: Heinz von Foerster's constructivism*, New York: Norton.

Shotter, J. (1984) *Social accountability and selfhood*, Oxford: Blackwell.

Shotter, J. and Gergen, K. J. (Eds) (1989) *Texts of identity*, London: Sage.

Shulman, B. H. and Watts, R. E. (1997) 'Adlerian and constructivist psychotherapies: An Adlerian perspective', *Journal of Cognitive Psychotherapy*, 11: 181–193.

Soffer, J. (1993) 'Jean Piaget and George Kelly: Toward a stronger constructivism', *International Journal of Personal Construct Psychology*, 6: 59–77.

Soldz, S. (1988) 'Constructivist tendencies in recent psychoanalysis', *International Journal of Personal Construct Psychology*, 1: 329–347.

Soldz, S. (1993) 'Beyond interpretation: The elaboration of transference in personal construct therapy', in L. M. Leitner and N. G. M. Dunnett (Eds), *Critical issues in personal construct psychotherapy* (pp. 173–192), Malabar, FL: Krieger.

Soldz, S. (1996) 'Psychoanalysis and constructivism: Convergence in meaning-making perspectives', in K. T. Kuehlwein and H. Rosen (Eds), *Constructing realities: Meaning-making perspectives for psychotherapists* (pp. 277–306), San Francisco, CA: Jossey-Bass.

Solomon, J. (1994) 'The rise and fall of constructivism', *Studies in Science Education*, 23: 1–19.

Spence, D. P. (1982) *Narrative truth and historical truth*, New York: Norton.

Spence, D. P. (1990) 'The rhetorical voice of psychoanalysis', *Journal of the American Psychoanalytic Association*, 38: 579–604.

Spencer-Brown, G. (1969) *Laws of form*, London: George Allen & Unwin.

Steffe, L. P. and Gale, J. (Eds) (1995) *Constructivism in education*, Hillsdale, NJ: Lawrence Erlbaum Associates, Inc.

Steier, F. (1991) 'Introduction: Research as self-reflexivity, self-reflexivity as social process', in F. Steier (Ed.), *Research and reflexivity* (pp. 1–11), London: Sage.

Stern, D. B. (1985) 'Some controversies regarding constructivism and psychoanalysis', *Contemporary Psychoanalysis*, 21: 201–208.

Stern, D. B. (1997) *Unformulated experience: From dissociation to imagination in psychoanalysis*, Hillsdale, NJ: The Analytic Press.

Stevens, C. D. (1998) 'Realism and Kelly's pragmatic constructivism', *Journal of Constructivist Psychology*, 11: 283–308.

Stewart, V. and Stewart, A. (1981) *Business applications of repertory grid*, Berkshire: McGraw-Hill.

Stojnov, D. (1996) 'A personal construction of war in Yugoslavia. Transition as a way of life', in D. Kalekin-Fishman and B. M. Walker (Eds), *The construction of group realities: Culture, society, and personal construct psychology* (pp. 95–102), Malabar, FL: Krieger.

Stojnov, D. and Butt, T. (2002) 'The relational basis of personal construct psychology', in G. J. Neimeyer and R. A. Neimeyer (Eds), *Advances in personal construct psychology: New directions and perspectives* (pp. 81–110), Westport, CT: Praeger Publishers/Greenwood Publishing Group.

Stone, R. (2006) 'Does pragmatism lead to pluralism?: Exploring the disagreement between Jerome Bruner and William James regarding pragmatism's goal', *Theory & Psychology*, 16: 553–564.

Stringer, P. and Bannister, D. (Eds) (1979) *Constructs of sociality and individuality*, London: Academic Press.

Sullivan, H. S. (1953) *The interpersonal theory of psychiatry*, New York: Norton.

Sussman, M. B. (2007) *A curious calling: Unconscious motivations for practicing psychotherapy* (2nd edn), Lanham, MD: Jason Aronson.

Taylor, P. C. (1998) 'Constructivism: Value added', in K. G. Tobin and B. J. Fraser (Eds), *The international handbook of science education* (pp. 1111–1123), Dordrecht, The Netherlands: Kluwer Academic Publishers.

Thomas, F. N., Waits, R. A. and Hartsfield, G. L. (2007) 'The influence of Gregory Bateson: Legacy or vestige?', *Kybernetes*, 36: 871–883.

Thomasson, A. L. (2005) 'First-person knowledge in phenomenology', in D. W. Smith and A. L. Thomasson (Eds), *Phenomenology and philosophy of mind* (pp. 115–139), Oxford: Oxford University Press.

Tomkins, S. A. (1970) 'Affect as the primary motivational system', in M. B. Arnold (Ed.), *Feelings and emotions* (pp. 101–110), New York: Academic Press.

Toukmanian, S. G. and Rennie, D. L. (Eds) (1992) *Psychotherapy process research: Paradigmatic and narrative approaches*, London: Sage.

Tschudi, F. (1977) 'Loaded and honest questions: A construct theory view of symptoms and therapy', in D. Bannister (Ed.), *New perspectives in personal construct theory* (pp. 321–350), London: Academic Press.

Tudor, K. and Worrall, M. (2006) *Person-centered therapy: A clinical philosophy*, Hove, UK: Routledge.

Vaihinger, H. (1965) *The philosophy of 'As if': A system of the theoretical, practical and religious fictions of mankind* (2nd edn), London: Routledge & Kegan Paul. (Original work published 1911.)

Varela, F. J. (1976) 'Not one, not two', *The CoEvolution Quarterly*, 11: 62–67.

Varela, F. J. (1979) *Principles of biological autonomy*, New York: North Holland.

Varela, F. J. (1984) 'The creative circle:Sketches on the natural history of circularity', in P. Watzlawick (Ed.), *The invented reality: How do we know what we believe and know? Contributions to constructivism* (pp. 309–323), New York: Norton.

Varela, F. J. (1985) *The science and technology of cognition: Emergent directions*, Paris: CREA, École Polytechnique & Institut des Neurosciences (CNRS).

Varela, F. J. (1987) 'Laying down a path in walking', in W. Thompson (Ed.), *Gaia: A way of knowing* (pp. 48–64), Hudson, NY: Lindisfarne Press.

Varela, F. J. and Shear, J. (Eds) (1999) *The view from within: First-person approaches to the study of consciousness*, Thorverton, UK: Imprint Academic.

Varela, F. J., Thompson, E., and Rosch, E. (1991) *The embodied mind: Cognitive science and human experience*, Cambridge, MA: MIT Press.

Vasco, A. B. and Dryden, W. (1997) 'Does development do the deed?: Clinical experience and epistemological development together account for similarities in therapeutic style', *Psychotherapy: Theory, Research, Practice, Training*, 34: 262–271.

Vico, G. (1710) *De antiquissima Italorum sapientia ex linguae latinae originibus eruenda* [*On the most ancient wisdom of the Italians*] (Trans. L. M. Palmer), Neapolis: Stamperia de' Classici.

Viney, L. L. (1993) *Life stories*, London: Wiley.

Viney, L. L. (1996) *Personal construct therapy: A handbook*, Norwood, NJ: Ablex.

von Foerster, H. (1974) *Cybernetics of cybernetics*. Opening address of the Annual Meeting of the American Society for Cybernetics.

von Foerster, H. (1981) *Observing systems*, Seaside, CA: Intersystems Publications.

von Foerster, H. (1984) 'On constructing a reality', in P. Watzlawick (Ed.), *The invented reality: How do we know what we believe we know? (Contributions to constructivism)* (pp. 41–61), New York: Norton. (Original work published 1981.)

von Foerster, H. (1989) 'The need of perception for the perception of needs', *Leonardo*, 22: 223–226.

von Foerster, H. (2003) 'Cybernetics of epistemology', in H. von Foerster (Ed.), *Understanding understanding: Essays on cybernetics and cognition* (pp. 229–246), New York: Springer.

von Foerster, H. and Pörksen, B. (1998) *Wahrheit ist die Erfindung eines Lügners. Gespräche für Skeptiker* [*Truth is the invention of a liar: Conversations for skeptics*], Bonn: Bild-Kunst.

von Foerster, H. and von Glasersfeld, E. (1999) *Wie wir uns erfinden. Eine Autobiographie des radikalen Konstruktivismus* [*How one invents oneself: An autobiography of radical constructivism*], Heidelberg, Germany: Carl-Auer-Systeme Verlag.

von Foerster, H. and Bröcker, M. (2002) *Teil der Welt. Fraktale einer Ethik* [*Part of the World/Fractals of Ethics*], Heidelberg, Germany: Carl-Auer-Systeme Verlag.

von Glasersfeld, E. (1974) 'Piaget and the radical constructivist epistemology', in C. D. Smock and E. von Glasersfeld (Eds), *Epistemology and education* (pp. 1–24), Athens, GA: Follow Through Publications.

von Glasersfeld, E. (1977) *The concepts of adaptation and viability in a radical constructivist theory of knowledge.* Paper presented at the 7th Annual Symposium of the Jean Piaget Society, Philadelphia.

von Glasersfeld, E. (1980) 'Viability and the concept of selection', *American Psychologist*, 35: 970–974.

von Glasersfeld, E. (1982) 'An interpretation of Piaget's constructivism', *Revue Internationale de Philosophie*, 36: 612–635.

von Glasersfeld, E. (1984) 'An introduction to radical constructivism', in P. Watzlawick (Ed.), *The invented reality: How do we know what we believe we know? (Contributions to constructivism)* (pp. 17–40), New York: Norton. (Original work published 1981.)

von Glasersfeld, E. (1985) 'Il complesso di semplicità' [The complex of simplicity], in G. Bocchi and M. Ceruti (Eds), *La sfida della complessità* [*The challenge of complexity*] (pp. 103–111), Milano: Feltrinelli.

von Glasersfeld, E. (1991) 'Knowing without metaphysics: Aspects of the radical constructivist position', in F. Steier (Ed.), *Research and reflexivity* (pp. 12–29). London: Sage.

von Glasersfeld, E. (1993) *From determinism or reductionism to constructivism: Brief therapy theoretical perspective.* Paper presented at the Seminar on 'Philosophy and art of brief therapy', Arezzo, Italy.

von Glasersfeld, E. (1995) *Radical constructivism: A way of knowing and learning*, London: Falmer Press.

von Glasersfeld, E. (September 8–10, 1996a) *The conceptual construction of time.* Paper presented at the congress *Mind and Time*, Neuchâtel.

von Glasersfeld, E. (1996b) 'Farewell to objectivity', *Systems Research*, 13: 279–286.

von Uexküll, J. and Kriszat, G. (1934) *Streifzüge durch die Umwelten von Tieren und Menschen: Ein Bilderbuch unsichtbarer Welten* [*Exploration through the individual worlds of animals and men*], Berlin: J. Springer.

Vygotsky, L. S. (1962) *Thought and language*, New York: Wiley.

Warren, B. (1998) *Philosophical dimensions of personal construct psychology*, London: Routledge.

Waddington, C. H. (1957) *The strategy of the genes*, London: Allen & Unwin.

Walker, B. M. (1993) 'Looking for a whole "mama": Personal construct psychotherapy and dependency', in L. M. Leitner and N. G. M. Dunnett (Eds), *Critical issues in personal construct psychotherapy* (pp. 61–81), Malabar, FL: Krieger.

Walker, B. M. (1997) 'Shaking the kaleidoscope: Dispersion of dependency and its relationships', in G. Neymeyer and R. A. Neimeyer (Eds), *Advances in personal construct psychology* (Vol. 4 pp. 63–100), Greenwich, CN: JAI Press.

Walker, B. M. (2003) 'Making sense of dependency', in F. Fransella (Ed.), *International handbook of personal construct psychology* (pp. 171–180), Chichester, UK: Wiley.

Walker, B. M. and Winter, D. A. (2007) 'The elaboration of personal construct psychology', *Annual Review of Psychology*, 58: 453–477.

Walker, B. M., Ramsey, F. L. and Bell, R. C. (1988) 'Dispersed and undispersed dependency', *International Journal of Personal Construct Psychology*, 1: 63–80.

Warren, W. G. (1985) 'Personal construct psychology and contemporary philosophy: An examination of alignments', in D. Bannister (Ed.), *Issues and approaches in personal construct theory* (pp. 253–265), London: Academic Press.

Warren, W. G. (1989) 'Personal construct theory and general trends in contemporary philosophy', *International Journal of Personal Construct Psychology*, 2: 287–300.

Warren, W. G. (1990a) 'Is personal construct psychology a cognitive psychology?', *International Journal of Personal Construct Psychology*, 3: 393–414.

Warren, W. G. (1990b) 'Psychoanalysis and personal construct theory: An exploration', *Journal of Psychology*, 124: 449–463.

Warren, W. G. (1991) 'Rising up from down under: A response to Adams-Webber on cognitive psychology and personal construct theory', *International Journal of Personal Construct Psychology*, 4: 43–49.

Warren, W. G. (1998) *Philosophical dimensions of personal construct psychology*, London: Routledge.

Watts, R. E. (Ed.) (2003) *Adlerian, cognitive, and constructivist therapies: An integrative dialogue*, New York: Springer.

Watts, R. E. and Phillips, K. A. (2004) 'Adlerian psychology and psychotherapy: A relational constructivist approach', in J. D. Raskin and S. K. Bridges (Eds), *Studies in meaning 2: Bridging the personal and social in constructivist psychology* (pp. 267–289), New York: Pace University Press.

Watzlawick, P. (Ed.) (1984) *The invented reality: How do we know what we believe we know? (Contributions to constructivism)*, New York: Norton. (Original work published 1981.)

Watzlawick, P., Beavin, J. and Jackson, D. (1967) *Pragmatics of human communication: A study of interactional patterns, pathologies, and paradoxes*, New York: Norton.

Wedge, M. (1996) *In the therapist's mirror: Reality in the making*, New York: Norton.

Weiner, M. L. (1975) *The cognitive unconscious: A Piagetian approach to psychotherapy*, Davis, CA: International Psychological Press.

Whitaker, R. (Ed.) (1998) *Encyclopaedia Autopoietica: An annotated lexical compendium on autopoiesis and enaction*. Retrieved December 7, 2008, from www.cybsoc.org/EA.html#constructivism

White, M. (1995) *Re-authoring lives: Interviews and essays*, Adelaide: Dulwich Centre Publications.

White, M. and Epston, D. (1990) *Narrative means to therapeutic ends*, New York: Norton.

Wilkinson, S. J. (1981) 'Constructs, counterfactuals and fictions: Elaborating the concept of "possibility" in science', in H. Bonarius, R. Holland and S. Rosenberg (Eds), *Personal construct psychology: Recent advances in theory and practice* (pp. 39–46), New York: St. Martin's Press.

Winnicott, D. W. (1960) 'Ego distortion in terms of true and false self', in D. W. Winnicott (Ed.), *The maturational processes and the facilitating environment* (pp. 14–52), London: Hogarth Press.

Winograd, T. and Flores, F. (1986) *Understanding computers and cognition: A new foundation for design*, Norwood, NJ: Ablex.

Winter, D. A. (1992) *Personal construct psychology in clinical practice*, London: Routledge.

Winter, D. A. and Viney, L. L. (Eds) (2005) *Personal construct psychotherapy: Advances in theory, practice and research*, London: Whurr.

Wittgenstein, L. (2001) *Philosophical investigations*, Malden, UK: Blackwell. (Original work published 1953.)

Wortham, S. (1996) 'Are constructs personal?', *Theory & Psychology*, 6: 79–84.

Wylie, R. C. (1961) *The self concept*, Lincoln, NE: University of Nebraska Press.

Yalom, I. D. (1980) *Existential psychotherapy*, New York: Basic Books.

Young-Eisendrath, P. (1997) 'Jungian constructivism and the value of uncertainty', *Journal of Analytical Psychology*, 42: 637–652.

Zetzel, E. (1956) 'Current concepts of transference', *International Journal of Psycho-Analysis*, 37: 369–376.

Author index

Subject index

For Product Safety Concerns and Information please contact our EU
representative GPSR@taylorandfrancis.com
Taylor & Francis Verlag GmbH, Kaufingerstraße 24, 80331 München, Germany